Earth's Changing Climate

Earth's Changing Climate

Roy A. Gallant

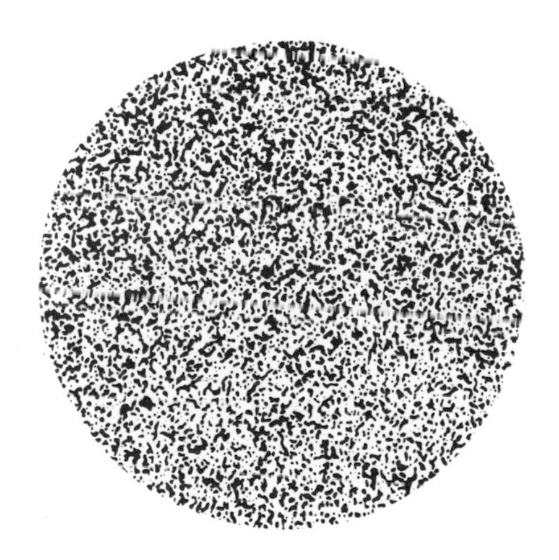

Four Winds Press
New York

LIBRARY OF CONGRESS CATALOGING IN PUBLICATION DATA

Gallant, Roy A

Earth's changing climate.

Bibliography: p.

Includes index.

SUMMARY: Discusses climate and explores reasons for changes in climate, including sunspots, cosmic dust clouds, and man-made factors. Analyzes the economic, social, and political effects of these changes.

1. Climatic changes—Juvenile literature.

[1. Climatic changes] I. Title.

QC981.8.C5G34 551.6 78-22124

ISBN 0-590-07447-4

PUBLISHED BY FOUR WINDS PRESS

A DIVISION OF SCHOLASTIC MAGAZINES, INC., NEW YORK, N.Y.

PRINTED IN THE UNITED STATES OF AMERICA

LIBRARY OF CONGRESS CATALOG CARD NUMBER: 78-22124

1 2 3 4 5 83 82 81 80 79

For L. S. H.

"The atmosphere is universal. It belongs to no one. At the same time, it belongs to everyone. . . . Climate modification, if ill-conceived and conducted without consideration of all mankind, could lead to catastrophe. The collaboration of all nations is needed so that such an event will never come to pass."

—Louis J. Battan
Harvesting the Clouds

Acknowledgments

I wish to thank several individuals and publishers, in some instances for reading and commenting on various chapters when this book was in the manuscript stage, and in other cases for permission to use already-published materials. In those instances where selected quotations were extremely brief and permission to use them, therefore, was not required, I acknowledge the source for those readers who may wish to refer to the original document in its entirety.

The quotations from Louis J. Battan are from his book *Harvesting the Clouds,* Copyright © 1969 by Doubleday & Company, Inc. I wish to thank my own publisher, Four Winds Press, for permission to excerpt brief passages from my books *How Life Began: Creation Versus Evolution,* Copyright © 1975 by Roy A. Gallant, and *Beyond Earth: The Search for Extraterrestrial Life,* Copyright © 1977 by Roy A. Gallant. I also wish to thank Grolier Incorporated and its *New Book of*

Knowledge for permission to use a brief excerpt from an article written by me and titled "Winds and Weather." My thanks also for permission to use a brief selection from *The Wonderful World of Prehistoric Animals,* by William Elgin Swinton, Copyright © 1961, by Rathbone Books, Ltd., with a new revised edition, Copyright © 1969, by Aldus Books, Ltd., London, and published in the United States by Doubleday & Company, Inc. My thanks to Alfred A. Knopf, Inc. for permission to use three brief excerpts from *The World of Ice,* by James L. Dyson, Copyright © 1962 by James L. Dyson.

The section on the Plains Indians culture and the drought during the fourteenth century is based on material in *Climates of Hunger,* by Reid A. Bryson and Thomas J. Murray, Copyright © 1977 by The Regents of the University of Wisconsin System and published by The University of Wisconsin Press. My thanks to Doubleday & Company, Inc. for permission to use two brief quotations from *Times of Feast, Times of Famine,* by E. L. Ladurie, Copyright © 1971 by E. L. Ladurie. Thanks also to *Mother Earth News,* March, 1976, for permission to use brief quotations from an interview with Reid A. Bryson. I am also grateful to the Worldwatch Institute for permission to use brief quotations of Erik Eckholm and Lester R. Brown, appearing in *Worldwatch Paper 13,* "Spreading Deserts: The Hand of Man," Copyright © 1977 by Worldwatch Institute. Thanks also to another of my publishers, Ginn and Company, for permission to adapt a passage titled "Case of the Unwelcomed Dam," an account of the ecological consequences of building Africa's Kariba Dam, in the Ginn Science Program, Intermediate Level C, by Roy A. Gallant and Isaac Asimov, Copyright © 1980 by Ginn and Company.

The chart titled "Environmental Effects of Man-Made Ground Emissions" appearing on page 173 is reprinted by permission of the Fund for the Republic, Inc. The chart originally appeared in *World Issues*, Vol. 1, No. 1, October/ November, 1976, published by the Center for the Study of Democratic Institutions.

My special thanks to environmentalist Dr. Reid A. Bryson, Director of the Institute for Environmental Research, University of Wisconsin, Madison, for furnishing materials relating to drought in the Sahel and climatological consequences of artificial manipulation of the environment; to astronomer Dr. Mark R. Chartrand, Chairman of The American Museum —Hayden Planetarium, for reviewing the entire manuscript; to geographer Dr. Val L. Eichenlaub, Western Michigan University, and to biologist Dr. Edward J. Kormondy, the Evergreen State College, both for reviewing the entire manuscript; and to biologist Dr. Steven M. Stanley, Johns Hopkins University, for furnishing valuable material relating to the diversity of floral and faunal communities through various geological periods. My special thanks also to my editors, Mary Lee Stevens and David Reuther, for their many extremely helpful comments at the manuscript stage.

Contents

Icebergs like this giant, photographed by the U.S. Coast Guard in Baffin Bay, are reminders that from time to time our planet is gripped by centuries of intense cold that we call an ice age.
U.S. COAST GUARD PHOTOGRAPH

1

A Rendezvous with Ice

A LAND OF "PERMANENT" SNOW

Greenland is a gleaming land of snow capped with an ice sheet that began to form some 100,000 years ago. Today this ice sheet is nearly 3 kilometers (about 2 miles) thick in places. But Greenland has not always been ice-covered, nor will it always be. Each day giant chunks of ice "calve," or break, off the west coast of Greenland's ice cap and plunge into the sea as mammoth icebergs. Every year an estimated 500 cubic kilometers (125 cubic miles) of ice plunges into the frigid waters of Baffin Bay along Greenland's west coast. In only a few minutes Rink Glacier, for example, may dump 500 million tons of ice into Baffin Bay. Some of this ice forms icebergs a mile or more long and towering 100 meters (300 feet) above the water. In a very active year, from 10,000 to 15,000 icebergs may break loose from Greenland's frigid shores.

Icebergs are said to "calve" off the ends of glaciers leading to the sea. The large berg that just broke off the end of Jacobshavn Glacier, Greenland, plunged into Baffin Bay. It is about eight kilometers (five miles) wide. Many of the icebergs shown here are equal in size to several city blocks. U.S. COAST GUARD PHOTOGRAPH

THE VOYAGE OF ICEBERG X

Perhaps it was on Tuesday, June 8, 1909 that one such giant slab of ice calved off the end of one of Greenland's numerous glaciers and plunged into the dark waters near Melville Bay. A mammoth iceberg was born. Although we can compute a date for this event, no one will ever know the *exact* place or the date when this event occurred, but occur it did.

At a pace of about four kilometers (2.5 miles) a day, this small mountain of ice began drifting southward on a three-year journey that was to shock the world. First it drifted across Baffin Bay toward the east coast of Baffin Island, a journey taking about six months. Here it was caught up and moved along a little faster by the cold, southward-flowing Labrador Current, which flows down out of the Arctic Ocean. Six months later it had been carried down through the Davis Strait and into the Labrador Sea off the north coast of Newfoundland. Two years from the time it had started its journey, it was a few hundred kilometers due east of Gander, Newfoundland. By this time it had traveled a total of some 3,000 kilometers (1,800 miles). Though it had lost much of its bulk through melting, it was still a floating mountain of ice, a pilotless "ship" passively moving southward ever nearer the busy North Atlantic shipping lanes.

There we will leave our titan of ice and turn to a titan of a different sort.

The world's newest, largest, and most luxurious ocean liner sailed on her maiden voyage from Southampton, England, on April 10, 1912. She was the White Star liner, *Titanic,* 274 meters (883 feet) long and displacing 66,000 tons of water. She was described as "a Victorian palace afloat." According to a London *Times* editorial, "everything had been done to make the huge vessel unsinkable, and her owners believed her to be so."

On leaving Southampton, she crossed the English Channel to France and then steered a course for Newfoundland. Aboard her were 1,315 passengers and 885 crew, although there is some confusion about these exact numbers. Her skipper was 60-year-old Edward J. Smith, a veteran of 40 years at sea. He was to retire after the *Titanic's* maiden voyage.

For several weeks before the *Titanic* had sailed, the United States Navy's Hydrographic Office in Washington had been aware of large fields of ice drifting southward from Greenland and into the shipping lanes which the *Titanic* had now entered. The first alarm about icebergs crackled into the *Titanic*'s radio room at 9:00 A.M., Sunday, April 14: "WESTBOUND STEAMER *CARONIA* REPORTS BERGS AND FIELD ICE IN 42°N FROM 49° TO 51°W APRIL 12. COMPLIMENTS." The *Titanic* was on course only a few kilometers south of that position. The ship's chief radio operator acknowledged the message. At 11:45 A.M. the *Amerika,* another liner, informed the *Titanic* it had just passed "two large icebergs" just south of the position reported by the *Caronia.* Again the *Titanic* acknowledged. At 1:42 P.M. the Greek steamer *Athenia* reported seeing icebergs directly along the *Titanic*'s course. Then at 9:40 P.M. the steamer *Mesaba* advised the *Titanic* of "much heavy pack ice and great numbers of large icebergs."

After spending several months drifting southward from their source in Baffin Bay, icebergs weather and assume shapes of sculptured works of art. U.S. COAST GUARD PHOTOGRAPH

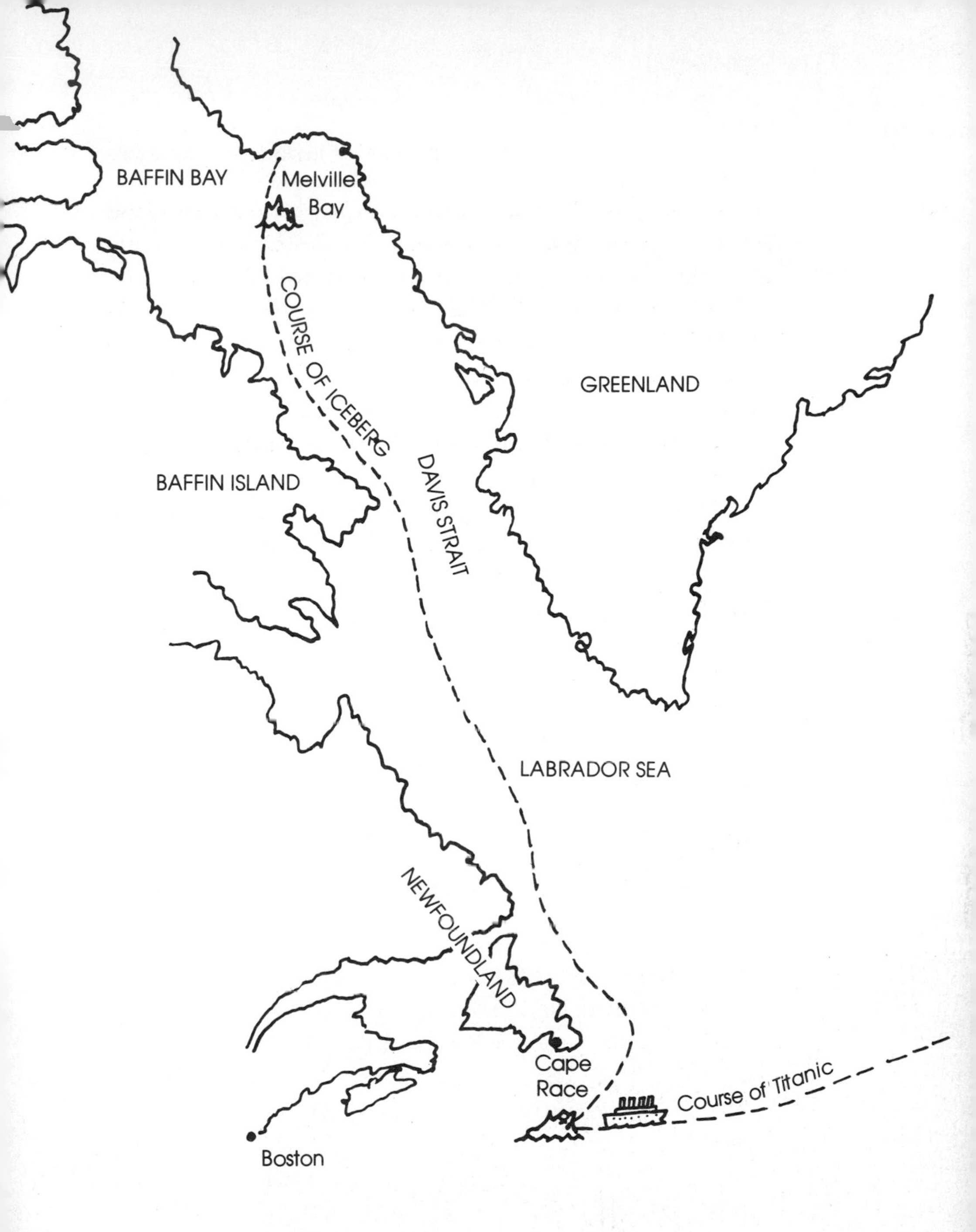

The map shows the probable source and course of the giant iceberg with which the Titanic *collided with disastrous results. The distance from Melville Bay to the impact point is about 3,000 kilometers (1,800 miles). It took the iceberg about three years to rendezvous with the* Titanic.

In spite of these several warnings, neither the owner of the *Titanic,* who was among the passengers, nor others on board showed much concern. They finally held to their belief that this titan of the sea was unsinkable. The night was clear and the *Titanic* continued to plow ahead, nearly at top speed.

At 11:40 P.M. a lookout sighted an iceberg dead ahead and immediately informed the bridge officer. Chief Officer William M. Murdoch instantly ordered "Hard a-starboard! Engines full astern!" But so massive was the *Titanic* that it would take 30 seconds for her to respond to full right rudder. It would also take her 4 minutes, over a distance of half a nautical mile, to come to a stop. The *Titanic* did not have that kind of time on her side.

She kept her fated rendezvous and collided with that mountain of ice which three years earlier had begun its slow voyage from the waters of Baffin Bay. Although melting had reduced the size of Iceberg X during its voyage, at the time of the collision the berg displaced an estimated 200,000 tons compared with the *Titanic*'s 66,000. The collision took place 650 kilometers (400 miles) south of Cape Race, the southern tip of Newfoundland.

The impact was almost gentle, but it was enough to cut open a 93-meter (300-foot) gash in the *Titanic*'s starboard side well below the waterline. She soon began to take on water more rapidly than her pumps could remove it. During the collision chunks and shavings of that prehistoric ice heap tumbled onto her decks.

Not until 30 minutes after the collision did Captain Smith, recovering from utter disbelief over the seriousness of the matter, decide to radio for help. By that time it was five minutes past midnight, and many passengers were still below decks in their rooms. Several ships heard the *Titanic*'s distress calls and replied that they were on their way to her. Meanwhile, the order to man the lifeboats was given, with "women and children first." The fact is that there were not enough lifeboats for all, so sure had her owners been of her unsinkability, and many of those lifeboats launched were filled to only half their capacity.

At 2:20 A.M., Monday, April 15, the unsinkable *Titanic* slipped beneath the calm, black sea. First her bow nosed under, then for a brief moment she was poised with her stern straight up, as though in one last salute. People in lifeboats reported seeing her that way, her propellers plainly visible. Then she silently slipped beneath the calm sea to the bottom, where she remains to this day.

The *Carpathia* was first to arrive on the scene. By this time it was 3:30 A.M. and the frigid waters had claimed those unable to swim to the lifeboats helplessly standing by. Of the total of 2,201 on board the *Titanic*, 700 were saved. By the time the rescue ships had done all they could and left with the handful of survivors, all that remained was scattered debris and a small mountain of ice with a chip taken out of its side, a relic of the past formed some tens of thousands of years ago.

2

100,000 Years of Ice

GLACIERS ARE NOT THE RULE

The ice-capped polar regions of Earth are familiar to us, and icebergs are common, but the fact is that we are now living in a temporarily warm interlude of an ice age. An ice age is an uncommon condition in Earth's long history. For 90 percent of the last 550 million years Earth's polar regions have been free of ice. (What conditions may have been like before that time is the subject of a later chapter.) But ice is a common Earth feature today, as it has been over the past million years. During that time, for example, at least seven ice ages have come and gone. The most recent one was at its peak only 18,000 years ago.

Climatologists are hard pressed to explain what triggers an ice age, or what causes the onset of a warming period, although they have offered some convincing arguments. One thing they can say for certain is that throughout Earth's history climate has continually changed. And there is no reason to suppose that it will not continue to change. One big question climatologists are asking is what the future holds in store for us in the way of climate during the next 50 years, and during the next 50,000 years.

WHAT IS "NORMAL" CLIMATE?

We happen to be living in a portion of that small 10 percent of the time over the past 550 million years when a substantial amount of Earth's water supply is locked up as polar ice and mountain glaciers. If we narrow that large time span down to only the last 70,000 years, the picture is rather different. Climatologists generally agree that from 1900 to about 1950 we had a relatively warm and stable world climate. But the climatologist Cesare Emiliaini warns that such favorable periods have existed during perhaps a mere 5 percent of the last 70,000 years, and usually they have ended quickly. Most often they have lasted for less than a hundred years. The American climatologist Reid A. Bryson adds that the balmy period we have recently been enjoying "has been the most abnormal of the last thousand years." "An exceptionally warm and stable climate over the last 50 years has lulled the world's people into a false sense of security," agrees the American climatologist Iben Browning. He says our climate hasn't been "normal," as we call it now, since the year 1200.

All three scientists agree that we are due for a change, as recent climate upheavals of the 1970s have hinted—parched croplands in northern France, the Soviet Union, Minnesota, the Dakotas, and California, and devastating drought across parts of Africa and India. Such dramatic turns of events have thrust the subject of climatology into news headlines the world over. And the subject of future climate change has become a leading topic among climatologists.

The big question, of course, is what kind of change? Are we headed for another mini ice age? Or is it going to get warmer? A slight change either way would bring about dramatic changes in our lives. A mini ice age would cause the onset of mass starvation for a substantial number of the world's people. And only a slight warming period, according to some climatologists, would melt the polar ice caps and so raise the sea level by about 80 meters (260 feet). In such an event coastal cities such as New York, London, Tokyo, and many others would become sunken cities for future underwater archaeologists to explore. Many climatologists foresee highly changing weather for many years ahead because our climate has seemingly been heading into a cooling period. They also see awesome times for world food production, social order, and economic stability. According to Browning, " 'normal' is climate that is just terrible. And what's happening now is that we're going back to that kind of 'normal.' "

"During stable times, planners tend to inherit the Earth," Browning explains. "They can count on predictable weather and good crops year after year, allowing them to plan for welfare programs, wars, or whatever. Unstable [weather] times are hard times. You see them throughout history. The rules change. People with food tend to keep it for themselves. The others become very hard to compromise with when their babies are starving. We have now entered one of those rough, tough periods."

The possibility of millions of the world's people starving to death as a result of climate change is one of the chief concerns of climatologists. And they point worriedly to the failure of the Indian monsoon over a six-year period, beginning in the late 1960s and lasting into the early 1970s. According to *Science* magazine, "wary of crying wolf too soon and critical of a few individuals who have publicly predicted disasters ahead,

A lowering of only 2°C or so could cause a relatively rapid melting of the polar ice caps. This large-scale melting would raise the world sea level by about 80 meters (260 feet). Coastal cities such as New York, London, Tokyo, and many others would be submerged and would become sunken cities for future underwater archaeologists to explore. New York City, shown here from South Ferry, would be submerged to about the depth shown by the shaded area.

---

climatologists . . . have nonetheless been expressing growing concern to each other and to government officials. . . . Climate, they say, especially the remarkably uniform and favorable climate of the period 1955 to 1970, cannot be taken for granted."

CLIMATE–WE'RE DUE FOR A CHANGE

While many climatologists agree that we are due for a change in climate, they are by no means in general agreement about what kind of change is in store for us, or just when it will come. According to Bryson, climate can change "quite suddenly." It may take only a century or less for an ice-age climate to grip us. Widespread drought conditions take less time, only 10 or 20 years, as in the case of the great drought in the American Southwest from 1271 to 1285, which killed or displaced many Indian communities. Climate change involving seasonal rains, such as a failure of the monsoons, can occur in only a few years and turn once fertile land into deserts. For example, from the late 1960s through 1973 failure of the monsoon across part of a northern strip of Africa caused the death of more than 100,000 people and the destruction of pasturelands and grains, which resulted in the loss of more than one third of the cattle. Wells and rivers alike dried up. A later chapter takes a detailed look at these and other climate calamities.

WHAT CAUSES CLIMATE CHANGE?

What causes long-term and short-term changes in climate is a key question. If we knew the answers, we would be in a better position to say what the climate of the next decade or the next century may be like.

Many causes of climate change have been named, but again there is more disagreement than agreement about which causes may be the more important ones. Astronomers are asking if the Sun from time to time changes the amount of energy it emits and so brings on climate change, with ice ages during times of low energy output, and tropical climates during times of high-energy release. Is it possible that active volcanoes on Earth release great amounts of dust into the atmosphere and so block some of the Sun's energy and bring on mini ice ages? The amount of atmospheric water vapor and carbon dioxide, changes in the shape of the land surface, growth and decay of polar ice, and many other things have been blamed for climate change. In Chapter 8 we look at some of these in detail.

Today every climatologist is wondering to what extent man's activity on this planet may be bringing about climate change. For example, the many pollutants—heat, carbon dioxide, dust, and numerous chemicals—that we release into the atmosphere may well be making conditions right for climate change. Unfortunately, at this stage in our study of climate there are far more questions than answers. One of the many questions: If climate takes a turn for the worse, what, if anything, can man do to control climate to his liking? In the concluding chapter of this book, a number of schemes to bring about climate change have been proposed—one, for example, to melt the Arctic ice cap!

In any study of climate, the best place to begin is with the many bits and pieces that make up that complex process we call climate.

3

What Is Climate?

A CHILLING SCENARIO

Suppose for a moment that a burned-out star known as a *black dwarf*—a cold object about the size of Earth but very much denser—passed through the Solar System. Suppose further that it came within about 1.5 million kilometers (930,000 miles) of Earth, passing between us and the Sun and then on out of the Solar System. No one feels the effect of this cosmic visitor. But its approach and departure are observed for several nights amid much excitement and are the cause of many newspaper headlines and TV "specials." Astronomers are the first to capture the attention of the media. During TV interviews they explain with the aid of diagrams that a rare "near-miss" has occurred, that we were lucky to have escaped a collision that would have shattered our planet to bits. But we did not get off scot-free. The close approach of the burned-out star seriously disturbed, or perturbed, Earth's orbit about the Sun.

Previously, the astronomers explain, Earth circled the Sun at an average distance of 150,000,000 kilometers (93,000,000 miles) and traced a nearly circular orbit about the Sun. Although Earth's distance from the Sun varied, it did not vary by much. On July 4, when Earth was at its greatest distance from the Sun, it was about 152,000,000 kilometers (94,500,000 miles) away. On January 2, when nearest the Sun, it was about 147,000,000 kilometers (91,000,000 miles) away. But the near-miss of the intruder black dwarf changed all that. Gravitational attraction acting between Earth and the black dwarf pulled Earth somewhat "off-course," just as the black dwarf also was pulled somewhat off its course. The result is that Earth's orbit was changed, the astronomers explain.

The diagram shows the imagined situation described in the text. A black-dwarf star sweeps in close to Earth ($Earth_1$). The mutual gravitational attraction acting between the black dwarf and Earth pulls Earth into a new orbit ($Earth_2$). The new orbit is an elongated one, alternately taking Earth much farther away from the Sun than before and then bringing it significantly closer than before. The black dwarf leaves the Solar System on a new course due to the gravitational attraction exerted on it by the Sun.

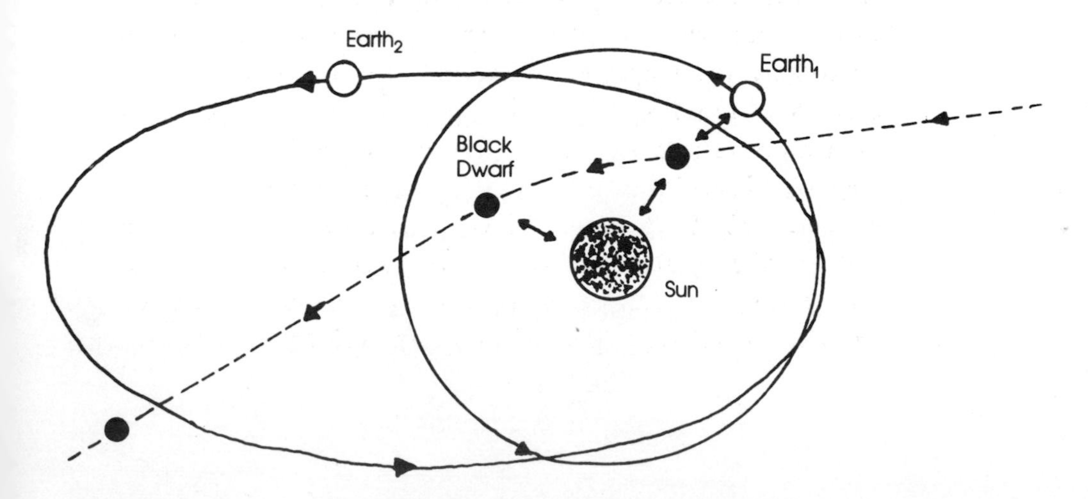

Earth's new orbit is a considerably stretched-out course that will take us several millions of kilometers closer to the Sun for part of the year, and many more millions of kilometers farther away from the Sun when Earth reaches the far end of its new orbit. Although it is too early to come up with precise figures, the astronomers explain, it now seems that Earth's closest approach to the Sun will be about 120,000,000 kilometers (74,000,000 miles) and its farthest point about 180,000,000 kilometers (111,600,000 miles). Another interesting feature of Earth's new orbit, the astronomers hasten to point out, is that our planet will spend about two-thirds of its time in the extreme regions of its new orbit *away* from the Sun and only about one-third of its time *near the* Sun.

Most people watching this interview with the nation's leading astronomers resent their "prime evening time" being taken up by astronomy professors drawing complex diagrams on a blackboard and reciting a lot of big numbers that don't mean anything to the average person. So they switch channels and tune in to their favorite sports program or family situation comedy. But others begin to sense the urgency of what the astronomers are saying.

The consequences of such an orbital switch are not difficult to imagine. And the climatologists would be the next ones to capture the attention of the media. Within weeks, they tell us, we will begin to detect the effects of the new orbit. As we near our closest approach to the Sun, Earth's atmosphere will begin to receive much more energy from the Sun than it did before, with the probable result of rapid atmospheric heating, but slower heating of the oceans and land. While this heating may be devastating in tropical and semitropical regions, the climatologists point out, the effects will be felt much less in middle latitudes and high latitudes.

They go on to explain that on a long-term basis the increased length of time Earth will be spending at its newly remote distance from the Sun will determine the long-term change Earth's climate will undergo. This is so, they explain, because more than three-quarters of the time Earth will be far removed from the Sun, during which it will undergo extremely long and cold winters. The relatively brief and hot summers, even though much hotter than summers past, will be so brief that they will not be able to reverse a continuing cold trend.

The climatologists warn that within a century or two Earth could be all but totally covered with ice. The long times our planet would be spending at the remote ends of its orbit would cause a marked cooling and gradual spreading of the polar ice caps. Although there will be some melting during summer in each hemisphere, they go on to explain, the winter buildup of snow and ice will be greater than the amount of summer melting.

SOLAR RADIATION FOR EARTH—HOW MUCH?

Although this little scenario is far-fetched (the probability of a starlike object entering the Solar System being extremely remote), the consequences of such a near-miss are not. Earth indeed could be pulled into a new orbit and one that would have profound effects on our planet's climate. The purpose of this hypothetical case of a black-dwarf near-miss is to introduce and emphasize one of the most important regulators of Earth's climate—the amount of energy reaching Earth from the Sun. This energy is called *insolation,* short for "incoming solar radiation."

Astronomers the world over have made measurements of the amount of solar radiation reaching Earth. They must take into consideration the depth of the atmosphere, which is greater over the equator than it is over the polar regions, the angle at which the Sun's rays enter the atmosphere and strike Earth's surface, and several other factors. When all such factors are taken into account, no matter from where on our planet the amount of energy striking a given patch of the top of Earth's atmosphere is measured, the amount of solar radiation is the same. Each minute, every square centimeter patch of the top of Earth's atmosphere receives very nearly an average of almost exactly 2 calories (1.95) of energy. That important quantity is called the *solar constant.* Until recently it was thought to have changed very little over the past half billion years of the Sun's life. But we'll have more to say about the so-called solar "constant" when we take up the causes of climate change in a later chapter.

As a unit of energy, one *calorie* is the amount of energy needed to raise the temperature of one gram of water one degree Celsius. Or if you prefer a more graphic description: one calorie is the amount of energy liberated when a fleet of 41,900,000 mosquitoes flying at cruise speed collide with a stone wall.

Energy from the Sun reaches us in the form of waves. As the diagram shows, some of these waves are long, while others are short. Near one extreme is infrared, or the long-wave radiation we call heat. Radio waves are still farther down at this long-wave end of the energy spectrum. Next come the various wavelengths of visible light—red having the longest waves and violet the shortest. Of still shorter wavelength are ultraviolet rays, which are the ones that give us sunburn and that in excessive amounts can cause skin cancer.

As energy of all of these wavelengths rains down on Earth continuously at the rate of two calories per square centimeter per minute, various things happen to the energy as it first enters and then filters down through Earth's cocoon of atmosphere. To find out what happens to all this energy, we is compressed into a layer about 30 kilometers (about 20 miles) deep. Take our atmosphere away and there would be no trees, no animals, no clouds or colorful sunsets, and no sound. Ours would be a dead planet like Mercury and the Moon. By day the direct rays of the Sun would heat everything to the boiling point of water. By night temperatures would plunge a few hundreds of degrees below the freezing point.

As a greenhouse provides heat to the plants it houses, our atmosphere serves as a blanket that prevents much of Earth's stored heat from escaping into space by radiation.

The atmosphere is a mixture of gases and dust. Most of the air—78 percent—is made up of nitrogen, an element that is important as a food for plants, but which is not used directly by us. Most of the remaining gas is oxygen, which nearly all of Earth's organisms depend on for life. The remaining 1 percent of atmospheric gases is a mixture of water vapor, argon, helium, neon, ozone, carbon dioxide, and still other substances. As you will find in later chapters, carbon dioxide and water vapor play important parts in helping to shape Earth's climate. In addition to the gases just mentioned, the air carries large amounts of dust particles, salt crystals from the oceans, bits and pieces of rocks and sand, pollen from plants, ash from volcanoes, and meteor dust. About a ton of meteoric dust falls to Earth's surface each day.

We can picture the atmosphere as a high stack of feather pillows. The weight of the pillows higher up tends to squash, or compress, those pillows lower down. This results in a greater pressure exerted on the lower pillows. That is why the air pressure at ground level is greater than the pressure at higher altitudes. And that is why high-flying aircraft must provide their occupants with pressurized cabins.

We can picture the atmosphere as being made up of layers,

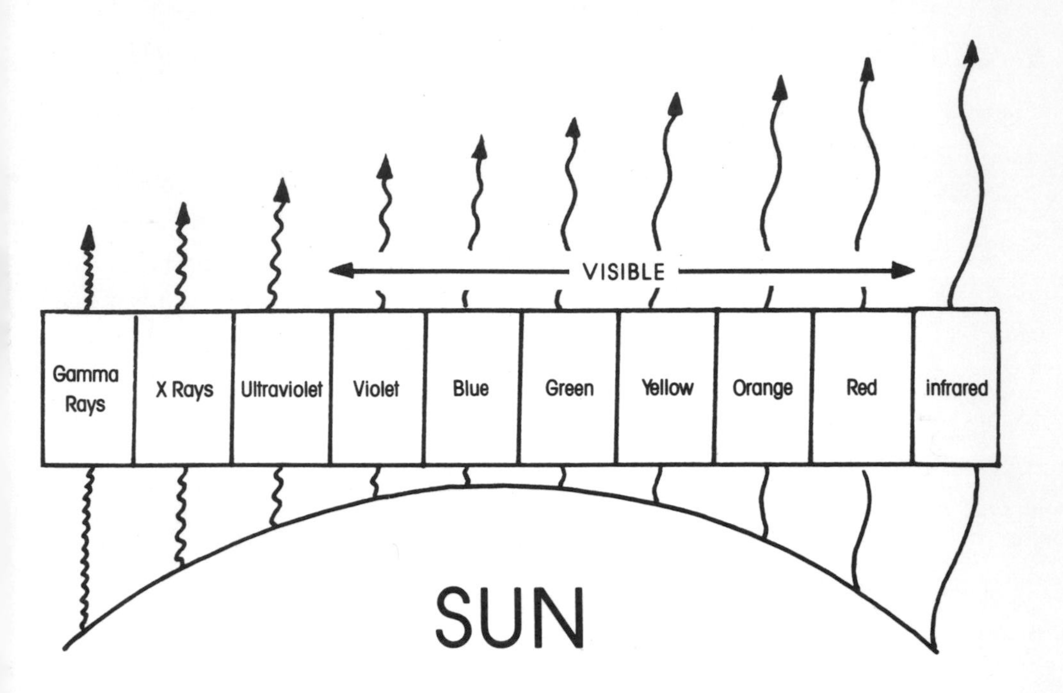

Energy from the Sun reaches Earth in various wavelengths. Near one extreme is the long-wave energy we call heat. At the other extreme are the short-wave gamma rays, which are highly destructive to living material. In the middle are the visible wavelengths of energy that we call "light."

must examine the atmosphere, which is another of the "pieces" that make up climate.

OUR OCEAN OF AIR

We can imagine ourselves as living on the floor of an ocean of air. At the bottom we are safe and comfortable, but drawn up near the top we would die. Held captive by Earth's gravity, our ocean of air surrounds the planet to a depth of hundreds and thousands of kilometers. But 99 percent of the atmosphere each layer having its own pressure and temperature oddities that make it different from the other layers.

The Troposphere. This is the first and lowest layer. It is the most crowded with gas molecules and is where almost all of our weather takes place. Over the United States the troposphere reaches up to about 12,500 meters (about 40,000 feet), or nearly 13 kilometers (8 miles). On a hot August day, the air temperature at the bottom of the troposphere may be 35°C (95°F), but at the top it will be −57°C (−70°F). The temperature of this air layer falls off at an average rate of 6°C for every 1,000 meters (or about 3.5°F per 1,000 feet). The reason for this temperature *gradient*, or change with altitude, is that radiant heat given off by the ground warms the air next to the ground more than it warms the air higher up.

Air in the troposphere moves over the land as winds. As the Sun heats large, flat areas of land, the air becomes lighter and rises, so vertical air currents also occur. While the lower troposphere contains large amounts of water vapor—water molecules in the form of a gas rather than in liquid form—the top layer of the troposphere contains relatively little water vapor.

The Stratosphere. This second layer of the atmosphere begins wherever the troposphere ends and goes up to a height of about 50 kilometers (about 30 miles). Like the upper troposphere, the lower regions of the stratosphere are swept with strong winds and are extremely cold. Higher up, however, the winds die and the temperature gradually rises, except over the polar regions in winter. Here the stratospheric polar night jet stream attains high speeds at an altitude of about 50 kilometers (30 miles). At the top of the stratosphere the temperature is about −1°C (30°F). The cause of this sudden warming is a layer of the gas ozone (about which we will have much more to say in Chapter 9). Ozone is a form of oxygen consisting of three atoms (0_3) instead of two (0_2), which is the form of oxygen we breathe. A blanket of ozone in the upper stratosphere blocks out most of the high-energy ultraviolet radiation from the Sun. Without the protective ozone layer, living organisms exposed to the full force of ultraviolet radiation would be seriously harmed. Atmospheric pressure at the top of the stratosphere is only 1/1,000 the pressure at sea level, which makes it about the same as being in deep space.

The Mesosphere. Resting on top of the stratosphere is the mesosphere, an air layer about 30 kilometers (about 20 miles) deep. The negative temperature gradient resumes in the mesosphere, the temperature at its base being about −1°C (30°F) but then falling off to about −90°C (−130°F) near the top. At this altitude the air is so diffuse, or thin, that hardly any light is scattered about by the decreasing numbers of gas molecules. The result is that the sky no longer appears blue, but nearly black.

The Thermosphere. Topping the mesosphere is the fourth major layer of air—the thermosphere. It is the borderline of space. At the lower level of the thermosphere the temperature begins to rise again. It increases from −90°C (−130°F) at the base to more than 1,093°C (2,000°F) at its upper boundary, an altitude of more than 30,000 kilometers (20,000 miles). But you must not confuse this high temperature with the heat you feel on a hot summer day. Since there are so very few gas molecules at thermosphere altitudes, there is no transfer of heat from the air to any object in the air. The temperature we are talking about now simply expresses the speed at which the gas molecules up there are moving about. Any living creature taken up into the thermosphere and exposed to its tenuous air would perish by being broiled to death on the side facing the Sun and frozen to death on the side in shadow.

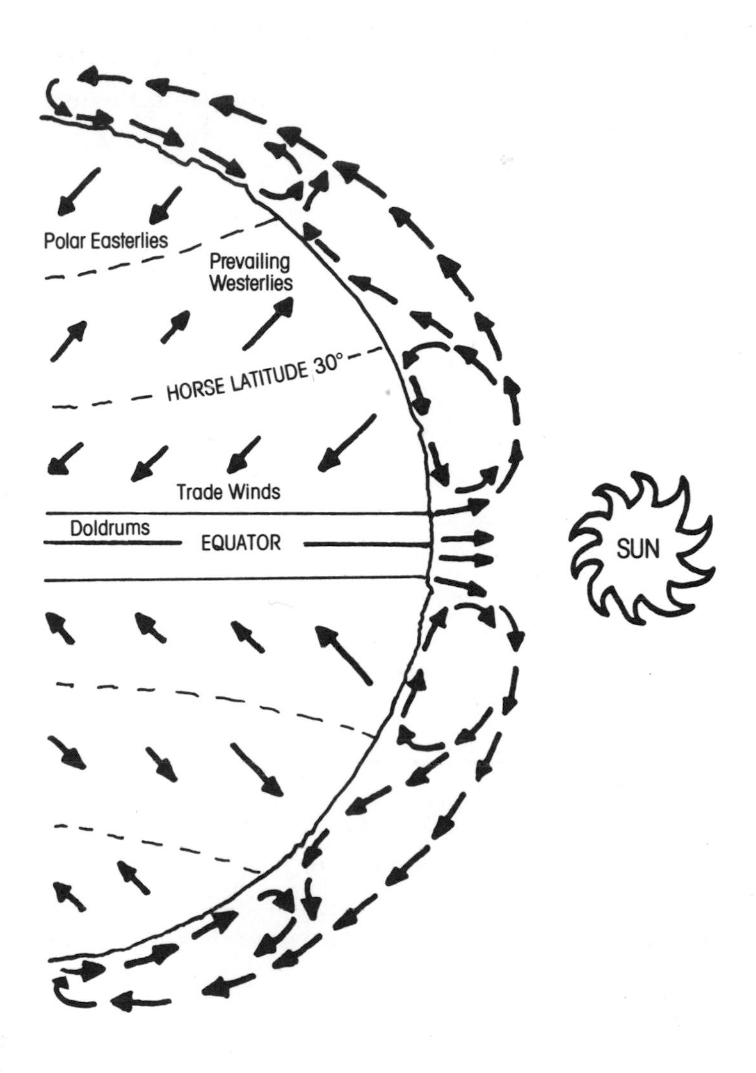

Earth's atmosphere is set in motion by energy from the Sun. Large belts of global circulation of the air are kept in motion as shown in the diagram.

THE ATMOSPHERE IN MOTION

The air surrounding our planet is continually moving. And for the most part we can count on it to move in certain predictable ways. While there are local motions of air, such as vertical currents and winds, there also are large wind systems that move in fairly regular patterns around Earth.

The major wind systems accounting for the general circulation of air around the globe occur in seven belts, as shown in the diagram. We count the Equator as one belt. In addition, there are three belts in the Northern Hemisphere and three more in the Southern Hemisphere.

Throughout the year, the Sun's energy falls most intensely on a broad belt extending just northward and southward of the Equator. All along the sunlit section of this belt, over land and sea alike, Earth's surface and the air above it are heated. This heating sets up a low-pressure system of rising air.

Much the same thing happens above a living-room radiator. Heat from the radiator causes the air just above to expand and rise, setting up a local low-pressure system in one part of the living room. As the Equator's low-pressure system of air rises to great heights, the air is cooled, becomes heavy, and tends to sink back to the ground again. But a steady flow of hot, rising air pushing up from below prevents it from doing so. This hot, rising air is laden with moisture (water vapor). As it is cooled at a higher altitude, the water vapor condenses into clouds and then into rain, providing the land areas of the Equatorial belt with abundant rainfall.

The belt of air girdling the Equator is carried along at the rotational speed of Earth's surface at the Equator. That speed is about 1,600 kilometers (1,000 miles) an hour. So, relative to the Equatorial belt, the air above the Equator has very little motion, except for its upward motion. What little wind blows is usually light and variable, and those parts of the Equatorial belt of air that lie over the oceans are often dead calm. Masters of those grand sailing ships of old dreaded this part of the ocean, where for days on end they would find themselves becalmed under the blistering tropical Sun. They called this belt of calm the *doldrums.*

As the Equatorial air rises aloft, some of it streams northward toward the North Pole while some of it streams southward toward the South Pole. At about 30° North and South latitudes some of the air curves downward toward Earth's surface. Here it tends to pile up and form a high-pressure system called the *horse latitudes.* In general, the air here is fairly calm, or if there are winds, they are light and variable. The climate of the horse latitudes is generally sunny, hot, and dry. Some of the world's great desert areas—northern Mexico, northern Africa, and northern India—lie along this belt.

The high-pressure air at the horse latitudes doubles back and flows close to Earth's surface toward the Equator, replacing the equatorial air rising aloft. This outward-flowing air forms a broad belt of wind called the *trade winds,* which blow rather steadily. Because this air is not keeping pace with Earth's rotational speed at this latitude, the trade winds blow at a slant instead of looping straight back to the Equator. In the Northern Hemisphere they blow from northeast to southwest and are called the *northeast trades.* In the Southern Hemisphere they blow from the southeast to the northwest and are called the *southeast trades.* This slanting effect, caused by Earth's rotation, is called the *Coriolis effect.* The slant of the trade winds also affects the course of the ocean currents.

From about 35° North and South latitudes to about 55° is another wind belt, called the *prevailing westerlies.* In the Northern Hemisphere they blow from the southwest to the northeast. In the Southern Hemisphere they blow from the northwest to the southeast. The air forming this wind belt has its source in the mainstream of air flowing northward and southward from the Equator. In the latitudes of the westerlies this air is moving faster than Earth's rotational speed; so, like the trade winds, the westerlies blow at a slant, but in the opposite direction.

Like the trade winds, the westerlies blow steadily day and night at Earth's surface. But we feel their effect most at altitudes where the airliners fly. A jet liner eastward bound from New York to London is carried along by the westerlies and can make the trip in about two hours less time than it can on the return flight from London to New York.

Mountains, valleys, plains, and other features of Earth's surface interfere with the flow of the westerlies at ground level. This is one reason that we do not feel the steady force of the westerlies at the surface. Warm, moist air moving up from the south, and cold, dry air moving down from the north meet in the path of the westerlies. This contributes to the ever-changing winds and variety of storms that make the westerlies our most active weather belt. Whenever the path of the westerlies over certain regions of Earth changes temporarily, marked changes in weather occur. In a later chapter we find out how the mystery of the decline of the once-flourishing Mycenaean civilization of Greece 3,000 years ago was solved, and how the mystery of vanishing American Indian cultures also has been solved recently by climatologists. It now appears very likely that a shift in the westerlies simply dried up the land and forced its inhabitants to move elsewhere or perish.

Some of the hot, moist air that begins its poleward journey from the Equator reaches the polar ice caps. But by the time it arrives at the top and bottom of the world, it has been cooled and nearly all of its moisture has been wrung out. This air tends to pile up at the poles where it forms a high-pressure cap. Because the speed of this air is slower than Earth's rotational speed at these high latitudes, the *polar easterlies*, as they are called, blow in the same slanting direction as the trade winds; that is, they are northerly winds at the surface.

Between the polar easterlies and the prevailing westerlies in the Northern Hemisphere is a belt separating these two zones. But it is not a belt of calm, as are the horse latitudes. In the northern polar belt the climate is stormy and the winds variable in both speed and direction.

These, then, are the major wind systems girdling Earth. But they have been described as "ideal" systems, that is, without considering the many variations of land features, the seasons, and the oceans, all of which tend to disrupt the neat profile we have drawn.

HOW THE LAND SHAPES CLIMATE

People who live in mountain regions are well aware of how local land features, or topography, can affect climate. By day the sunny slope of a mountain heats up faster than the areas farther down the slope and at some distance from it. As the slope air is heated and becomes lighter, it rises. Cooler surrounding air is drawn toward the mountain and flows up the slope, replacing the warmer, rising air. At night this pattern is reversed. Because of the greater altitude, air next to the slope cools more rapidly than air over the lower and surrounding land. As it cools, it becomes heavy and flows down the mountain. If there are small valleys leading into a main valley corridor, the cold, downward-flowing air spills into the valleys and meets in the main corridor, sweeping through it with great force.

If there are mountains near a coast, cold, high-pressure air from the slopes sweeps down through the valleys toward the coast, where there is warmer, low-pressure air. Much the same thing happens in winter where there are plateaus. Cold air tends to collect on the plateau, then slips down the slopes, causing a gentle or moderate breeze. Such winds from plateaus and from coastal mountains are called *drainage winds*. One of the best-known drainage winds in the United States is called the *Santa Ana*, a hot and dry wind. It is a strong wind that sweeps through southern California's Santa Ana Canyon and spills out over the coastal lowlands. The *bora*, one of Europe's best known drainage winds, is a cold, strong wind that sweeps the shores of the northern Adriatic at speeds greater than 130 kilometers (about 80 miles) an hour.

To the east of the Rocky Mountains, particularly in Montana and Wyoming, is a wind called the *chinook*. Moist air of the prevailing westerlies moves eastward across the United States from the Pacific Ocean. As it crosses the mountains it is forced aloft where it is cooled and loses its moisture. By the time it crosses the Rockies this air is cold and dry. On the eastern side of the Rockies it flows down the slopes, warming along the way and absorbing moisture from the ground and trees. So well known is its "hunger" for moisture that in winter the wind is called the "snoweater." Because of its dryness and relative warmth, this wind can be very unpleasant. In Europe, where it is called the *foehn*, it is quite common on the northern slopes of the Alps. During a foehn, people tend to become depressed, irritable, and complain of headaches. A foehn (or chinook) announces itself by a rise in temperature and a drop in humidity.

BALANCING EARTH'S HEAT BUDGET

During the daytime about 29 percent of the Sun's energy entering Earth's atmosphere is reflected back to space by clouds and dust and so is not available to heat the atmosphere. Another 4 percent is reflected back to space by Earth's surface and so is lost. Another 19 percent is absorbed by water vapor,

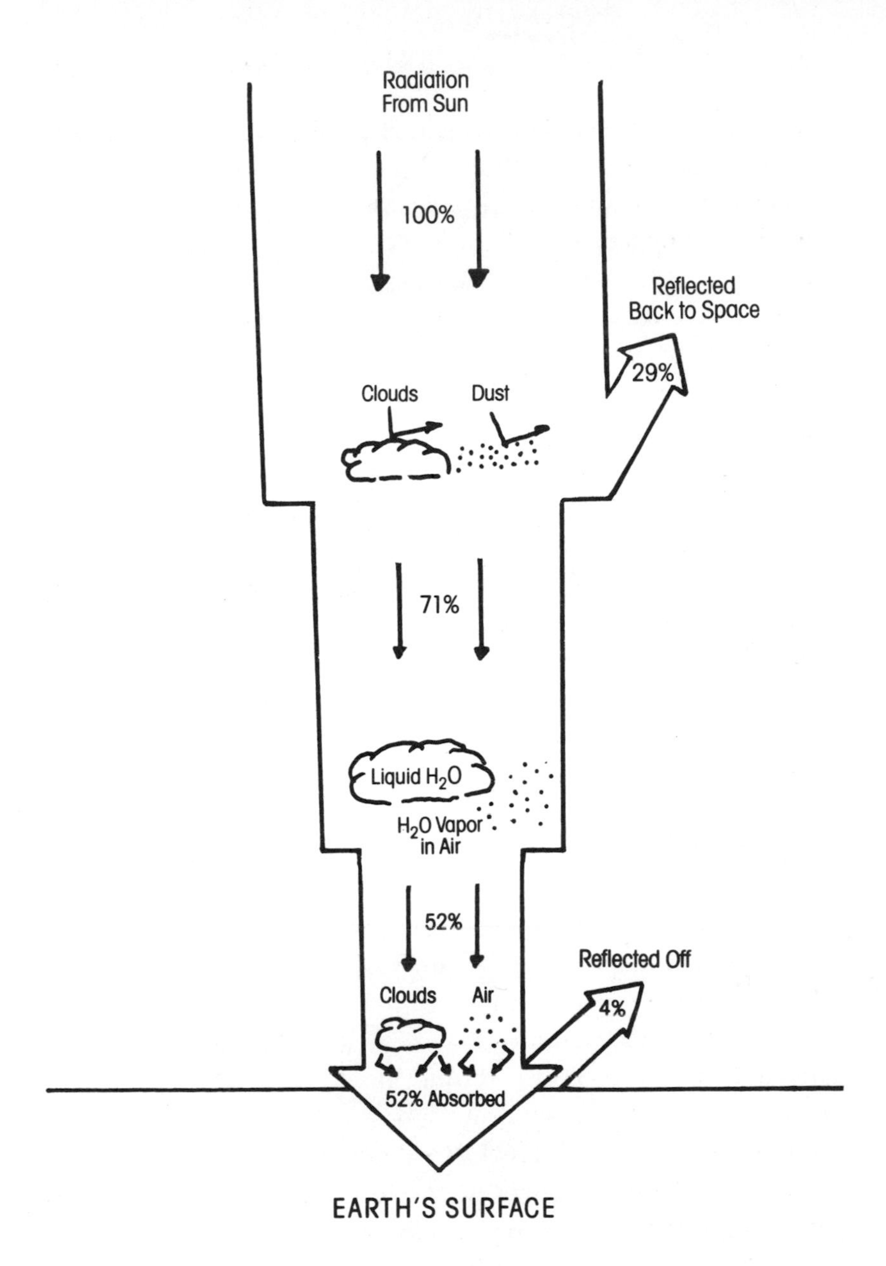

About two-thirds of the solar energy arriving at Earth is retained by Earth while one-third is lost back to space.

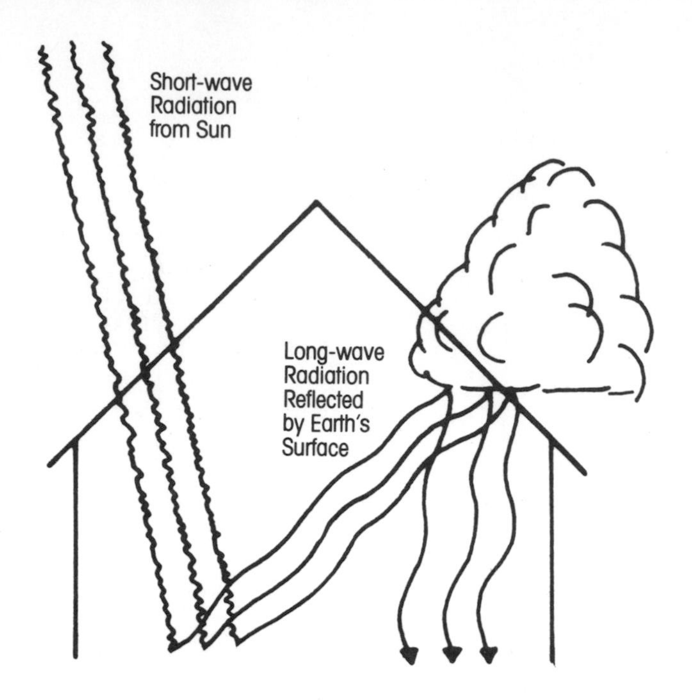

Short-wave radiation striking Earth's surface is absorbed and re-emitted as long-wave (heat) radiation. This long-wave radiation is reflected by clouds back to Earth's surface. The same thing occurs in a greenhouse, where the glass roof permits the passage of short-wave radiation but traps the long-wave radiation.

---

liquid water in clouds, and dust. Twenty-nine percent of the total insolation is absorbed directly by Earth's surface. An additional 23 percent, scattered by the atmosphere and clouds, reaches the surface indirectly and is absorbed there. So of the total of 100 percent of insolation, about 52 percent is absorbed by Earth's rocks, soil, oceans, and vegetation. That amount plus the 19 percent absorbed by the atmosphere means that approximately two-thirds of the insolation is kept by Earth while one-third is lost back to space.

If Earth kept on absorbing that 52 percent of insolation reaching us, our planet would gradually heat up. Since it is not observed to be heating up, then we conclude that Earth's surface gives off heat. The energy that Earth reradiates is of the long wavelength kind, the infrared. While some of this reradiated heat energy is lost to space, some is kept by Earth. The amount kept is absorbed by carbon dioxide and water vapor in the air and part is reradiated back toward the surface again. This heat-trapping action of the air is called the *greenhouse effect.*

The amount of insolation received in Galveston (Texas), London, Buenos Aires, or any other place on Earth at a certain time depends on several things: the energy output of the Sun at that time, the amount of light-blocking activity of dust in the atmosphere, length of the day at that location, and the angle at which the Sun's rays happen to be striking the surface at that location.

Two imaginary beams of solar energy strike Earth's surface at two different locations with different results. Because the high-latitude beam strikes the surface at an angle its intensity is weakened since it is spread out over a wider area than a beam of the same size striking the Equator. Thin arrows represent energy reaching Earth's surface from the Sun. Heavy arrows represent energy reemitted back to space by Earth's surface.

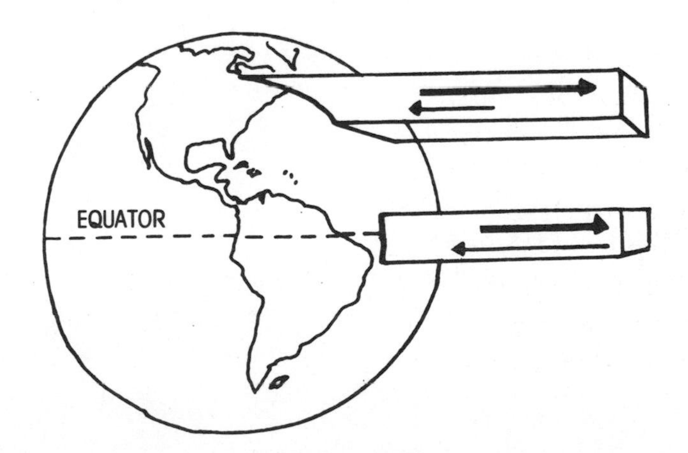

The last point is worth considering for a moment. As the diagram shows, the Sun's rays strike Earth at different angles at different latitudes. At the Equator they always strike directly and so are most intense there. But at higher latitudes they slant through a greater thickness of the atmosphere and slant at a smaller angle, which causes their energy to spread out over a larger area.

How Well Different Parts of the Planet Absorb the Sun's Energy

Kind of Surface	Percent of Energy Absorbed*
Oceans	93–77
Forests	80
Savanna	85
Desert	70
Snow and ice	20
Rock	85
Wheat field	80

* These percents are broad estimates and are given for comparison only.

So far, we have considered only two pieces of the climate puzzle—the atmosphere and Earth's heat budget. Although there are well over 20 more, we will consider only three of them—seasonal change, circulation of the oceans, and Earth's water cycle.

CAUSE OF THE SEASONS

Realizing that Earth's distance from the Sun varies by a few million kilometers from one year to the next, we might suspect that this varying distance from the Sun is the cause of our seasons. But as you found earlier, that cannot be the case since

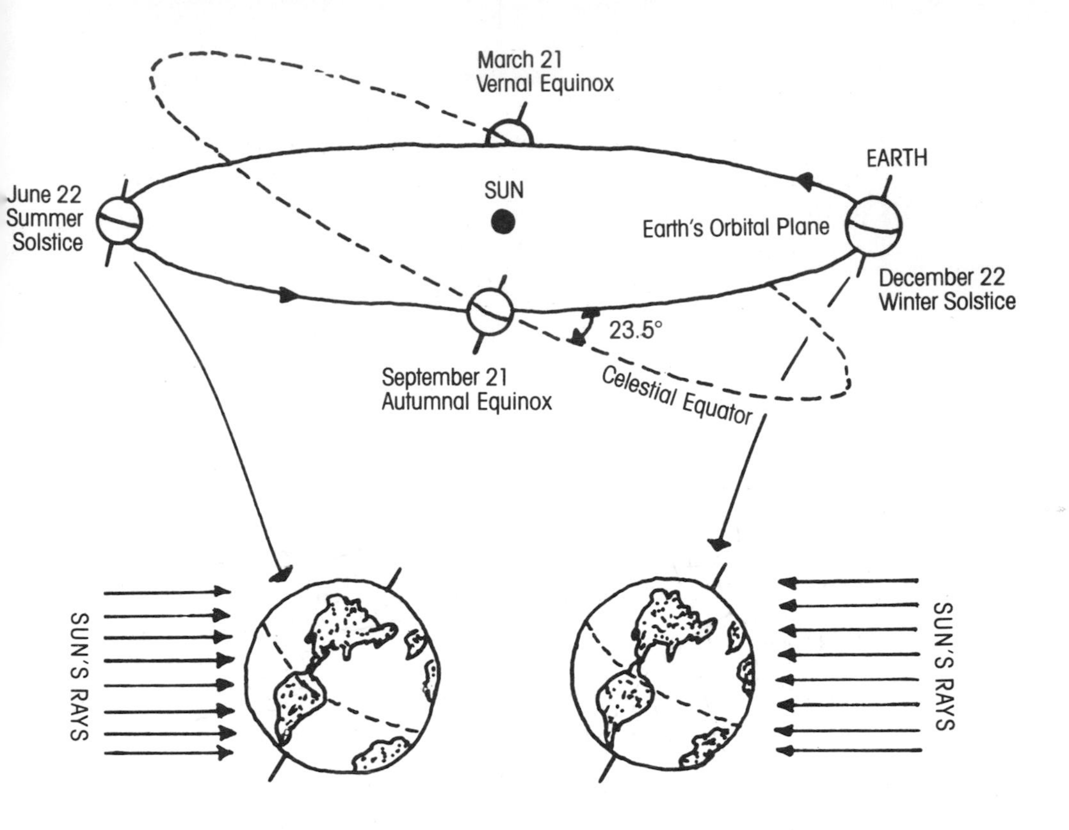

The seasons are caused by Earth's obliquity, or the amount by which it is tilted in space. As a result of its obliquity, a given location on Earth's surface receives varying amounts of insolation at different times of the year. See text for details.

---

we are nearest the Sun early in January and farthest from it early in July. The cause of the seasons lies not in Earth's distance from the Sun but in the way it faces the Sun.

The diagram here shows that Earth is tilted a bit in space. This tilt is called its *obliquity*. The solid-line disk in the diagram represents the plane of Earth's orbit. Notice that because Earth is tilted by a certain amount, a line drawn through its equator intersects the orbital disk at an angle of 23.5°.

Because of this tilt, the Sun's rays strike a given location on Earth's surface at different angles—and so with changing intensities—at different times of the year depending on where Earth happens to be in its orbit around the Sun.

As winter gives way to spring, and spring to summer, each day the noontime Sun appears a bit higher in the sky than on the previous day. Because of the Sun's higher overhead position, and because the days gradually become longer, each day grows a little warmer, at least in theory! It is warmer because the Sun's rays are striking us from more directly overhead than before. Then as summer gives way to fall, and fall to winter, each day the noontime Sun appears a bit lower in the sky, and each day the air grows a little cooler, again in theory.

In the Northern Hemisphere summer begins on June 22 (see diagram), at which time the noontime Sun appears at its highest point in the sky. That marks the official beginning of summer and is the day when we in the Northern Hemisphere have the greatest number of daylight hours. After that the days begin to grow shorter and the nights longer, until at official autumn, about September 21, day and night are equal. Because Earth remains tilted in the same direction in space, the Northern Hemisphere begins to tilt away from the Sun over the next three months. By about December 22, it is tilted back in its farthest position. Because it is, the noonday Sun reaches its lowest point in the sky and the Northern Hemisphere now receives the Sun's rays at the lowest angle, which means the least amount of heating. This first day of winter marks the shortest day of the year, after which the days begin to grow longer as the Sun appears progressively higher in the sky each day. South America now receives the direct rays of the Sun and enjoys long summer days.

Three months later, about March 21, the length of day and night again are equal, marking the arrival of spring. Each day the noonday Sun is seen to climb higher in the sky and the days gradually grow warmer. You might want to draw your own diagram to show what would happen to our seasons if Earth were not tilted at an angle of 23.5° but instead had its north-south polar axis straight up-and-down in relation to its orbital plane.

Earth has not always been tilted at an angle of 23.5°, nor will it always be, an important fact we return to in a later chapter when we discuss the causes of climate change.

As Earth spins around on its axis it wobbles, as does a spinning top that is running out of spin energy. The reason is that Earth is not a perfect sphere. Because it rotates on its axis, it has developed a slight bulge at the Equator and slight flattening at the poles. The diameter at the Equator is some 43 kilometers (27 miles) greater than the polar diameter. And because the Equator is tilted over at an angle of 23.5°, the Sun's

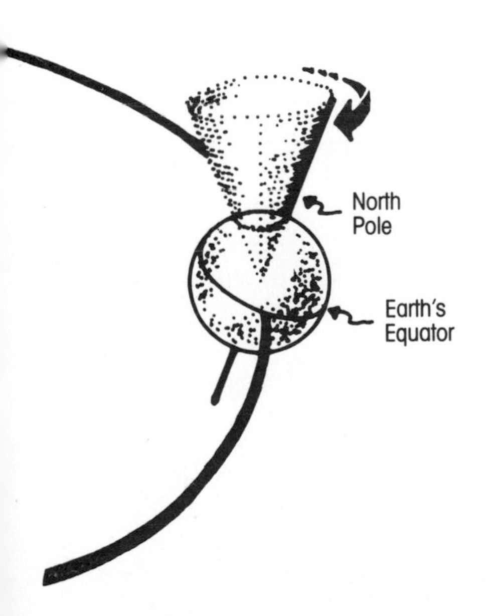

Earth wobbles as it spins on its axis, just as a top does as it loses rotational speed. Called precession, *this wobbling motion gradually changes the pattern of Earth's seasons. For example, about 10,500 years ago the Northern Hemisphere winter occurred not in December but in July. One complete precessional wobble takes about 26,000 years.*

and Moon's gravitational tugging on our planet are not in line with each other. What happens is that Earth's axis slowly gets twisted around in a circle, one circle being completed every 25,800 years. This means that the North Star, presently Polaris, is not always the same star. In 3000 B.C., for example, the star Thuban seen in the constellation Draco, was the North Star; in A.D. 7000 it will be the star Alderamin in the constellation Cepheus. This wobbling of our planet is called *precession*. Because of it, about 13,000 years ago Earth was closest to the Sun during the Northern Hemisphere summertime rather than in the wintertime as it is now. Theoretically, summers then should have been hotter than they are now, and winters colder. Precession, then, is another important piece of the climate puzzle, one associated with long-term climate changes.

CIRCULATION OF THE OCEANS

Like the atmosphere, the ocean currents follow a general pattern of circulation, and one that is closely related to the atmospheric circulation. And like the atmosphere, Earth's oceans are extremely important climate regulators. One reason is the ability of water to absorb heat, store it, and then carry it from one place to another as the currents move. Water in motion is about five times a better storer of heat than is soil, especially dry and loose soil. Also, water in motion can be heated to much greater depths than soil can. That is why at night the temperature of the ground may become much lower than it is during the day, while the temperature of the surface water of a lake or the oceans changes hardly at all. This ability of water to store heat accounts for the generally mild winter temperatures along the coasts compared with harsh temperatures inland away from large bodies of water. It also accounts for those cool ocean breezes on a hot summer day.

"Water is the driver of nature," said Leonardo da Vinci

some 500 years ago. Water is also the most abundant single substance on Earth's surface. Nearly all of Earth's water is salt water of the oceans. And by far most of that ocean water is in the Southern Hemisphere. The next largest amount of water —but only a drop compared with the oceans—is locked up as ice (fresh water) in the polar ice caps and as scattered mountainous glacial ice.

The World's Water

	Percent of All Water	Salt or Fresh
Oceans	97.0	Salt
Ice	2.3	Fresh
Underground water		Fresh
Surface water	0.7	Fresh
Water vapor in the air		Fresh

Like the atmosphere, the oceans are ever in motion. Great rivers of water that we call currents wind their way around the globe, curving this way and that. When we trace the course of one of these currents—the Gulf Stream, for example—we can see what important climate regulators the currents can be.

THE GULF STREAM AS A CLIMATE REGULATOR

The Gulf Stream begins as a narrow current of warm water, about 25°C (77°F), flowing out of the Gulf of Mexico off the tip of Florida. Off southern Florida it moves at the rate of about 150 kilometers (90 miles) a day. The Gulf Stream next swings northeast and up along the eastern U.S. coast at an average rate of about 130 kilometers (80 miles) a day. Off Cape Hatteras (North Carolina) it has cooled a bit to some 22°C (72°F) and begins to branch. When south of Nova Scotia, the

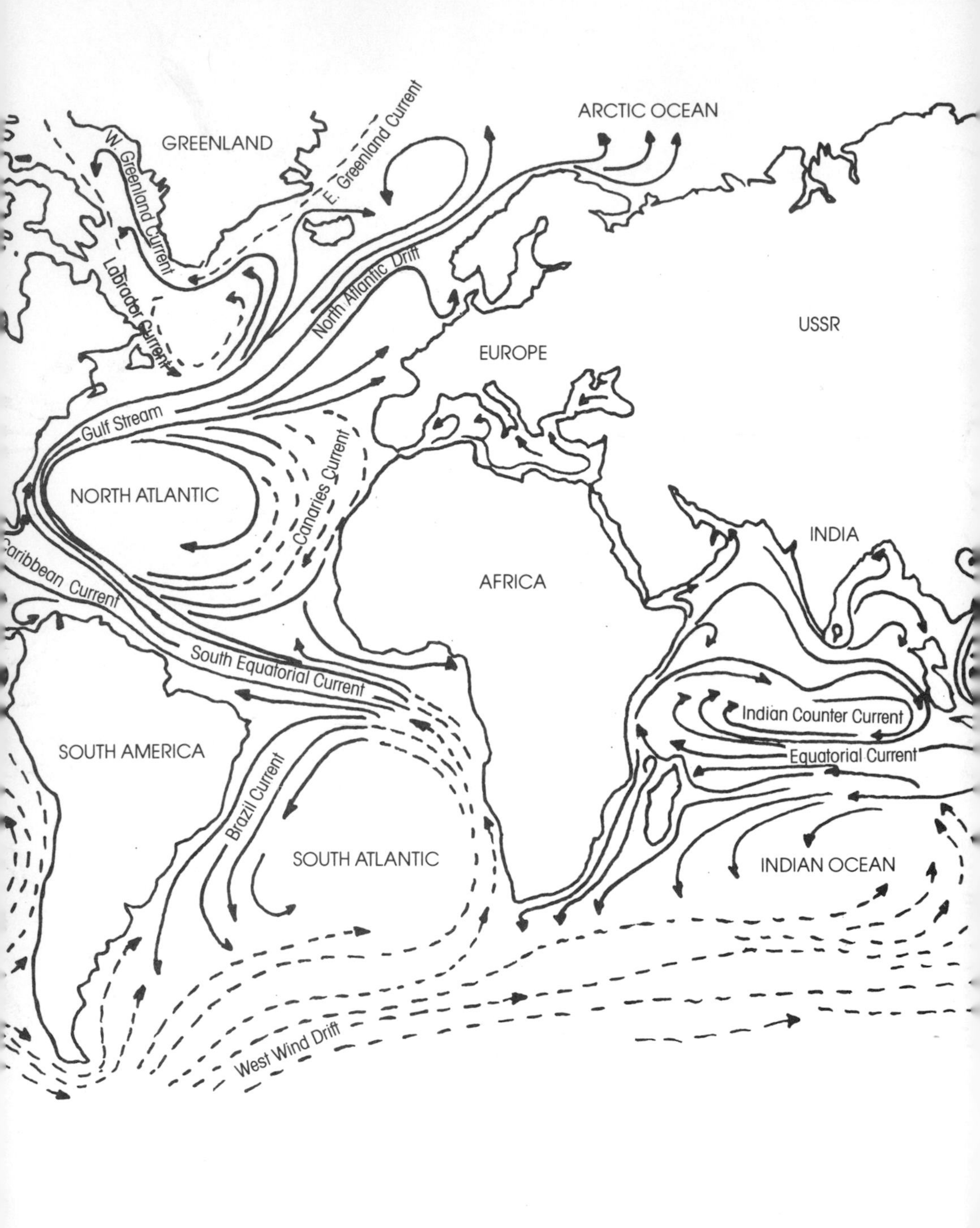

ARCTIC OCEAN
GREENLAND
W. Greenland Current
E. Greenland Current
Labrador Current
North Atlantic Drift
EUROPE
USSR
Gulf Stream
NORTH ATLANTIC
Canaries Current
Caribbean Current
AFRICA
INDIA
South Equatorial Current
Indian Counter Current
Equatorial Current
SOUTH AMERICA
Brazil Current
SOUTH ATLANTIC
INDIAN OCEAN
West Wind Drift

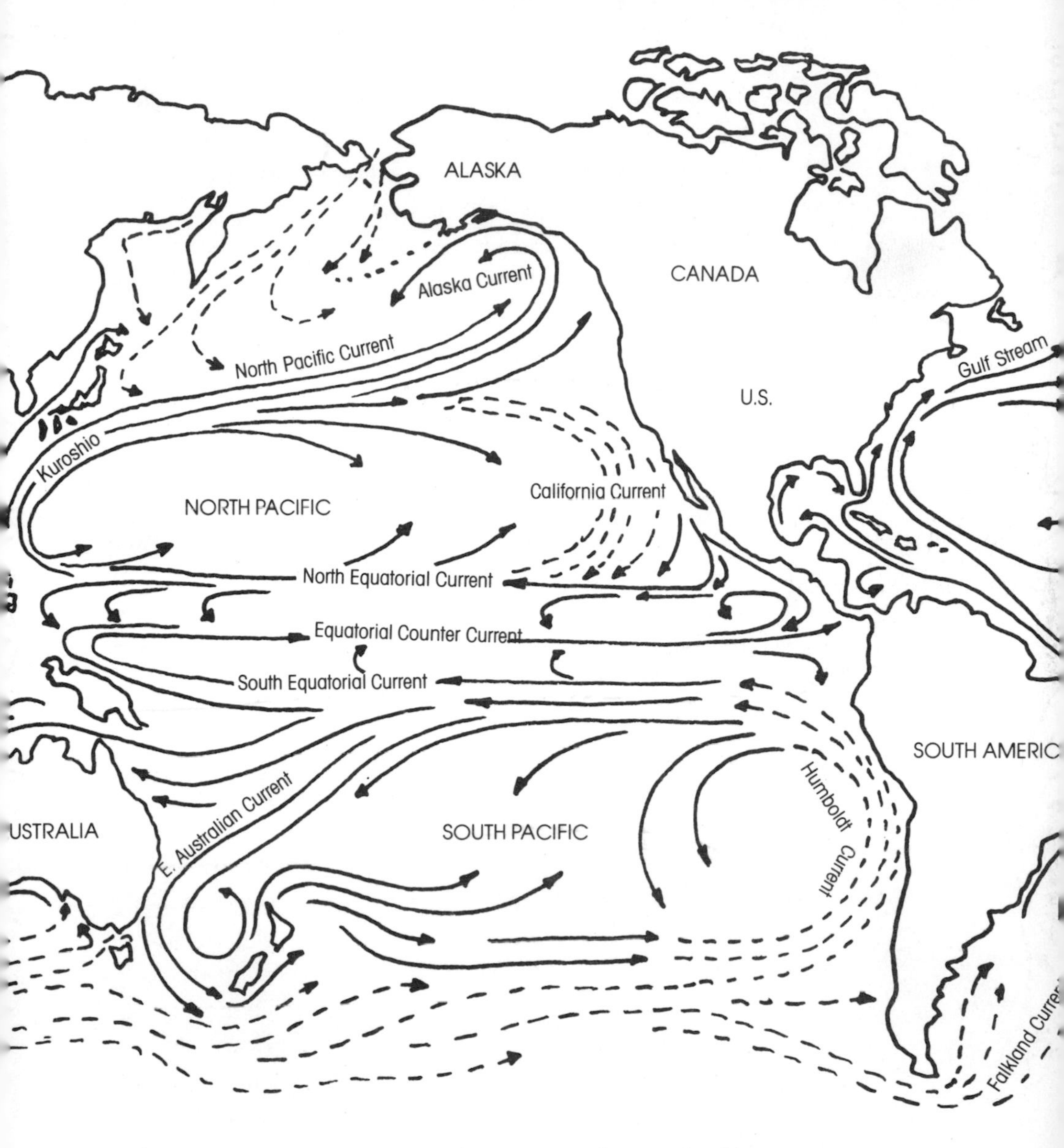

Earth's ocean currents continually transport heat and cold over the globe in predictable patterns. Solid arrows represent warm currents, while broken arrows represent relatively cold currents. Generally, the major ocean currents are driven by and follow the pattern of global wind circulation.

now broadened Gulf Stream has slowed to about 70 kilometers (45 miles) a day. Near Newfoundland its northern section meets the cold Labrador Current flowing down from the Arctic Ocean and the Gulf Stream's water is cooled to about 15°C (60°F). Off the Grand Banks of Newfoundland the northern arm of the Gulf Stream loops around and flows toward western Greenland. Here its warming effect speeds the decay of ice brought southward by the East Greenland Current. Another branch of the Gulf Stream veers off in a northeast direction and flows to the southwest shores of Iceland. Although cooled now to 8°C (46°F), it has a warming effect on Iceland's climate.

The main arm of the Gulf Stream flows nearly due east and branches in two before reaching the European coastal network. The northern arm moves off in a northeasterly direction as a relatively warm current at a speed of about 20 kilometers (12 miles) a day. It bathes the shores of Ireland, England, Scotland, and Norway. The harbors of Norway are kept ice-free by this warm Atlantic water while the harbors of Labrador, which is farther south than Norway, do not benefit from Gulf Stream water and are iced over for several months of the year. The last of this northern branch of the Gulf Stream is lost in the Arctic Ocean, but not before providing a relatively favorable climate to Spitsbergen, a group of Norwegian islands in the Arctic Ocean, and keeping their west coast nearly free of ice.

The southern arm of the Gulf Stream loops down toward the northwest coast of Africa as a relatively cold current. Speeded up somewhat by the northeast trade winds, this arm of the Gulf Stream joins westward-flowing equatorial water and is carried back to Florida again where it completes its cycle.

Most of our geography books describe the Gulf Stream as a

river of warm water flowing toward the western coasts of Europe. Oceanographers prefer to think of the Gulf Stream as a "barrier current" that separates the warm, blue water of the Sargasso Sea in the central North Atlantic from the cold, green waters to the north.

What climate changes would occur if the Gulf Stream became weaker, or disappeared? According to the British oceanographer J. C. Swallow, "If it weakened, the climate of Europe would possibly become warmer because the warm Sargasso Sea water would be free to spread farther north and east. But we have too little knowledge to answer such questions with certainty."

HOW CURRENTS REGULATE CLIMATE

The Gulf Stream is a good example of global surface current patterns. The general pattern is one of nearly closed loops that turn clockwise in the Northern Hemisphere and counterclockwise in the Southern Hemisphere. The major currents tend to follow the pattern of the prevailing winds. When we realize that half the transfer of heat from equatorial regions toward the Arctic and Antarctic is due to ocean currents, we can begin to understand the importance of ocean currents to climate change.

There are many examples of the ways in which ocean currents affect climate (and more immediately the weather). They do so by carrying large amounts of heat or cold from one place to another. In winter, air near the seacoast generally is warmer than air inland. As we saw earlier, this is due to the ocean's ability to store heat for longer periods than the land can. Britain's mild winter climate is a good example of a land area that is kept warm in winter and cool in summer by surrounding seawater. In Maine, Massachusetts, Oregon, Washington, and northern California, people living near the coast generally do not experience temperatures as low as the temperatures reached farther inland.

A CURRENT THAT RAN AWAY

In 1925 the cold, northward-flowing Humboldt Current off the coast of Peru moved seaward and so touched off a chain reaction of climate-related events. The shift permitted warm equatorial waters to move down along the Peruvian coast, and consequently the temperature of the coastal water quickly rose by 5°C (9°F). This sharp rise turned out to be a killing temperature for the normally rich supply of tiny plant and animal organisms, called *plankton,* living in those waters. The warmer water also disturbed many small fish, which also have a small temperature-tolerance range. So large numbers of this important link in the food chain died either of too much heat or as a result of their plankton food supply being depleted. Larger fish that depended on the smaller fish for food were the next to go; their dead remains littered the shores for scores of kilometers. Thousands of sea birds living on the coast and nearby islands also died, since their food supply of the larger fish was also cut off.

But this was not the end link in the chain of ecological events. For years the Peruvians had "mined" many tons of the bird droppings, called *guano,* as a highly valued natural fertilizer. As long as the birds were abundant there was a plentiful supply of this economically important resource. The "small" change in the surface temperature of the water was enough to cause unusually heavy rains, which washed many tons of the guano deposits into the sea and so made it unavailable for human use. The rains gullied the neighboring dry land. It destroyed crops, buildings, roads, and many of the local plant and animal populations. In only a few weeks the current change had brought about dramatic changes on land and sea alike. Although a few months later the Humboldt Current moved back to its former position, years passed before the land recovered.

EARTH'S WATER CYCLE

More and more these days we read about a growing freshwater shortage. As the world's population continues to soar and as industrial development continues, there is an ever greater demand for fresh water by factories and people. Areas such as the Arab countries, southern California, and metro-

---

Earth's water cycle operates continuously as energy from the Sun evaporates water from the oceans and various land features. Then water vapor condenses as clouds and returns to Earth's surface in the form of precipitation.

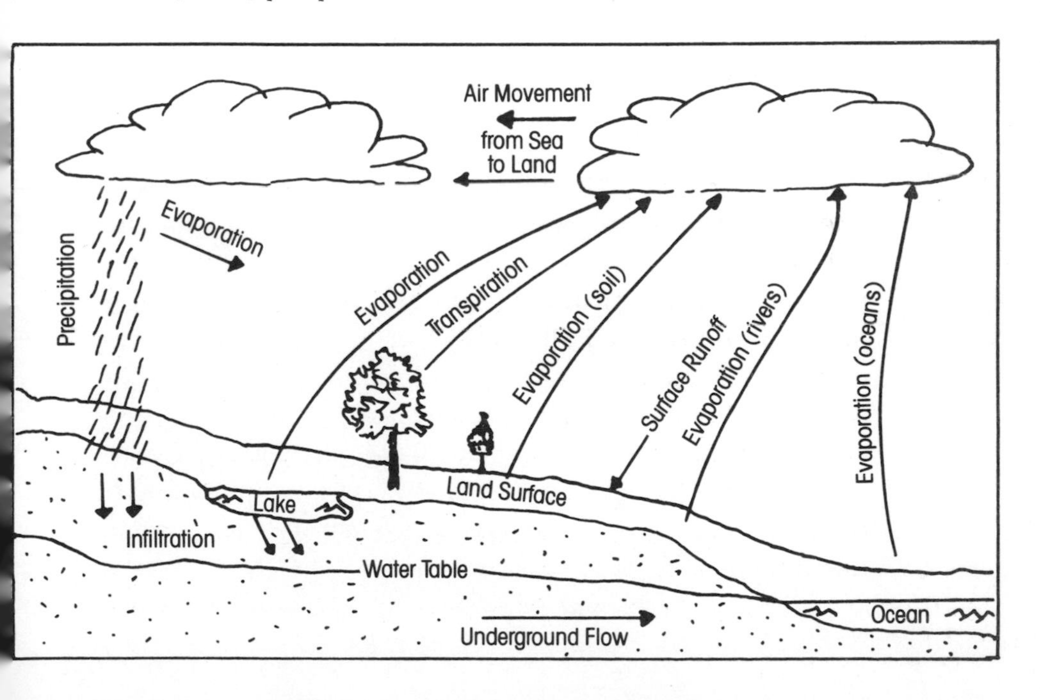

politan New York have experienced water shortages several times over the past two decades.

Earth's water originally was formed in a chemical reaction between oxygen and hydrogen deep within our planet hundreds of millions of years ago. It was then forcefully expelled into the air as water vapor by volcanoes. On cooling in the atmosphere it condensed into liquid water and fell as rain. This marked the beginning of what we call the *hydrologic cycle,* or water cycle.

Earth's supply of water is limited, although it is ever being exchanged between the atmosphere and surface through evaporation and condensation. Nearly all of the water in the atmosphere comes from the evaporation of ocean water into water vapor. On rising into the atmosphere, this warm, moist air is cooled and its water vapor condenses into fine water droplets that we see as clouds. When enough of these fine water droplets fuse into larger droplets they become heavy enough to fall out of the cloud as rain; they may be cooled enough to turn to snow crystals. When this liquid water reaches Earth's surface, some is absorbed by the ground, some evaporates again as water vapor, and some flows back to the sea as rivers and streams. While about 40 percent of our precipitation flows directly into the sea as runoff, the remaining 60 percent is returned to the atmosphere as water vapor. These are global average figures and do not apply to specific areas such as a tropical rain forest or the Sahara Desert.

If the 2.3 percent of Earth's water that is locked up as ice were to melt, it would cause a rise in sea level of about 80 meters (260 feet), a possibility we return to in a later chapter. By far most of Earth's water is stored in the ground, most of it being so deep beneath the surface that it is not available to the water cycle.

The water cycle, then, is another of those more than two

dozen pieces making up the climate puzzle. Any change in the water cycle is bound to bring about a change in climate. And changes in the circulation of Earth's atmosphere trigger regional changes in the water cycle since changes in atmospheric circulation involve the redistribution of moisture. Coupled with changes in the distribution of moisture is that of heat, carried either by the atmosphere or ocean currents. Where both heat and moisture are plentiful the water cycle is active and the region usually will be characterized as rainy tropics. Where atmospheric moisture is lacking but heat is plentiful, a region will be tropical desert and the water cycle nearly inactive. In very cold climates, moisture may be plentiful but heat in short supply, so the water cycle here tends to be limited. For example, heat carried by warm ocean currents into the polar regions is responsible for precipitation there. And energy from the Sun is the driving force of the entire system.

SORTING IT ALL OUT—OR TRYING TO

The main purpose of this chapter has been to describe briefly some of the more important ingredients of climate, and equally important, to suggest that each ingredient is ever changing and related to every other ingredient in the climate system. Since each ingredient is a changeable one, or a *variable* as the climatologist calls it, the job of trying to predict how a change in one variable might affect two or more other interacting variables is a monstrous one. It keeps several computers humming day and night as climatologists attempt to build mathematical models of our climate system. The mass, composition, and circulation of Earth's atmosphere, the movements of ocean currents, the topography of the land, Earth's rotation, insolation, and the hydrologic cycle are only a handful of climate variables that the computer must cope with.

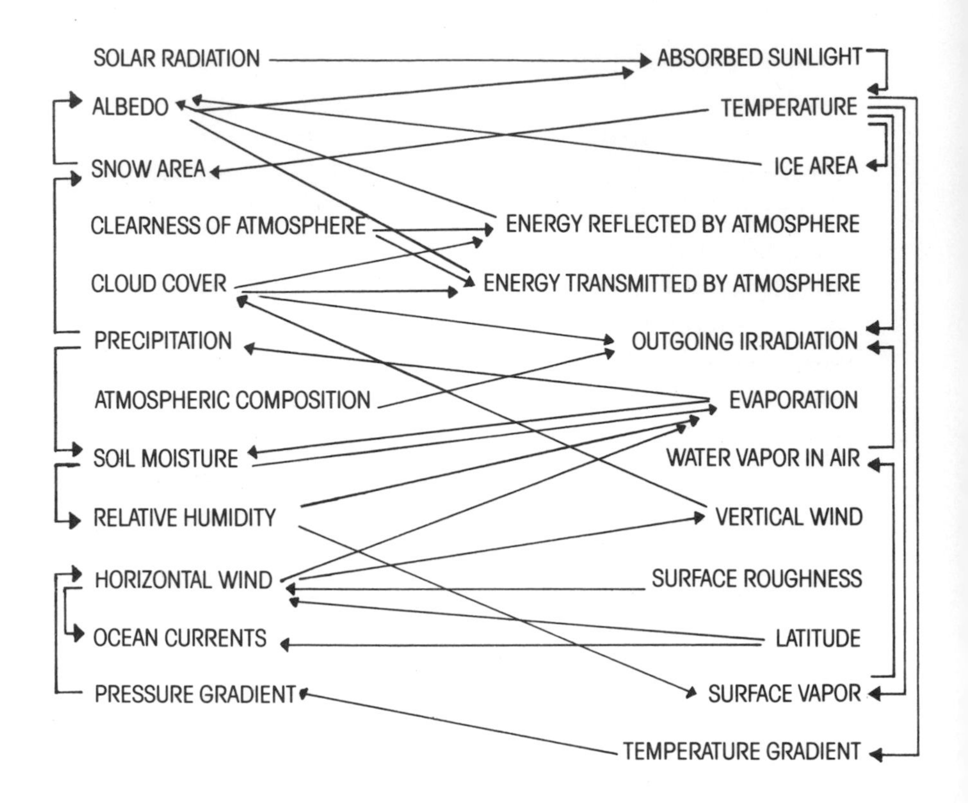

There are numerous variables, or changing conditions, that determine climate in a given area. Any one of these variables is related directly or indirectly to all the others. One of the tasks faced by climatologists is trying to predict how a change in one variable might affect two or more other interacting variables. AFTER W. W. KELLOGG AND STEPHEN H. SCHNEIDER

The world's population continues to increase wildly. So do man's industrial activities in order to keep pace with the growing numbers of people. Such runaway growth means that we release more and more heat into the atmosphere each year. Does this mean that the average global temperature of the atmosphere will steadily rise? Maybe; but maybe not. At this stage we cannot say for certain. The increased heat *might* cause the evaporation of more ocean water which would cause an increased amount of cloud covering, which in turn would reduce the amount of solar heating of the surface, which would tend to counteract the heating.

Or consider this possibility: If the heating happened to be concentrated in the Arctic or Antarctic, it *might* cause widespread melting of glacial ice and snow and so expose a greater surface area of water to sunlight. This would mean the absorption of an increased amount of solar energy by the newly exposed water area. Because water absorbs heat so much better than ice does, and stores it so well, this might result in a runaway warming. Or the effect of an increased cloud cover, which probably would result, might cancel out the effect of the melting ice or snow. "The range of possible interactions is staggering," according to W. W. Kellogg and Stephen H. Schneider, members of the Climate Project of the National Center for Atmospheric Research, Boulder, Colorado.

Before coming to grips with ways in which man may well be on the way to altering Earth's climate by releasing vast amounts of heat, carbon dioxide, and other agents in wholesale fashion into the atmosphere, we will first look into two intriguing aspects of Earth's climate: first, how Earth formed originally and evolved a primitive climate, and second, how Earth's climate has changed over the past hundreds of millions of years.

4

In the Beginning...

Earth's climate has not always been as it is today. It is characterized by change, not stability, just as our planet's animals and plants, mountains and rivers, and the very shapes and positions of continents have changed over the hundreds of millions of years of Earth's history.

In our search for a creation scheme that can account for the formation of planet Earth, we must not lose sight of the fact that Earth is but one of many members of a larger aggregate of matter, the Solar System. This Solar System is comprised of at least nine planets (plus a recently discovered miniplanet between Saturn and Uranus) accompanied by a total of at least 34 known satellites; thousands of rock fragments, called *asteroids,* occupying orbits between Mars and Jupiter; meteoroids; comets; and the Sun itself. Any hypothesis that attempts to account for the origin of any one of these components of the Solar System but ignores the others is of little use to us.

WHEN WAS EARTH FORMED?

Were the Sun, planets, and other objects in the Solar System formed at about the same time? Or did they come into being at different times? Evidence favors the first idea, that the Sun, Earth, and the other planets originated at about the same time out of the same cosmic "soup" of raw materials.

Astronomers take a number of approaches to this problem. One is to examine the Sun. First they can compute the amount of hydrogen fuel the Sun has available to keep its nuclear furnace going. They can also compute how rapidly the Sun is using up its fuel supply. Dividing the second quantity into the first shows that the life-span of a star like the Sun is about ten billion years. But the life-span of the Sun is not its age. By "age" astronomers mean the length of time the star or planet has been just about as we see it now—for example, the length of time the Sun has been pouring out energy at its present rate.

Unfortunately, we cannot reach out and tear a chunk out of the Sun to measure the age of its material. Instead we must be content to examine pieces of Earth rock, Moon rock, Mars rock, and cosmic stuff that rains down on Earth as meteorites. Geologists have measured the age of rock samples from every corner of Earth. The oldest rocks yet found from Earth's crust are from Greenland and are 3.8 billion years old. Rocks from other regions—for example, near the Great Lakes and in certain parts of Europe—are 3.5 billion years old. It is very unlikely that Earth crustal rocks will turn up that are much older than the oldest samples presently known. But that does not mean that Earth was formed only 3.8 billion years ago. That age is for rock that went through its most recent geological change that long ago. Earth's various rocks are continually changing as they are worn down by rain, wind, and other agents. In the process of being worn down, they turn into sediments such as sand and clay, which are then carried to the sea by streams and rivers. Millions of years later the sediments are thrust up as new mountains, such as the Rockies, which in turn are worn down as sediments again. While Earth has a recorded history going back at least 3.8 billion years, its history before that, or *prehistory*, is unknown to us by means of direct investigation.

The oldest Moon rocks that have yet been examined have a geologic history going back nearly a billion years earlier than the oldest Earth rocks. This makes sense if Earth and the Moon were formed at about the same time, because the Moon is smaller and would have cooled faster. Meteorites now appear to be the "senior citizens" of the Solar System. Many stony and iron meteorites show an average age of about 4.6 billion years. (How geologists find the age of rocks, meteorites, and other very ancient substances is examined later.) If we accept 4.6 billion years as an approximate age of the Solar System, then Earth went through about one billion years of geological and chemical evolution before a crust of solid rock developed. So all the evidence points to an age somewhere around five billion years for the formation of the Sun, planets, and other objects of the Solar System.

HOW WAS EARTH FORMED?

Around the mid-1700s, ideas suggesting how the Sun and planets were formed began to appear. The several hypotheses can be grouped into two main classes—*catastrophic* and *nebular*. Those of the catastrophic school imagine a ready-made Sun that was disturbed by a passing star or other large object that strayed close to the Sun. During the fly-by, gravitational attraction caused a great cloud of material to be torn out of both objects. The planets and all other objects of the Solar System presumably were formed out of this cast-off material.

Such an encounter would give rise to *two* planetary systems, one for each star.

During the 1940s, the catastrophic school began to fall out of favor with astronomers. The chances of two starlike objects colliding are very small, astronomers reasoned, so small that planetary systems formed in this way would be extremely rare events. On the other hand, according to the nebular hypothesis, the formation of planets is a natural result of star formation.

THE NEBULAR HYPOTHESIS

The nebular hypothesis starts with a large, cold cloud of gas and molecular dust out of which the Sun, Earth, and other planets were formed some five billion years ago. At that time the cloud is thought to have extended about 16 billion kilometers (ten billion miles) in diameter, which is about five billion kilometers (three billion miles) greater than the Solar System's present diameter. It also contained somewhat more matter than the Sun does today. Under gravitational attraction, the hypothesis goes on, the cloud gradually closed in on itself, spinning and flattening until it eventually became a huge rotating disk. About 95 percent or more of the cloud's gas and dust formed a sphere at the center of the disk. It was this densely packed globe of matter that eventually began to glow a dull red as it heated up and became a new star.

A great wheel of leftover material extended outward from the Sun's equator to a distance of about five billion kilometers (three billion miles)—about the present distance from the Sun of the planet Neptune. Like a phonograph record, the gas and dust making up the disk spun around the rotating solar hub. Within the disk many whirlpools formed, broke up, and formed again, but some of the larger and denser ones did not break up. They held together and swept up large amounts of surrounding gas and dust, growing more massive in the process. At least eight such whorls formed, each taking the shape of a sphere and eventually becoming one of the planets known to us today.

At first, the young Sun was a cool globe of gas that gradually drew large amounts of nearby disk material into itself. However, farther out in the disk at about the present distance of Jupiter, where the Sun's gravitational attraction was weaker because of the greater distance, large amounts of disk material remained. This would account for the fact that Mercury, Venus, Earth, and Mars are relatively small planets compared with the more distant and massive Jupiter, Saturn, Uranus, and Neptune.

Internal gravitation of the young Sun caused it to collapse in on itself. In the process, material in the core region was packed together with tremendous force. As the material became more and more tightly packed, the Sun continued to heat up and became increasingly brighter.

During these early years in the formation of the Solar System, astronomers picture the young Sun as a relatively cool red object producing energy in a way quite different from the way it does now. Surrounding the new Sun was a dense fog of gas and dust through which the newly forming planets moved. Space throughout the Solar System at this time must have been opaque. As this gas and dust was continually being swept up by the young planets, hydrogen (H) atoms in the fog probably were combining with carbon (C) atoms and producing the gas methane (CH_4). Hydrogen also would be combining with nitrogen (N) atoms to produce ammonia (NH_3), and with oxygen (O) atoms to produce water vapor (H_2O).

Evidence for such a process of the building up of heavier groupings of atoms comes not only from the laboratory, but from our studies of the giant planets Jupiter and Saturn. Because of their large mass, gravity on those planets is much stronger than on Earth. This means that while Earth could not hold on to its primitive atmosphere, having lost more than 90 percent of it, Jupiter and Saturn probably kept most of theirs. To this day the atmospheres of those giant planets probably are the same as when the planets were formed. They are known to consist of methane, ammonia, water vapor, hydrogen, and helium. But by far most of their matter is hydrogen and helium.

YOUNG EARTH AS A HOT PLANET

According to scientists, after Earth condensed from a sphere of gas and molecular dust, its gravitation would have caused its matter to pack more and more tightly around the core. This compaction, accompanied by heating resulting from radioactive materials, would have heated up the planet rapidly to a temperature of about 1,200 K (2,000°F). Such heating would cause iron and other heavy materials to sink toward the core region. Lighter-weight materials, such as the silicate rocks presently forming Earth's crust, would tend to float in the soup of denser materials. During some such process of separation, many gases would bubble out of solution and collect above the new planet as a primitive atmosphere. Among such gases would be large amounts of hydrogen (H), water vapor (H_2O), nitrogen (N_2), methane (CH_4), hydrogen sulfide (H_2S), and ammonia (NH_3).

As more and more water vapor collected in the atmosphere, it would be cooled, condense out, and fall as rain. Because Earth's surface probably was still hot during this period, the new rains would vaporize on contact with the ground. But gradually as the crust cooled, the torrential rains would begin to form pools that in time developed into local ponds and then lakes and then seas. Meanwhile, ultraviolet energy from the Sun would have broken down some of the complex gases of the atmosphere. For example, ammonia would be changed into free hydrogen and molecules of nitrogen (N_2), methane into carbon and hydrogen, and water vapor into hydrogen and oxygen. The free hydrogen would be so light that most of it would escape Earth's gravitational grip. Many of the free oxygen atoms would have joined and formed ozone (O_3). And gradually a layer of ozone would block out most of the ultraviolet energy, a condition essential to the development of life.

Many such reactions would have been taking place in Earth's primitive atmosphere, which in no way resembled Earth's atmosphere today. So, if earth scientists are correct, some 400 million years after our planet had developed a solid, cool crust, it accumulated its first seas and had an atmosphere made up mainly of methane, ammonia, and water vapor. That atmosphere was more like the present atmospheres of Jupiter and Saturn.

So about 4.5 billion years ago, Earth had primitive seas in which currents could move about; it had a primitive atmosphere to be put into circulation by energy of the Sun; and it rotated on its axis (and very likely much more rapidly than it does today). In short, it had all the ingredients necessary for climate evolution.

THE FIRST LIVING THINGS

Biologists have discovered fossils of primitive algaelike organisms that lived about 3.5 billion years ago. These organisms play an important part in our story about Earth's climate. They may have contributed significantly to climate change as they gave rise to more advanced organisms that caused Earth's atmosphere to evolve in an important way. Unlike their 3.5 billion-year-old ancestors who relied on ready-made food in their environment, these newer organisms made their own food (a form of sugar called *glucose*) through a process called *photosynthesis*. Just as all green plants do today, these ancient organisms combined carbon dioxide from the atmosphere with water by using energy from the Sun to drive the chemical reaction. In the process they gave off free oxygen (O_2) as a by-product:

CO_2	+	H_2O	→	$[CH_2O]$	+	H_2O	+	$O_2\uparrow$
Carbon Dioxide		Water Vapor		Glucose		Water		Oxygen

The accumulating supply of free oxygen in the atmosphere would have acted on the remaining methane by breaking it down and changing it into carbon dioxide and water vapor. This free oxygen also would have broken down ammonia and changed it into free nitrogen and water vapor. Eventually, that would have led to our present atmospheric mixture of about 78 percent nitrogen and 21 percent oxygen.

Changes in atmospheric composition must eventually lead to climate change. One of the large questions climatologists are now asking is *how much* of a change in atmospheric composition does it take to trigger a change in climate? The answer is not yet known. Let's consider two extreme (by Earth standards) cases in atmospheric change bringing about dramatic changes in climate—the planets Venus and Mars.

THE CLIMATE OF VENUS

Venus is very nearly the same size as Earth. And because it was formed in essentially the same region of space as Earth was, it must also have condensed out of the same original materials as Earth did. It therefore seems likely that Venus's structure and composition might be rather similar to those of Earth. But there the similarities end.

Venus happens to have 90 times more atmospheric pressure

As viewed by Mariner 10 *in February, 1974, Venus's clouds are seen as a pattern of swirls. This photograph was taken from a height of about 5,800 kilometers (3,600 miles) and was made at ultraviolet wavelengths. The dark regions in the cloud deck are not the planet's surface but some substance that absorbs ultraviolet radiation.* JET PROPULSION LABORATORY

---

at the surface than we do! Where the bulk (78 percent) of Earth's atmosphere is nitrogen, nearly all (97 percent) of Venus's air is carbon dioxide gas. Venus's upper clouds contain traces of carbon monoxide (CO) and some water vapor. The carbon monoxide is a result of carbon dioxide molecules being broken down into carbon monoxide, and oxygen being given off. The energy source driving this chemical breakdown is ultraviolet radiation from the Sun. For each part of carbon monoxide formed, there should also be one part of oxygen released ($CO_2 \rightarrow CO + O$). In other words, we would expect to find 50 percent carbon monoxide and 50 percent oxygen. But we don't. Instead there is 50 times less oxygen than that!

Although there are traces of water vapor in Venus's upper atmosphere, the relative humidity seems never to reach even as much as 1 percent, so Earth-like showers cannot occur on Venus. Instead, Venus's clouds are composed of highly corrosive sulfuric acid! In addition, there is hydrogen chloride and hydrogen fluoride. When dissolved in water, these two agents make two other highly corrosive substances—hydrochloric acid and hydrofluoric acid. If these substances were in our atmosphere, they would soon combine with the rocky material at the surface and be neutralized. How those acids stay in Venus's atmosphere as clouds is a mystery. The planet's surface must be very different from Earth's.

Russia's *Venera 8,* which landed on Venus's surface in 1972, measured winds aloft blowing at more than 320 kilometers (200 miles) an hour. At the surface, however, the winds were gentle. From an altitude of about 30 kilometers (20 miles) above Venus's surface a light rain or mist of acid falls through the dense air and eventually to the ground. On Earth such an acid mist would quickly dissolve sulfur, mercury, lead, tin, and nearly all our surface rocks. Exactly what Venus's surface chemistry is like remains a mystery.

Venus's extremely dense and acid atmosphere acts as a heat trap for long-wave (heat) radiation from the planet's surface. As a result, there is a greenhouse effect that keeps the surface of the planet at a temperature of about 480°C (900°F). Earth's large organic molecules of living matter would quickly fall apart under such high temperatures. Venus, it now appears, has the hottest climate in the Solar System.

How can we account for Venus's dense atmosphere of carbon

dioxide? Although Earth has about as much carbon dioxide as Venus has, most of ours is locked up in rocks as carbonates. We can imagine a time when Venus more closely resembled Earth in atmospheric density and temperature. But something happened to change its atmosphere, and with devastating results to its climate. Because of Venus's closeness to the Sun, we can imagine a greenhouse effect gradually heating up the planet until temperatures at its surface become high enough to boil away the surface waters. Water vapor accumulating in the atmosphere would add to the greenhouse effect, trap heat radiation from the surface, and so cause the temperature to soar. Eventually, temperatures would be high enough to liberate the vast stores of CO_2 locked up in the rocks. Astronomers do not know if that is what actually happened, but it seems a possible explanation.

THE CLIMATE OF MARS

Like Venus, Mars also was formed in a region of space neighboring that of Earth, so Mars evolved compounds like those on Earth—for example, minerals made up of varying combinations of magnesium, silicon, iron, oxygen, and sulfur.

Like Earth, Mars acquired its primitive atmosphere by the venting of gases from the hot interior, but this "outgassing" activity on Mars was much less than on Earth. The gases involved include carbon dioxide, methane, nitrogen, hydrogen, and water vapor. Mars' low surface gravity (only four-tenths that of Earth's) allowed most of the planet's vented hydrogen, a lightweight gas, to escape. Gradually the atmosphere acquired more and more carbon dioxide, which is much heavier than hydrogen.

Today the Martian atmosphere is mostly carbon dioxide with about 2 percent argon (compared with Earth's 0.03 percent carbon dioxide and 1 percent argon), only 0.01 percent water vapor, and trace amounts of nitrogen. The original amount of nitrogen in the Martian atmosphere was probably ten times the present value. Nearly all of Mars' water supply is locked up in the planet's polar caps and permafrost (compared with between 2 and 3 percent for Earth). If the Martian ice could be released as liquid water, there would be enough to form a planet-wide layer nearly 14 meters (45 feet) deep. So there is not necessarily a "shortage" of water on Mars—the water just happens not to be available in a liquid state during this particular period in Mars' evolution as a planet. We can regard the planet as gripped in an ice age. The Martian atmosphere also contains trace amounts of ozone and hydrogen. Quite likely, along with the escape of free hydrogen from the top of Mars' atmosphere, oxygen, nitrogen, and carbon dioxide also are presently escaping.

The Martian atmospheric pressure at the surface amounts to only about 130 times that on Earth at sea level. This is so little pressure that a container of liquid water placed on Mars' surface would vaporize explosively, just as a container of liquid air vaporizes when exposed to sea-level pressure on Earth. At one time Mars' atmospheric pressure may have been about half that at sea level on Earth.

The amount of carbon dioxide in the Martian atmosphere varies from day to night and from season to season, as the temperature varies from about 24°C (75°F) at the Equator at noon down to about −100°C (−150°F) at the poles. Since carbon dioxide condenses at about that temperature, clouds composed of a mixture of water-ice, dry-ice (solid carbon dioxide), and dust are common.

When the polar temperatures increase during seasonal change, large masses of water vapor and carbon dioxide are vaporized, thus temporarily increasing the mass of the atmosphere. The denser atmosphere then is a better medium to transfer heat. This further warms the polar ice and so releases still more carbon dioxide and water vapor. This condition may temporarily build up the Martian atmosphere to densities approaching Earth values.

Has the Martian climate always been as it is today? We can

This spectacular Martian feature is the Tithonius Chasma, about 75 kilometers (47 miles) wide. Part of the Valles Marineris, an extensive canyon, the structure may have been formed as a result of crustal movement. The fingerlike projections may have been formed by running water in ages past when Mars may have had a dense atmosphere and abundant water. JET PROPULSION LABORATORY.

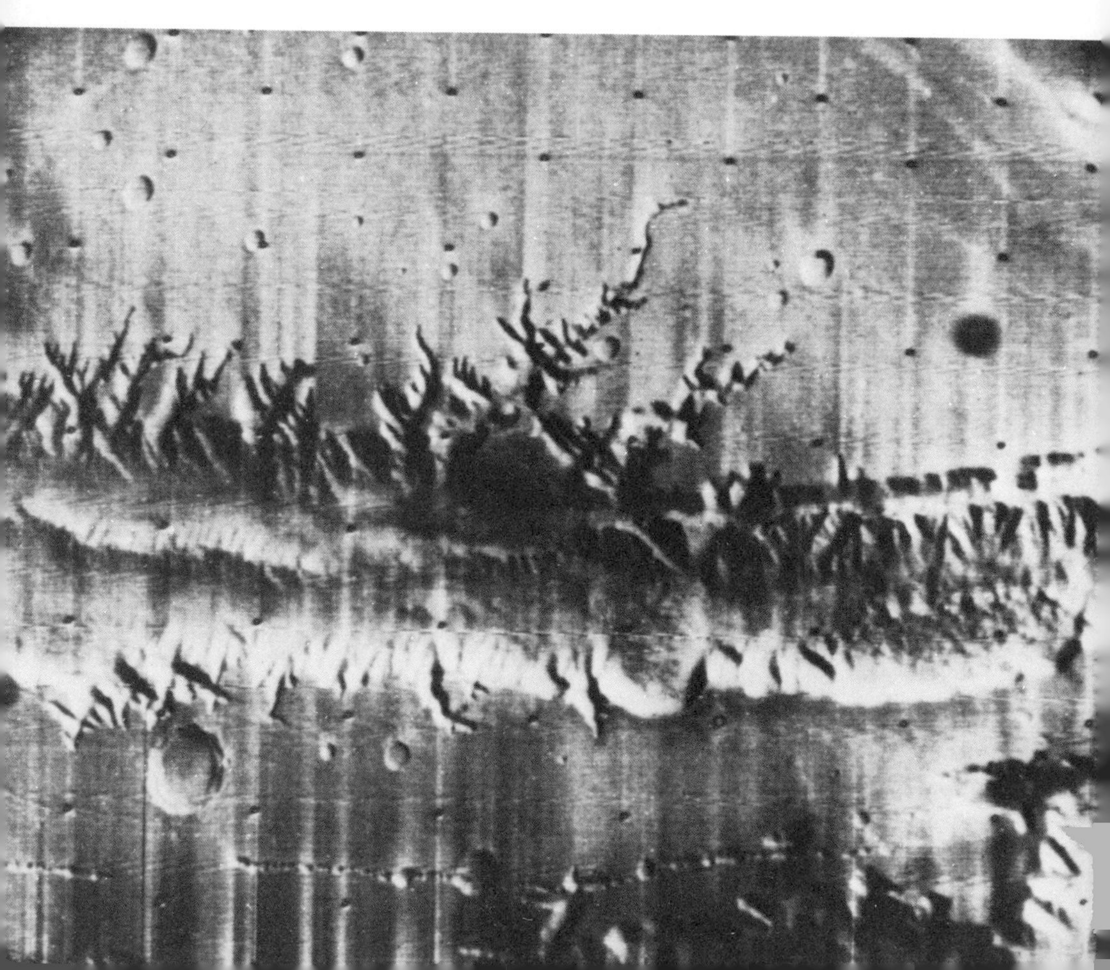

be certain that it has not. Evidence we can read in the surface features of the red planet point to a time when Mars had a climate not too unlike that on Earth today. But this possibility is still open to debate.

Like Earth, Mars has a precessional wobble. While it takes Earth about 25,800 years to complete one precessional loop, it takes Mars about twice that long. The astronomer Carl Sagan has suggested that Mars may now be in the grips of precessional winter, with an extensive polar ice cap in the Northern Hemisphere containing the bulk of the planet's potential atmospheric mass. If so, then 25,000 years ago the planet would also have been in the grip of precessional winter, but this time with the bulk of the atmosphere locked up in the Southern Hemisphere ice cap. But 12,000 years ago the planet would have been enjoying precessional spring and summer, "a time on Mars of balmy temperatures, soft nights, and the trickle of liquid water down innumerable streams and rivulets, rushing out to join mightily gushing rivers," according to Sagan. "If so," he goes on, "twelve thousand years ago was a good time on Mars for life similar to the terrestrial sort. If I were an organism on Mars, I might gear my activities to the precessional summers and close up shop in the precessional winters—as many organisms do on Earth for our much shorter annual winters. I would make spores; I would make vegetative forms; I would go into cryptobiotic repose; I would hibernate until the long winter had subsided."

We have taken this detailed look at the atmospheres of Venus and Mars because there is a lesson here for us Earth dwellers. To what extent can we keep pouring heat, carbon dioxide, dust, and other materials into our own atmosphere before triggering a pronounced change in climate? We return to this vital question in Chapter 9.

Meanwhile we have left Earth at an age of about a billion

or so years. We have evidence for the existence of primitive photosynthesizing life forms around that time. The presence of such life forms suggests a mean climate, neither extremely hot nor extremely cold. It also suggests the presence of liquid water and of an atmosphere that was gradually becoming oxygen-rich.

We then ask what happened to Earth's climate over the millions and hundreds of millions of years after that and what effects it had on an equal number of life forms that subsequently arose, lived, and died since those remote times. But first we should take a brief look at some of the methods scientists use to reconstruct Earth's distant past.

5

Uncovering Earth's Ancient Climates

THE STORIES FOSSILS TELL

Let us take a fossil and its piece of rock as an example. The fossil is a kind that we can find in a quarry near Liverpool, in England.

In this quarry, the rocks are a reddish color, which tells us that the rocks were made from a desert sand. At some time in the past, then, this place near Liverpool was a hot, sandy desert. If we look around, we might find a slab of this reddish rock that shows a change in the conditions long ago. On this slab we can see something which is very familiar. There are ripple marks on it, the same sort of marks we see on a wave-washed beach—but turned to stone. So the sand forming this slab of the rock was once part of a beach and, when the wind blew, the water rose up in waves and made these ripple marks.

Another slab of rock from this same quarry can show us something equally interesting. On the flat surface, where it has been broken out of the quarry, we may see the pitted marks of raindrops. If we can find several of these slabs and can work out their original position in the quarry, they will tell us the direction of the wind that blew the rain that made these pitted marks nearly 200 million years ago!

Not very far away from our quarry, we may come upon the footprints of a number of little animals. Some of these footprints are rather like a human hand: there are five fingers and one is bent back like a thumb. But if we find a trail of these footprints we may be very puzzled for the "thumbs" are on the outside of the print. When these little trails were first found scientists could not understand them. One even drew the animal walking with crossed legs so that its thumbs would be in the correct position! Later scientists realized that the fifth toe was not a thumb at all but a shorter outside toe that many reptiles have.

These footprints, then, were made by a little reptile. No one has found the bones of this reptile, but lots of footprints have been found and we have been able to work out much about the animal; where it lived and what it lived on, and therefore what it was looking for as it wandered about.

As well as these handlike footprints, we can find a number of much smaller footprints of little animals that apparently ran along in a lizardlike way. From other pieces of rock we can learn a little of the plants that grew in this sandy place.

In this way we can learn what it was like just outside Liverpool 200 million years ago: the plants that grew there, the animals that lived there, and what the climate was like.

—William Elgin Swinton (1961)

The major concern of this chapter is how scientists are able to reconstruct climate changes in Earth's past and determine the effects those changes have had on living organisms.

Our knowledge of Earth's past climates unfolds in much

the same way as the solution of a crime, step by step. The investigator first gathers all the clues he can find. One clue may not tell him very much, but a second, third, and still more clues begin to paint a picture of how the crime was committed, and eventually lead to the guilty one.

The scientific investigator, in this case the *paleoclimatologist* ("paleo" means *old*), also collects clues. Among them are fossils of plants and animals. For example, lots of fossil remains of different kinds of reptiles discovered in a certain rock layer would be an important clue to the paleoclimatologist. Reptiles are cold-blooded animals and so depend on heat from their surroundings to drive their body chemistry because they have no built-in way of regulating their own body temperature. Such a find would suggest that the region experienced a relatively warm climate, since these animals could not survive in a cold climate. Another clue would be the age of the rock in which the fossil had been preserved, and so on.

HOW FOSSILS ARE USED

Fossils also provide important clues about the changing positions of seas and land masses through geologic time, as you found from the Liverpool story. Because such animals as corals, brachiopods, and trilobites have lived only in the sea, any rocks that now contain traces of those organisms must at one time have been part of the sea floor. If we follow the curving shoreline of an ancient inland sea now marked by rock containing marine fossils, we can trace the outline of that sea and show its position on a map. The old stems of fossilized trees found where they originally grew tell us of a former land area. We then know that an ancient sea did not cover that area at the time the trees were growing there.

The discovery of fossil tree ferns and fossil magnolias in Antarctica and Greenland is clear evidence that those ice-covered regions once had temperate or even tropical climates and were located in changing positions on the globe. Coal deposits often contain tree ferns and other plants. The presence of these plants in a region that is now gripped by cold shows that at the time the plants were alive the region was warm and swampy.

It was the English surveyor and civil engineer William Smith who around 1800 discovered that a given rock layer usually contains only certain kinds of fossils. The younger rock layers above and the older rock layers below have different kinds of fossils. At about the same time, scientists in France were drawing much the same conclusions that Smith was. But they also observed that fossils from the higher and, therefore, younger rock layers were more like modern forms of life than those fossils from older rock layers located deeper in the ground.

The fact that one rock layer of fossils sandwiched between two other layers is older than the top layer but younger than the bottom layer tells us only the *relative* ages of the three layers. It tells us nothing about their *absolute* age, or their actual age in years. To find out how old this or that layer of rock is—and therefore any fossils it may contain—the scientist turns to another method.

TELLING GEOLOGIC TIME WITH ATOMIC CLOCKS

Our estimates of the age of Earth as a planet, and of various rock samples taken here and there at various places, is based on radioactive dating.

Early in this century earth scientists developed a means of measuring the absolute age of rocks and certain fossils. They use the atoms of certain elements as atomic clocks, a method called *radiometric dating*. In the 1800s scientists discovered that chemical elements such as uranium, potassium, and

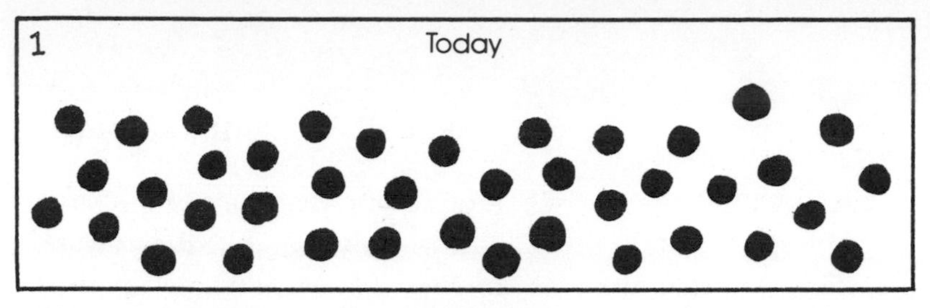

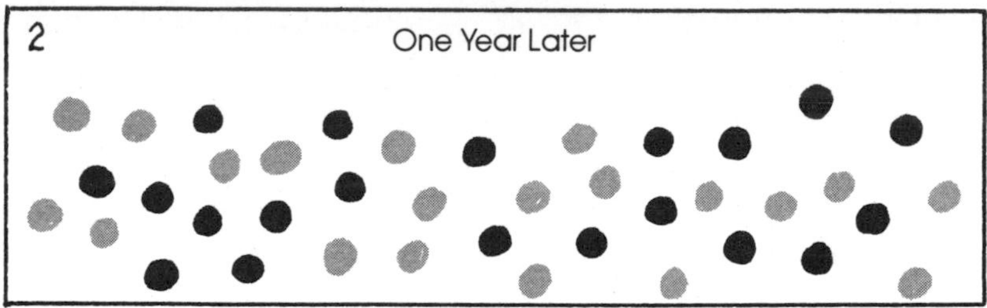

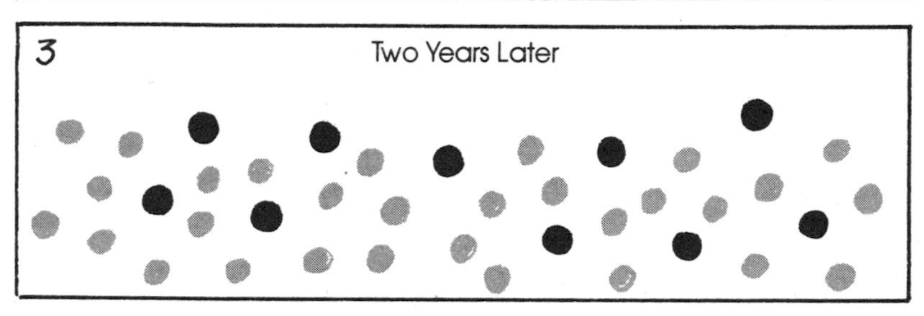

Measuring the Half-Life of a Radioactive Element
See text for details.

---

thorium are radioactive, that is, their atoms gradually break down by giving off certain particles. As they do, these atoms turn into the atoms of different elements. For example, both uranium and thorium turn into lead. Potassium turns into argon.

Here is a simple way of understanding how radioactive elements can be used as atomic clocks:

Suppose that you have a box containing 12,800 black marbles, as shown in the top diagram. You want to find out how old the box of marbles is. Imagine that the black marbles "age" by turning into gray ones. In one year, half of the black marbles turn to gray ones, as shown in the middle diagram. So at the end of that first year there would be 6,400 black marbles left and 6,400 gray ones. At the end of the second year, half of the remaining 6,400 black marbles have turned to gray ones, as shown in the bottom diagram. There would then be 3,200 black and 9,600 gray marbles. This process would go on until eventually there would be no more black marbles left to turn to gray. Our clock would have run down.

If you counted 800 black marbles and 12,000 gray ones, you would know that four years had gone by since the first black marble changed. But you would not need to go to all that trouble since you could use a sampling technique. Just scoop one thousand or so marbles out of the box and then count black and gray ones. You could then divide the number of black ones by the number of gray ones to get the black-to-gray ratio, as shown in the right-hand column of the table.

Telling the Passage of Time with Black Marbles Changing to Gray

Passage of Time in Years	Number of Black Marbles	Number of Gray Marbles	Black-Gray Ratio
0	12,800	0	0
1	6,400	6,400	1:1
2	3,200	9,600	1:3
3	1,600	11,200	1:7
4	800	12,000	1:15
5	400	12,400	1:31
6	200	12,600	1:63
7	100	12,700	1:127
8	50	12,750	1:255
9	25	12,775	1:511

This is how an atomic clock works. The scientist measures the ratio between the number of unchanged atoms of a radioactive element and the number of new, or "daughter," products that have formed. The amount of time needed for half of the atoms of a radioactive element to change is called the element's *half-life*. Nothing seems to affect the half-life of any radioactive element—neither changes in temperature nor changes in pressure. Since the scientist knows the half-life of the radioactive element, and since he can measure the ratio of the numbers of new and old atoms, he can then tell how long the clock has been "running."

Different radioactive elements have different half-lives. Shown here are five different radioactive elements that are used to tell the absolute age of rocks, the elements they change into, and their half-lives.

The Half-Lives of Five Radioactive Elements

This radioactive element . . .	changes into . . .	and has a half-life of
Uranium–238	Lead–206	4,510 million years
Uranium–235	Lead–207	713 million years
Potassium–40	Argon–40	1,350 million years
Rubidium–40	Strontium–87	6 million years
Rubidium–87	Strontium–87	47,000 million years

Usually, only very small amounts of a radioactive material are present in a rock being dated. This means that the slightest error in measurement may mean a large error in the ratio between the two elements. It would be like taking a sample of only ten marbles rather than 1,000. The point is that a sample of 1,000 is more representative of the total of the blacks and grays among 12,800 marbles than a sample of only ten marbles.

A slight error in measurement of a small radioactive sample may mean a difference of millions of years in the final absolute-age figure. Just a 5 percent error in a 100-million-year-old rock might mean an error of five million years. This would be just a little less than three times the age of all humanity itself.

Scientists make two assumptions when they date materials by the radioactive decay method. In the potassium-argon series, for example, they assume that potassium or argon atoms have not been added to the rock in question since it was formed. Secondly, they assume that argon atoms were not present in the rock originally. Although many rocks are known to have contained some of the "daughter" product (argon in our example), scientists can determine how much of the "daughter" product there was originally. They can then subtract that amount from the total amount of "daughter" product measured and so end up with a reliable measurement of the amount produced by radioactive decay. Because radioactive potassium is so common throughout Earth's crustal rock, it can be used to date many different kinds of rocks.

For the paleoclimatologist interested in very ancient climates, radiometric dating and a careful study of fossils are basic information. Knowing how fossils have changed during early geological history enables scientists to reconstruct the duration and range of past temperature and moisture conditions. To find out about climate change in more recent times, climatologists turn to other methods.

DATING ONCE–LIVING MATERIALS

Since all living matter known to us contains carbon, this element can be used as an atomic clock to date the remains of once-living materials. Ordinary carbon is in the form of carbon–12. The form used as a short-term atomic clock is carbon–14, which has a slightly more massive nucleus. Carbon–14 is continually being produced in the atmosphere out of nitrogen–14. This occurs as the nitrogen–14 is bombarded by energetic particles from space called *cosmic rays*. Green plants continually take in carbon–14 right along with carbon–12 as they take in carbon dioxide, which contains both forms of carbon, in the process of photosynthesis. So green plants, and all the organisms that depend on them for food, which includes almost all organisms, take in carbon–14. But carbon–14 does not remain as carbon–14 once it is a part of the organism. Instead it changes back into nitrogen–14.

When a plant or animal dies, it stops taking in carbon–14, so the amount of carbon–14 an organism contains immediately begins to decrease the moment the organism dies. When an old bone, shell, or other piece of organic material being dated is analyzed, the scientist looks for the ratio of carbon–14 to ordinary carbon. That ratio reveals the age of the organic sample. Since carbon–14 has a half-life of only 5,730 years, it is useful only for short-term dating (although recent reports suggest that carbon–14 may be used to date materials as old as 100,000 years).

The carbon–14 method has proved extremely useful in dating wood, charcoal, peat, bones, marine shells, and other organic materials. Scientists make two assumptions when they use carbon–14 as an atomic clock: (1) that all organisms take in carbon–14 at a more rapid rate than the rate at which it decays into nitrogen–14 in their living tissues; and (2) that the rate of carbon–14 production in the atmosphere is fairly constant, as is the ratio of carbon–14 to carbon–12.

THE TALES OF TREE GROWTH RINGS

Once the climatologist has dated the remains of an ancient fossil tree by the carbon–14 method, he can examine the tree's annual growth rings and find out about the rainfall pattern

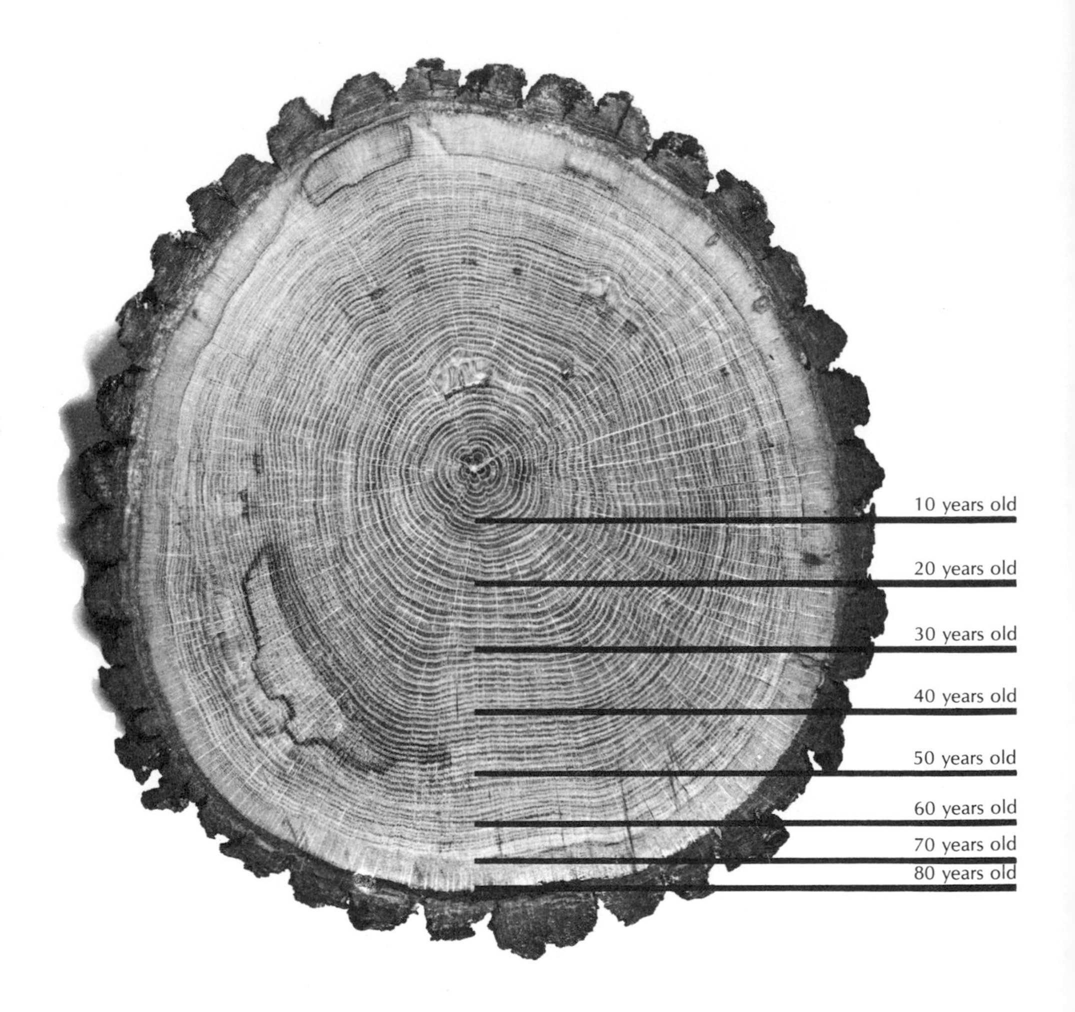

By examining the annual growth rings of certain trees, climatologists can estimate the rainfall pattern during the time a tree was alive. Thick rings indicate years of abundant rainfall. Thin rings indicate below normal rainfall. The total number of rings is a clue to the tree's age when it died.

during the time the tree was alive. Or, if the tree is still alive, he can find its age by counting the growth rings, a method called *dendrochronology* ("dendro" means *tree*; "chronology" means *time*). California's giant Sequoia trees reveal an age up to 4,000 years, and bristlecone pines to about 5,000 years. Records in tree rings for fossil trees go back even further in time, to about 8,000 years ago.

In some geographical areas, there happens to be a close relationship between a combination of the temperature and the amount of rainfall in a given year and the width of a tree's annual growth ring for that year. Plentiful rainfall and warm temperatures mean rapid growth and relatively wide growth rings; a cool season with little rainfall means little growth and relatively narrow growth rings. Tree-ring growth in the interior plains and plateaus of the United States and Canada reveals some interesting climate changes that have occurred over the past 850 years. For example, during nearly all of the thirteenth century the climate was dry, but then the fourteenth century had a stormy climate. The last 25 years of the sixteenth century was the driest period in the last 650 years. We will have much more to say about these periods of drought later.

Gleaning clues about ancient climates by examining tree rings is not as easy as it might seem because the width of the rings is affected by *both* rainfall *and* temperature. Does a thick ring suggest a season of plentiful rain or an unusually warm growing season with moderate rain? It is not easy to answer such a question. That is why climatologists rarely use tree-ring evidence all by itself. Rather they use it with as many other bits of information as they can gather from other sources.

Before leaving the subject of dendrochronology, it is worth mentioning this interesting fact. Carbon–14 dating of ancient trees does not always agree with annual growth-ring counts.

Since tree-ring counts have been carried back about 8,000 years, scientists can compare the carbon–14 method of dating with the tree-ring method that far back in time. All seems to be well for a tree sample up to about 2,000 years old. When both methods are used to date the sample, both show the same age—again, for tree samples up to about 2,000 years old. But for samples older than about 2,000 years, the two methods do not agree. For example, while a tree-ring count may put the age of a fossil tree at 4,600 years, the carbon–14 age turns out to be only 4,000 years. The age gap between the methods keeps widening from about age 2,000 to about age 6,000 years.

Why there should be such differences is not at all well understood. We have said that scientists using the carbon–14 method of dating make the assumption that the rate of carbon–14 production in the atmosphere is fairly constant, as is the ratio of carbon–14 to carbon–12. But is that actually the case? Possibly there have been several upsets in the carbon cycle of the atmosphere and oceans in the past. And perhaps there have been times of very active cosmic-ray activity alternating with times of little such activity. This would change the rate at which carbon–14 in the atmosphere is produced. Now consider the enormous amounts of oil, coal, and other fossil fuels we are burning each year, and have been burning since the late 1800s. Also consider that man keeps pouring carbon dioxide into the atmosphere at an ever-increasing rate. Now it just happens that all those fossil fuels are so old that the carbon contained in the carbon dioxide they release is virtually all carbon–12, since the carbon–14 these fuels once contained has long since decayed into nitrogen–14. In other words, the ratio of carbon–14 to carbon–12 may well not be "fairly constant." Another way the ratio may have been upset is by the testing of atomic bombs, which produce carbon–14. According to environmental scientist Arthur N. Strahler, "at one time this man-made radiocarbon raised the total atmospheric radiocarbon to a level 100 percent above the normal value, and at present it is about 60 percent above normal."

VARVES AS CLUES TO PAST CLIMATES

Another short-term means of deciphering past climates is by studying samples called *varves,* the built-up layers of silt and clay laid down on the bottoms of lakes and ponds year by year. Varves provide climate records going back only a few thousand years. And the bodies of water being studied must have been subject to seasonal freezing and thawing.

In summer all kinds of materials, including dust carried by the atmosphere, enter the lake and slowly settle down to the lake bottom. In winter, however, the surface ice prevents foreign matter from entering the lake. Only the fine clays already suspended in the water settle out and sink to the bottom. A long hollow tube pushed deeply into the soft bottom of a lake can bring up 20 or more varve layers representing an equal number of years' deposits. No two years produce quite the same thickness of varve layering. The thickness of a varve indicates the amount of silt deposited during summer, which in turn depends largely on the strength of the spring thaw and resulting flooding. Heavy rainfall during a summer will cause relatively large amounts of soil to be washed into a lake by runoff and so contribute to the thickness of varves.

Varve records also reveal quite accurately the dates of the recession of glaciers. This is because varves cannot form beneath glaciers any more than they can form beneath a lake permanently topped with a layer of ice. So a lake bed only recently exposed by the retreat of a glacier will have relatively young varves compared with an old lake bed long free of glacial activity. In Scandinavia, for instance, varve records go back about 13,700 years. Because the youngest varves are found in

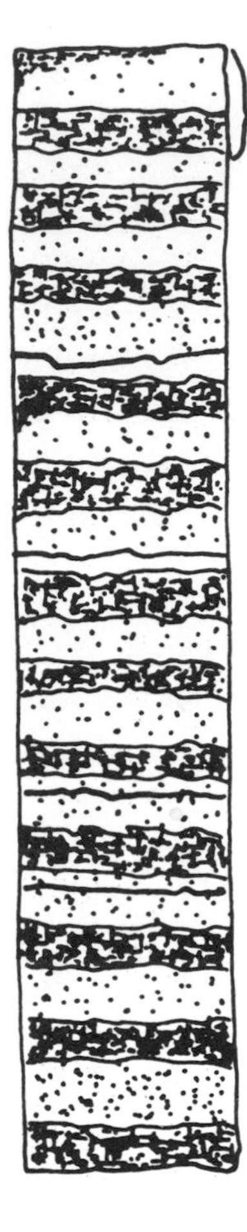

The dark bands in this schematic diagram of a varve represent silt and other matter deposited on a lake bottom during summer. The lighter bands represent deposits of clay that slowly settled to the bottom during winter when the lake was frozen over. So one dark band plus a neighboring light band represent one year's deposit.

the north and the oldest ones in the south, it is an easy matter to trace the history of the last ice sheet as it retreated northward.

There are also fossil varves. These are formed as the soft materials forming a lake bottom or ocean bottom are gradually compressed and over millions of years turned to rock. At some later period that rock is then thrust up as part of a new mountain. A geologist studying a sample of this fossil varve can read it in much the same way as he can read a fresh sample of varves removed from a lake bottom only yesterday. Scientists working in Alberta, Canada, have uncovered a fossil varve record 300 million years old and spanning a period of 900 years. Here is a record of climate change over a period of nine centuries during the upper Devonian, when most of North America was covered by shallow seas, a time known as "The Age of Fishes."

SOILS AS CLUES TO PAST CLIMATES

Ancient soils also serve as climate indicators, but only of the past million or so years. As varves show a sequence of differing layers, so does a core sample of soil. One such soil core taken in Czechoslovakia reveals the sequence of alternating warm and cool periods for nearly a million years. One of the clues is the presence in certain of the soil layers of tiny snails known to be of a cold-dwelling kind.

EVIDENCE FROM POLLEN

Rocks formed out of the clays, sand, and other sediments that rain down on a lake bottom or ocean floor are called *sedimentary rocks*. These are the rocks that contain fossils. Among the many different materials forming the sediments are countless billions of grains of plant pollen produced each growing season and carried far and wide on the wind. Since each kind of plant produces its own particular kind of pollen, scientists can tell what associations of plants grew at this or that time in Earth's history. Fossilized pollen and the various changes in types of plant association found in different locations are evidence that there have been a number of distinct changes in climate over the past 30,000 to 35,000 years.

THE RISE AND FALL IN SEA LEVEL

Again, one way we can trace the shorelines of ancient seas is to trace the extent of fossilized ripple marks and other such characteristics of old sea bottoms. Such studies reveal not only the locations of ancient seas but the rise and fall of shorelines. That is a very reliable indicator of climate change because a change in sea level tells us that something was happening to

World sea level rises during times of polar-cap melting and lowers during times of polar-cap growth. Evidence suggests that the world sea level has changed over the past 20,000 years as shown here. AFTER FAIRBRIDGE

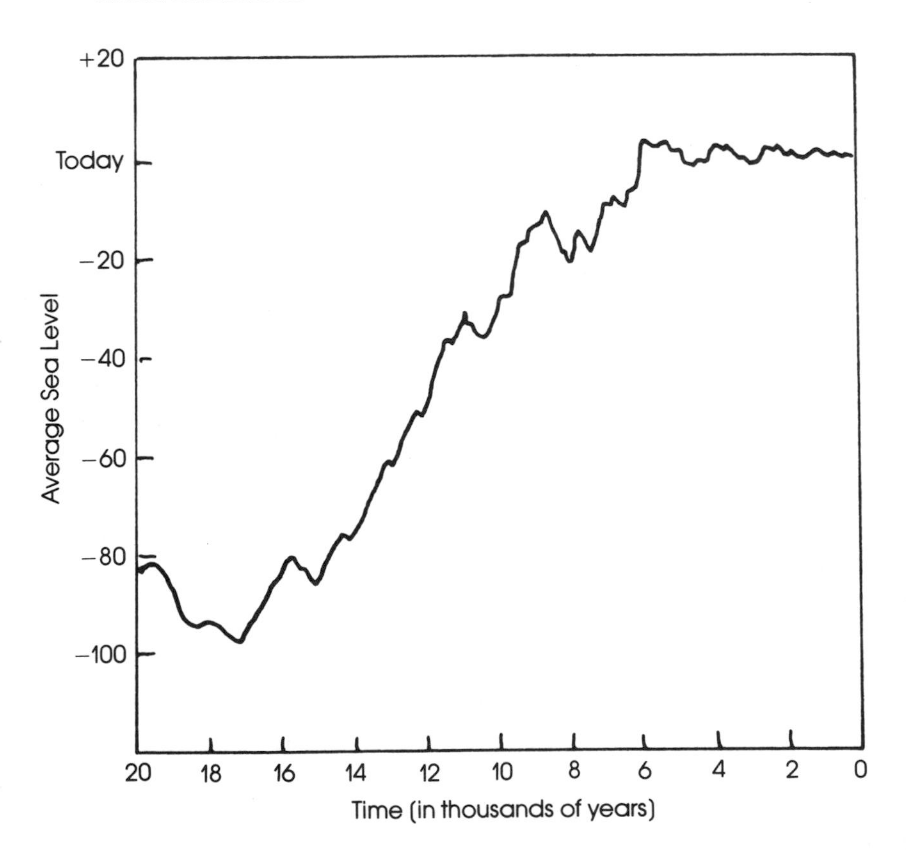

the ocean water. A lowering of the mean sea level would indicate that water is being removed to make glaciers. A rise would indicate that glaciers were going through a stage of melting. As the graph shows, about 17,000 years ago the mean ocean level was about 100 or more meters (about 300 feet) lower than it is today. So at that time there must have been extensive glaciers covering the continents, some up to three kilometers (two miles) deep.

USING OXYGEN TO DEDUCE PAST CLIMATES

Scientists have discovered that they can use "fossil" oxygen as a thermometer to measure the temperatures of ancient seas and the atmosphere. Most of the oxygen of the air and that dissolved in lakes, rivers, and oceans has an atomic weight of 16 ($^{16}0$). But there is a heavier form, $^{18}0$. One interesting thing about these two forms of oxygen is that the ratio of one to the other varies with the temperature of the water. For example, ocean water at 10°C (50°F) has a somewhat higher ratio of $^{18}0$ to $^{16}0$ than ocean water at 30°C (86°F). When water evaporates from the sea as water vapor, which then condenses out first as clouds and then as rain or snow, more of the lighter-weight $^{16}0$ tends to enter the air than does the heavier-weight $^{18}0$. So we would expect a shovelful of snow or a cloud to contain more $^{16}0$ than $^{18}0$.

Fossil shells of tiny marine animals (foraminifera) that lived many millions of years ago and that have been preserved in the ocean-bottom sediments still contain oxygen that they took in from the sea water in which they lived. By analyzing the $^{18}0$ to $^{16}0$ ratio, scientists have a thermometer telling them ocean temperatures millions of years ago. For example, measurements show that 32 million years ago Antarctica's ocean water was as warm as that now off the coast of Rhode Island. Waters of the Arctic were similarly warm at that time. Evidence for this comes from fossils that show that parts of Greenland that are now without trees were then sprawling forests of pine and spruce.

During an ice age much of the ocean water is lost to the atmosphere and is temporarily locked up as glacial ice. The relatively small amount of water that is left behind is richer in $^{18}0$ than was the larger amount of water previously. By comparing the relative amounts of $^{18}0$ in the shells of one group of marine organisms that lived earlier than another group, scientists can determine which group may have lived during an ice age and which may have lived during a warm period. In some cases this technique takes us back more than a million years.

How is the $^{18}0/^{16}0$ thermometer used to measure the temperature of the atmosphere many thousands of years ago? Glaciers are not formed directly by the freezing of ocean water. Instead they are formed through a gradual accumulation of snow that becomes compacted as ice. Since the air from which polar snows form in summer is warmer than the winter air from which snow also falls, we would expect the glacial ice formed from the compacted snow to occur in summer-winter layers. We could further expect these layers to be labeled as summer or winter layers by analyzing their $^{18}0/^{16}0$ ratio. And so they are. When scientists drill a deep core of ice from a glacier, they have a record of air temperatures going back to the time the ice was formed layer by layer. Ice cores taken in Antarctica and Greenland, extending down more than 305 meters (1,000 feet) give us an unbroken temperature profile of the past 10,000 to 100,000 years.

WHY STUDY ANCIENT CLIMATES?

When scientists ask how climates of the past have changed, they are concerned with three broad categories: (1) those distant periods going back millions and hundreds of millions of

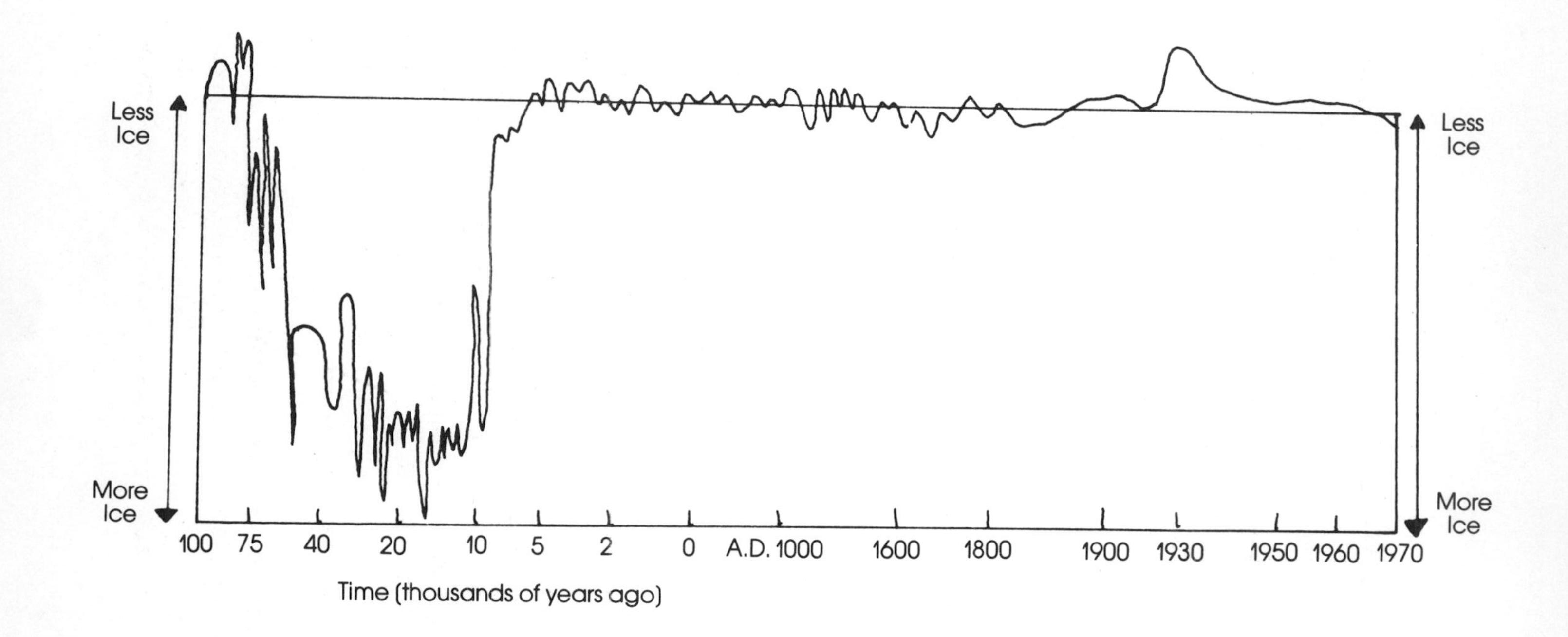

By analyzing the oxygen composition of successive layers of ice compacted over many centuries, climatologists are able to distinguish periods of cold from periods of warming. Analysis of core samples drilled out of the Greenland ice cap reveals the temperature record over the past 100,000 years. Notice that the curve is compressed at the left because the large time span is given less horizontal space than the period from A.D. *1000 to 1970.* AFTER W. DANSGAARD years; (2) more recent periods going back only a few thousands of years; and (3) climate change that has occurred since man has been making systematic observations and recording both short-term and long-term patterns of weather.

Examination of a core of varves, a core of ice, or a core of soil; dating organic remains by the carbon–14 method; analyzing the oxygen–18 to oxygen–16 ratio in a glacial sample; examining tree rings of a one-thousand-year-old Sequoia—all are means of reconstructing Earth's climate of thousands and millions of years ago. The climatologist can be certain that fossil vegetation marking a given region at a given time indicates that the region was then free of glaciation. But he would not be willing to say that a given region was both warm *and* moist, or either warm *or* moist solely on the basis of a fat growth-ring of a tree. He would want additional evidence and general agreement with several other techniques of investigating the climate of that region at the time the tree grew there.

We have hardly exhausted the many means used by climatologists to discover what Earth's past climates have been like. But at least we have touched on a few of the major ones and so have dispelled some of the "mystery" of how scientists are able to say with reasonable confidence that during such and such a time long ago certain plants and animals were living in association with each other and thrived amid "favorable" climate conditions.

It is now time to reconstruct Earth's climates of the past as paleoclimatologists view them today. As we do so, we should keep these two points in mind: first, that it becomes ever more difficult to be certain about this or that ancient climate the further back into Earth's history we probe; and second, even though it is difficult, it is important that we discover all we can about Earth's climatological history. What has occurred in the past is a key to the future.

6

Climates of the Past

THE PRECAMBRIAN PERIOD

In Chapter 4 we left Earth at an age of about one billion or so years old, or about 3.5 billion years ago. Simple photosynthesizing organisms had evolved and begun to change the atmosphere in an important way—by adding oxygen to it. At first the oxygen liberated during photosynthesis would not become free oxygen of the air. Instead it would quickly bond with iron and certain other elements in the primitive seas. Not until those "oxygen-hungry" elements of the seas had satisfied their chemical appetite for oxygen would the oxygen continuing to be liberated during photosynthesis enter the atmosphere as free oxygen.

This long period we have been talking about so far, since Earth's formation as a planet, is part of that geological period called the Precambrian. It began with the formation of Earth some 4.5 billion years ago and came to an end some 570 million years ago.

THE GEOLOGIC CALENDAR

<table>
<tr><th>Era</th><th></th><th>Period</th><th>Time (millions of years)</th><th>Duration (millions of years)</th></tr>
<tr><td rowspan="2">Cenozoic (from Greek words kainos, meaning "recent," and zoe, meaning "life")</td><td></td><td>Quaternary (meaning "fourth")</td><td>present to 2</td><td>2</td></tr>
<tr><td></td><td>Tertiary (meaning "third")</td><td>2 to 65</td><td>63</td></tr>
<tr><td rowspan="3">Mesozoic (from Greek words mesos, which means "middle," and zoe)</td><td></td><td>Cretaceous (from Latin word creta, meaning "chalk")</td><td>65 to 136</td><td>71</td></tr>
<tr><td></td><td>Jurassic (named after the Jura Mountains)</td><td>136 to 190</td><td>54</td></tr>
<tr><td></td><td>Triassic (from Latin word trias, meaning "three" and referring to a three-fold division of rock in southern Germany)</td><td>190 to 225</td><td>35</td></tr>
<tr><td rowspan="7">Paleozoic (from Greek words palaios, meaning "ancient," and zoe)</td><td></td><td>Permian (named after the Province of Perm in the Ural Mountains of Russia)</td><td>225 to 280</td><td>55</td></tr>
<tr><td rowspan="2">Carboniferous</td><td>Pennsylvanian (named after the coal regions of that state)</td><td>280 to 325</td><td>45</td></tr>
<tr><td>Mississippian (named after the limestone area near the junction of the Mississippi and Missouri Rivers)</td><td>325 to 345</td><td>20</td></tr>
<tr><td></td><td>Devonian (named after Devon, England)</td><td>345 to 395</td><td>50</td></tr>
<tr><td></td><td>Silurian (named after the Silures, an ancient tribe in Wales)</td><td>395 to 430</td><td>35</td></tr>
<tr><td></td><td>Ordovician (named after an ancient Celtic tribe, the Ordovices, in Wales)</td><td>430 to 500</td><td>70</td></tr>
<tr><td></td><td>Cambrian (from Cambria, the Roman name for Wales)</td><td>500 to 570</td><td>70</td></tr>
<tr><td colspan="3">PRECAMBRIAN</td><td>570 to 4,500 (?)</td><td>3,930</td></tr>
</table>

This geological time scale for Earth's history has been worked out by earth scientists. While the "period" is the most used division in this time scale, the different periods are grouped under larger divisions called "eras." Notice that most of the names assigned to the periods are place names of localities where rocks of that age were first studied and described. On the other hand, Tertiary and Quaternary are names retained from an earlier four-fold division of the rocks.

Primitive seas began forming early during the Precambrian. Evidence for the formation of such seas comes from the discovery of pebbles, sand, ancient mud, and other such sediments that had been washed into ancient sea beds by the action of streams and rivers. Unsorted mixtures of these sediments suggest that they were carried and deposited by ice. Such clues to an extensive Precambrian ice age suggest that from about

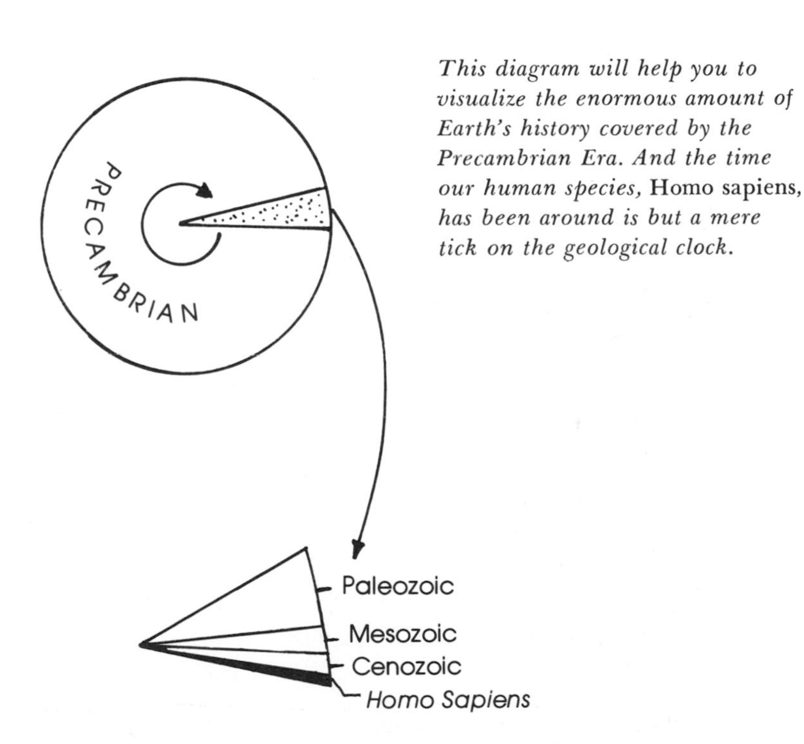

This diagram will help you to visualize the enormous amount of Earth's history covered by the Precambrian Era. And the time our human species, Homo sapiens, *has been around is but a mere tick on the geological clock.*

600 to 700 million years ago the Precambrian land mass was covered with a sprawling ice sheet.

At this time in Earth's history the present continents and oceans had not been formed. There was one supercontinent called *Pangaea* which later broke into a northern half, called *Laurasia*, and a southern half, called *Gondwana*. Still later these two in turn broke apart and eventually formed the continents and seas familiar to us today.

After this period of Precambrian glaciation, another major event occurred. Over a period of some 30 million years new living forms evolved at a dizzying pace. No one quite knows why, but there are theories. Some biologists feel that it was not until around Cambrian times that there was enough oxygen in Earth's atmosphere to permit the appearance of

---

It now appears that when Earth first established a solid crust there may have been but a single mammoth continent, called Pangaea. It later broke apart into two large land masses, Gondwana in the south and Laurasia in the north. These land masses in turn later broke apart into the continents we know today.

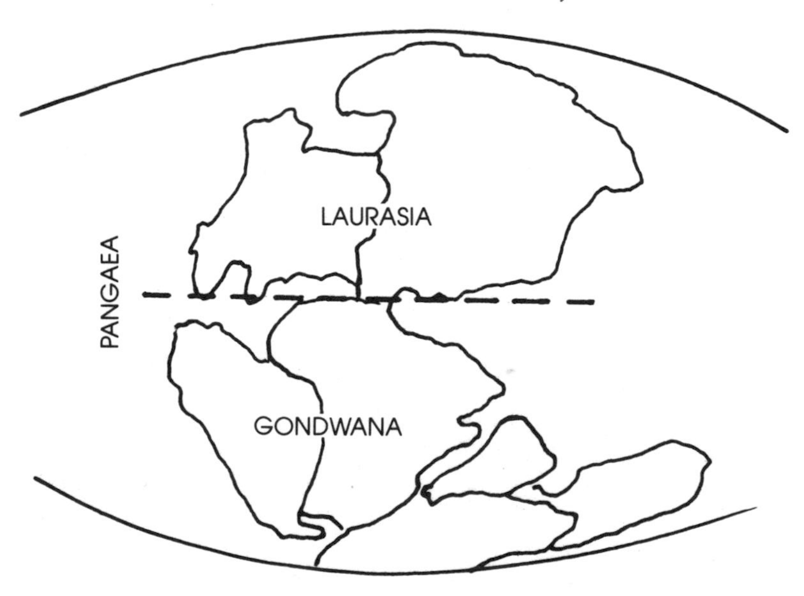

Called stromatolites, *these objects are limestone deposits made by Precambrian blue-green algae some two billion years ago. They are located at Great Slave Lake, Canada.* GEOLOGICAL SURVEY OF CANADA

---

many new forms of plants and animals—that for most of the Precambrian, living organisms consisted only of simple forms that did not require oxygen to drive their chemical activity.

Another theory has been offered by Steven M. Stanley of Johns Hopkins University. He pictures a time during the Precambrian when the algaelike organisms whose ancient fossils have been found dominated the living world. Perhaps for two billion years or more these organisms ruled as they grew and ever increased their numbers under favorable climate conditions. They were able to do this for two reasons. First, there were no plant-eating species around to reduce their numbers; and second, there were no other large populations of plant forms to compete with the sprawling, algaelike populations.

Stanley next pictures a time, after a long period of evolution, when populations of plant-eating organisms, perhaps single-celled "animals," evolved and established themselves. Then, as these "animals" increased their numbers, they began to decrease the numbers of the algaelike organisms. Here was an important step forward in paving the way for the evolution of new forms of plants and animals alike, Stanley suggests. It meant increased living space for other plant life that had been unsuccessful in competing with the successful algal forms. As new plant forms arose and prospered so did new animal forms. Stanley feels that some such sequence of events triggered the explosive evolution of new plant and animal life forms whose fossils became so numerous by the beginning of the Cambrian.

THE CAMBRIAN PERIOD

The fossil record is our evidence for the explosive appearance of numerous new life forms by the beginning of the Cambrian. Cambrian-age rocks are found in Wales and many

During the Cambrian, shallow seas (dotted areas) covered a large area of the supercontinents Laurasia and Gondwana.

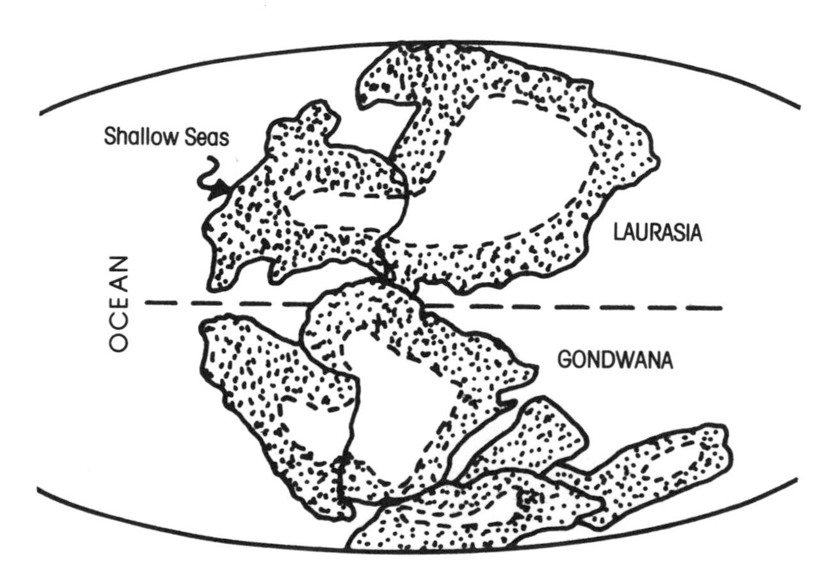

Among the primitive organisms abounding in the Cambrian's shallow seas were more than 1,000 species of trilobites, measuring from microscopic size to about 50 centimeters (about two feet) in length.
COURTESY: THE AMERICAN MUSEUM OF NATURAL HISTORY; PHOTO BY THE AUTHOR

---

other parts of the world, including the eastern United States and Canada. The early Cambrian climate seems to have had long cold spells that later were to be followed by warmer spells. Early in this period the central region of North America was dry land; but later in the period sinking of the land allowed shallow inland seas to form. By the end of the period almost all of the continent had been flooded.

These shallow seas abounded with many forms of life, including sponges, trilobites, brachiopods, graptolites, and other animals lacking backbones. At this stage in Earth's history neither plant nor animal life had yet invaded the land. Trilobites, extinct by the end of the Paleozoic Era, were especially abundant. There were more than 1,000 known species measuring from microscopic size to two cm (about one inch) and to 50 cm (about two feet long). These organisms were distantly related to the later-appearing crabs, shrimp, and insects.

The warm late-Cambrian seas teemed with different life forms—shallow-water organisms, deep-water forms, floating and swimming forms, and bottom dwellers. Such widespread diversity, or variety, means competition among species. And competition includes some predator-prey associations—animals eating other animals. Those Cambrian organisms tending to be the most successful in the survival game were those who had developed hard shells. But there also were soft-bodied forms including jellyfishes, worms, and sponges.

During the Cambrian in North America, Europe, and Asia, various long depressions on the continents were collecting and filling up with sedimentary "fill." Much later these sediment dumps were to be thrust up as mountain ranges. So it was during the Cambrian that our Rocky Mountains and the Appalachians, for instance, were in the first stages of formation.

THE ORDOVICIAN PERIOD

The Ordovician continued as a rich period for marine life. Trilobites reached their greatest numbers, as did bryozoans, graptolites, cephalopods, and crinoids. Mollusks included bivalves like today's clams and oysters. Animals with backbones appeared for the first time during the middle of this period. About 70 percent of the present-day Northern Hemisphere was flooded during this period. It was sometime during the Ordovician, according to Columbia University geologist Rhodes W. Fairbridge, that what is now the central Sahara Desert was then located at the South Pole and covered with glacial ice. Part of the evidence is great glacier-caused gouges extending hundreds of kilometers in the bedrock beneath the

Among the marine organisms abundant during the Ordovician were crinoids, animals that lived attached to the sea bottom. COURTESY: THE AMERICAN MUSEUM OF NATURAL HISTORY; PHOTO BY THE AUTHOR

desert sand. Later this section of continental crust migrated toward the Equator and eventually took up its present position.

THE SILURIAN PERIOD

Most of the present-day land area of the Northern Hemisphere continued to be covered by shallow seas during this 35-million-year period. The highly successful trilobites, numerous for more than 150 million years, began to die out in large numbers during the Silurian. Giant water scorpions measuring three meters (ten feet) were common. Far better fossils of animals with backbones are found for this period than for the previous one, but none had yet developed jaws. They were either surface feeders or bottom feeders that sucked in their food in vacuum-cleaner fashion.

Many of these early animals with backbones had bony armor as protection against predators. Others had thick protective scales. Near the end of the Silurian new types of backboned animals were evolving—the placoderms, fishes with jaws capable of biting, cutting, and crushing. This new feature made the placoderms especially successful predators.

It was during the Silurian that life seems to have taken its first hold on land. By this time weathering of the rocky surface had formed soil, a new medium for the evolution of climate and one that proved suitable for plants. The earliest known fossils of land plants have been found in Silurian rocks from Australia and Europe. Called psilopsids, they are a group that has survived up to present times. These leafless plants most likely were shallow-water plants that gradually developed features enabling them to survive as the level of the seas lowered from time to time. Photosynthesis in these leafless plants took place in the stems. Later, ferns were to develop and become abundant as early land plants.

Animal life also seems to have taken hold on the land during the late Silurian. The earliest forms yet identified are millipedes and scorpionlike organisms such as those air-breathers found preserved in late Silurian rocks from Scotland. It would seem that both forms were scavengers, eating the remains of marine organisms stranded on the beach at high tide or during storms.

During the Silurian there was much volcanic activity in

what is now Maine and the Canadian areas of New Brunswick and eastern Quebec. Land disturbances gave rise to a 6,450-kilometer(4,000-mile)-long mountain range extending from Wales through Scandinavia and westward to northern Greenland. At this time, it would have been possible to walk from Canada to Europe since there was no Atlantic Ocean.

The Cambrian, Ordovician, and Silurian periods can be grouped together as the early Paleozoic Era. It is very hard to deduce many specifics about climate as long ago as 400 million years and spanning 175 million years. Fossils provide us with the most important clues to climate that long ago, and that is why it is important to review the kinds of living organisms that lived period by period. Where there are few or no fossils, such as during large segments of the Precambrian, it is hard for us to say very much about climate conditions then.

And if we have as clues to climate during early geological time only extinct species, the problem is nearly as serious. For example, we know that modern reef-building corals, palm trees, and crocodiles thrive in warm climates, but not in cold ones; and that polar bears and penguins are found in cold climates but not in warm ones. Unfortunately, these organisms are relatively recent ones and are not found among the early Paleozoic assemblages of fossils. Although we can make some intelligent guesses, we do not know for certain what climate preferences trilobites, graptolites, and placoderms had.

So far no one has produced evidence of glacial activity during the early Paleozoic Era, so we can guess that the climate was generally mild. Although there seems to have been some glacial activity twice during the Precambrian—once about a billion years ago, then again some 750 million years ago—there probably was very little, if any, ice during the Cambrian, Ordovician, and Silurian periods.

Another reason for thinking that early Paleozoic climates

were generally mild is the *distribution* of fossils. Fossils of the same species are found rather widely spread both north and south, just as if there had been hardly any difference in climate in what is now southern South America and midlatitude Canada. Early Paleozoic fossils recently found north of the Arctic Circle differ very little from those found near the Equator. Again, the evidence points to a generally mild climate from the time Earth's first true cellular organisms arose up until about 300 million years ago, which puts us well into the late Paleozoic.

THE DEVONIAN PERIOD

The "Age of Fishes" is the name given to the Devonian Period, since these animals evolved into a bewildering variety of forms. Many were armored like their Silurian ancestors. Others were covered with small scales. Some were sluggish and cumbersome, others streamlined, fast-swimming, and sharklike.

There were four major groups of Devonian fishes—two left over from Silurian times and two newcomers. The two new types were the ancestors of modern sharks and the bony fishes. Some of these bony fishes had an air bladder that worked as a kind of lung. They also had powerful fins with a bony structure similar to an arm or leg. This structure enabled the animals to move about on the land, which they appear to have done when there was need to move from a pond that dried up during drought to a new area of water. This ability would have been very important to the survival of these animals since Devonian times had plentiful rain alternating with times of long drought conditions.

By late Devonian times amphibians similar to the animals just described had evolved. Traces or remains of them have been found in ancient swamps in Pennsylvania and Green-

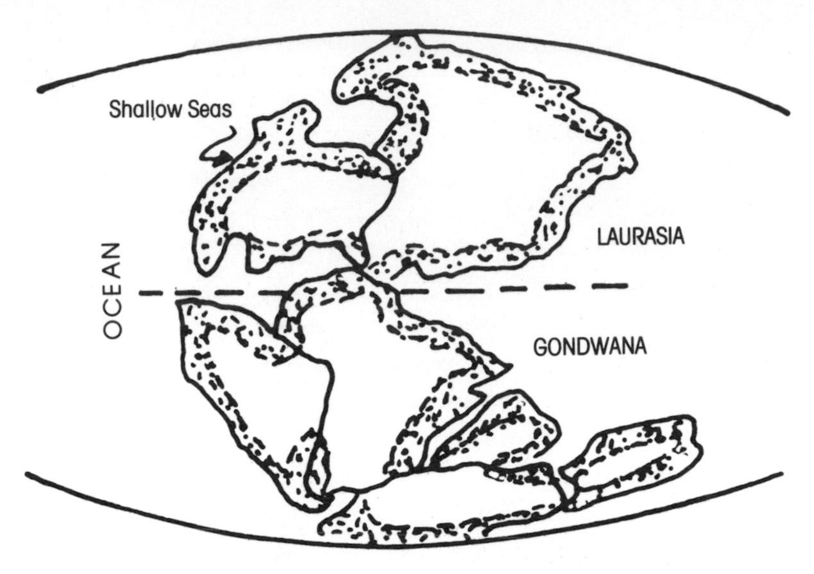

By Devonian times the shallow seas had retreated somewhat, exposing a much larger land area. Land plants and animals had evolved by this time and important geological changes were occurring on the land, including mountain formation in what is now New England, Quebec, and Nova Scotia.

---

land. By this time numerous other land organisms had evolved, including millipedes, scorpions, spiders, and the first insects, which were wingless. Among plant life were horsetail rushes, tall tree ferns with stems more than one meter (about three feet) thick, and forests of scale trees reaching heights of 15 meters (46 feet).

The trilobites and graptolites of earlier times began to die out during the Devonian. But the warm seas were abundant with reef-building corals, numerous lamp shells, mollusks, sponges, sea lilies, and starfish.

The Devonian Period was a time of important change on the land. High mountains were raised in what is now New England, Quebec, and Nova Scotia, as well as along the east coast of Australia.

THE CARBONIFEROUS PERIOD

Together, the Mississippian and Pennsylvanian periods, which span about 65 million years, are known as the Carboniferous. The land was changed in many important ways during this time, although shallow seas continued to cover much of the northern hemisphere early in the period. Extensive mountains were raised in western Europe, and the Ouachita Mountains of Oklahoma and Arkansas were formed.

Judging from the number of fossil teeth and fin spines, sharks were abundant in the warm waters of the early Carboniferous. Thirty-meter-high (100-foot) scale trees were common along the edges of pools, shallow lakes, and swamps, and below them was a dense undergrowth of ferns and other plants.

During the later Carboniferous some areas of the land alternately sank and rose, giving rise to large lakes and swamps. Gradually layer upon layer of this matted organic matter was compressed in the water and formed that substance we call peat, the first stages in coal formation. From time to time great areas of these peat-filled swamps sank just below the level of nearby seas. Time and again the land subsided, then rose above the sea again. Each time, old forests died and new ones took their place. With each lowering of the land, sea waters flowed over the peat, covering it with new sediment deposits often containing fossil remains. So today we find layers of coal alternating with layers of sedimentary rock. About half of the world's workable coal was formed during the Pennsylvanian, mainly from the giant scale trees.

The Carboniferous is called the "Age of Amphibians" since these animals dominated the land. They were the only dominant animals with backbones until the close of the period, when reptiles appeared. This was an important evolutionary change. Amphibians lay jelly-encased eggs in water, and so water is essential to them. Because each reptilian egg contains

The Carboniferous was a time of swamp formation. Matted organic material in these many swamps was compressed and formed peat, the first stages in coal formation. COURTESY: THE AMERICAN MUSEUM OF NATURAL HISTORY; PHOTOGRAPH BY THE AUTHOR its own water supply, it is not dependent on a water medium for development. This proved to be an important advantage, and during the next period life away from water took many new turns. In addition to amphibians and reptiles, there were Carboniferous land snails and hundreds of special cockroaches, some giant ones ten centimeters (four inches) long. There were also spiderlike animals such as centipedes and scorpions.

THE PERMIAN PERIOD

The Permian Period, which lasted nearly as long as the Carboniferous, also was a time of great change. The Appalachians south of New England were thrust up, and the Ural Mountains of Russia also were formed. Along the west coast of North America there was widespread volcanic activity. While the western United States was still covered by shallow seas during this period, in other parts of the Northern Hemisphere inland seas were drying up and leaving vast deposits of salt and potash.

Most of the Permian forests were made up of cone-bearing trees like our present-day pines, firs, and spruce. The giant horsetails and scale trees of earlier times became smaller, although ferns, tree ferns, and seed ferns continued to thrive. A general drying of the land is suggested by the huge success of reptiles and a gradual decline in amphibians. Without sufficient water in which to lay their eggs, amphibians could not be expected to thrive. So a significant climate change tipped the scales in favor of reptiles over amphibians.

The late Permian was a time of much dying among organisms living in the shallow seas. Over a period of only a few million years, 30 percent or more of the families of marine organisms died out. Gone were the trilobites, the ancient corals, most brachiopods, crinoids, and bryozoans. The cause of this mass extinction, the greatest known such event in the

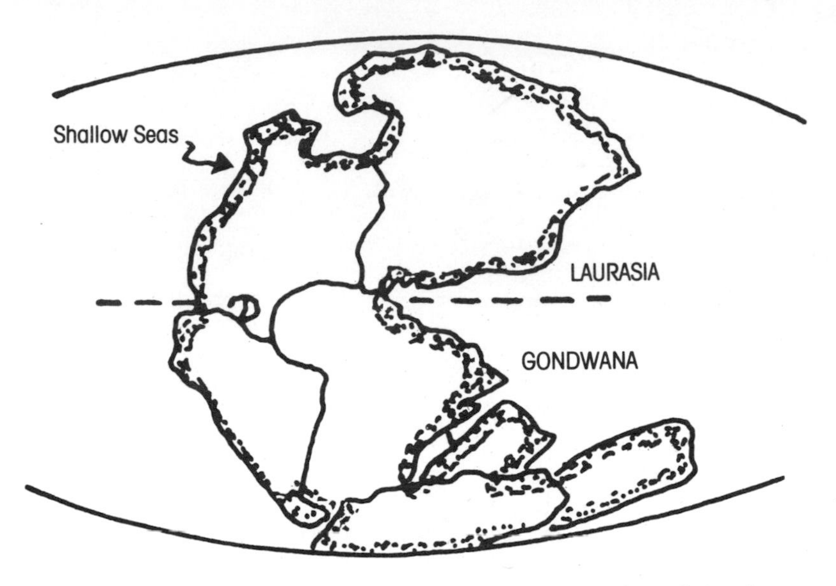

In Permian times, the land masses known as Laurasia and Gondwana had not yet begun to break apart, so there were few barriers to land plants and animals spreading over wide areas. During the Permian the shallow seas had nearly withdrawn from the land.

---

history of life on Earth, was for a long time a major biological mystery. But in recent years geological evidence for the continents being ever on the move seems to have solved the mystery. Near the end of the Permian, the coming together of the continents greatly reduced the total area of shallow seas. Also, it now seems that great depressions in the ocean floor also caused a general lowering of the ocean level. Possibly during late Permian times the sea level lowered enough to expose the continental shelves and so eliminate most of the shallow seas and the many life forms they supported.

The telltale mixture of sand, flat pebbles, and other sedimentary material mentioned earlier shows that the Southern Hemisphere was gripped in an ice age for about 50 million years. This widespread glaciation seems to have begun mid-

way through the Pennsylvanian, about 300 million years ago, and lasted midway through the Permian, about 250 million years ago. These sediments, called *tillite*, are composed of material picked up by glaciers as they creep along. Later, when the glaciers melt, they drop the material. So areas where such a mixture of sediments is found were at one time covered by an ice sheet. Once picked up by a moving glacier, small rocks at the bottom of the ice are smoothed and polished as flat pebbles as the ice grinds them along the bedrock and so leaves telltale scratches in the bedrock.

The interesting thing about this late Paleozoic ice age is that those parts of South America showing evidence of the ice age are now in tropical and semitropical regions. Geologists regard this as important evidence that the continents indeed have wandered in the past as they can be shown to be wandering today.

Ice sheets covered not only South America but also South and Central Africa, India, Australia, and Antarctica. Now if those land masses were once joined as Gondwana, the great southern continent which had drifted southward, then we could reasonably expect it to be covered with ice. It now seems that large-scale glaciation can occur only when a large con-

The Mesozoic was a time of dramatic change in life, environments, and geography. It is known as the "Age of Reptiles" and was the time when dinosaurs ruled the land. Numerous species are shown here, ranging in size from the giant Tyrannosaurus *to lizardlike animals about the size of a collie dog.* COURTESY: PEABODY MUSEUM OF NATURAL HISTORY

---

tinent is situated in a polar position for a sufficiently long time. That seems a more reasonable explanation than supposing that ice sheets are capable of forming at tropical and semitropical latitudes. That would require rather large temperature changes, for which there is no evidence.

THE MESOZOIC ERA

Where the Paleozoic Era spanned some 400 million years, the Mesozoic spanned a much smaller interval of about 160 million years. It was a time of extraordinary change in life, environments, and geography. Including the Triassic, Jurassic, and Cretaceous periods, it is known as the "Age of Reptiles." The old reptiles of the Permian died out and were replaced by new forms. Some, such as ichthyosaurs and nothosaurs, were marine animals. Others, weighing up to 20 tons or so, lived in shallow lakes. And still others, such as the huge

Tyrannosaurus, preyed on other smaller animals and were land dwellers. These were the dinosaurs, all of which appear to have evolved from a small collie-sized ancestral type, called *thecodont*.

By the late Triassic, most of the modern groups of insects had appeared, and almost all of the amphibians of the Paleozoic had become extinct. The bony fishes of the Triassic more closely resembled modern fishes than their earlier ancestral types.

It is not until the Jurassic Period that the fossils of true mammals first appear. They were tiny animals not much larger than a rat. Flying reptiles, the pterosaurs, and the earliest known true birds appeared during the mid-Mesozoic.

The Jurassic was the time the first fossils of true mammals were formed. About the only clues to what these animals resembled are several tiny jawbones (top left). Similar to shrews, the animals were about the size of a rat, or close to the size of a large dinosaur egg. AFTER M. WILSON

The Jurassic landscape seems to have been one of warm and moist conditions favoring numerous swamps and forests in contrast with the drier climate of the Triassic. Flowering plants appear during this era and were common later during the Cretaceous Period. Certain insects associated with the pollination of plants also appear. By the end of the Mesozoic, giant sequoias had become common in the conifer forests. Sharks became plentiful; and snakes make their first appearance.

At the close of the Mesozoic the dinosaurs became extinct after ruling the land for 150 million years. Their passing marked the second period of great dying, and the cause for it has yet to be learned. Again, perhaps the drifting continents hold the answer. Some biologists estimate that some 25 percent of all animal families perished! However, the mammals survived and were to become the dominant land forms during the next and present era, the Cenozoic. "Dominant" here means by size. By sheer numbers the insects would have to be considered "dominant."

It is worth probing a bit deeper into the possible cause(s) of these periods of great dying. The answer has to be found in marked environmental change and the inability of plant and animal organisms to adjust to the change. But to what part(s) of the environment do we look? Could changes in the amount of free oxygen in the atmosphere have taken place? Could the Sun's energy output have changed temporarily? Could there have been a temporary marked increase in ultraviolet radiation, or of cosmic rays? Could there have been "foreign" organisms temporarily taking over and wiping out large groups of plants and animals because they had no natural defense against those foreign organisms? Could there have been a temporary shortage, or excessive amount, of essential nutrient elements normally present in fixed amounts in both the soil and sea? Or, as we have already suggested, could changes in climate be the cause? Climate has most often been cited, although some argue against climate being the sole cause. They say that we have been gripped in glacial conditions off and on over the past several millions of years, yet we have no evidence of wholesale extinctions resulting from this relatively severe climate change.

The Triassic was a period of extensive outpourings of molten rock to the surface. The famous Palisades of New York and New Jersey were formed, as were similar rock formations in South America, southern Africa, Australia, and Antarctica. In contrast, the Jurassic was a period of relative quiet. Although the Sierra Nevada Mountains were formed and sinking of the land took place along the western edges of both North and South America, in a way the Jurassic was a stage-setting period for the great activity during the next period, the Cretaceous.

Cretaceous seas covered most of Europe, much of Asia, and nearly half of North America. The Gulf of Mexico received nearly 4,000 meters (13,000 feet) of sediment during this period. The Rocky Mountains of North America and the Andes of South America were thrust up. By this time the continents had begun to acquire their present-day shapes.

We almost begin to feel at home by the end of the Mesozoic. Numerous groups of plants and animals then living closely resemble similar types living today. And since they are closely related, we can be more confident of the kinds of environmental conditions that they needed to survive—temperature of both seas and land, for instance. It is only since the Mesozoic Era that we have reliable paleotemperature records. They suggest that the tropics were at an average of 25° to 30°C (77° to 86°F) and that both polar regions were very much warmer than they are today—between 8° to 10°C (46° to 50°F). The

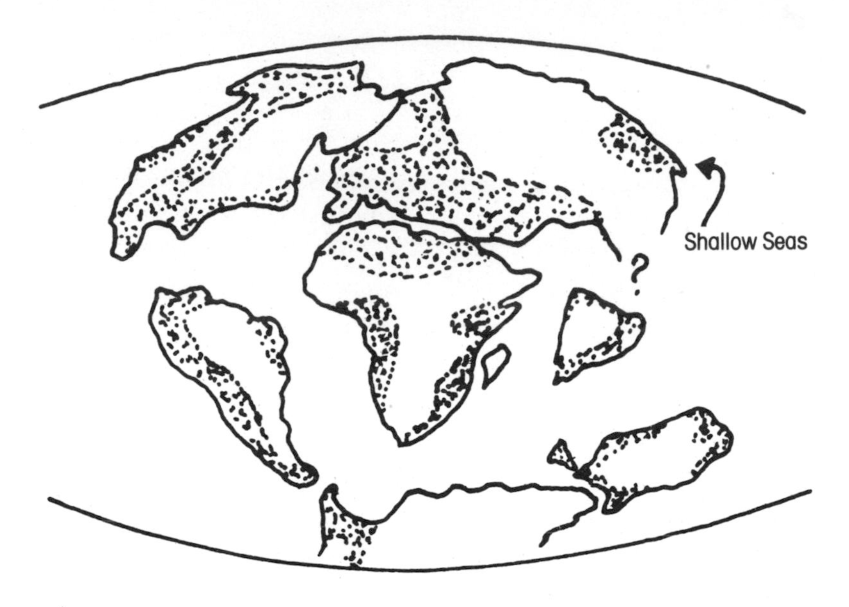

By the end of the Mesozoic the continents had drifted apart to about where they are now. But shallow seas continued to cover much of the land. Europe, for example, was nearly totally covered by water.

subtropical belt in the Northern Hemisphere may have reached all the way up to the present Canadian border.

Climatologists tell us that during more than 90 percent of the 570 million years since Cambrian times, the north and south polar regions of the planet probably were free of ice. During this time the average world temperature seems to have been about 22°C (72°F). Palm trees grew in most parts of what is now the United States, and New York State then had Florida's present climate. Periods of ice were to dominate for long —by human standards—spells, however. First there was a glacial period about half a billion years ago, followed by a 100-million-year-period of glaciation during the late Precambrian. Then the Gondwana glaciation lasted for about 50 million years during the Pennsylvanian-Permian periods. Earth was then to be free of glacial periods for nearly another 250 million years. That brings us to the Triassic Period, only ten million years ago.

THE CENOZOIC ERA

During the Tertiary Period, which takes up most of the Cenozoic Era, there was widespread volcanic activity in the western United States. Mounts Shasta and Rainier were formed, and continental drifting gave rise to the great Alpine-Himalayan mountain chain. There also was volcanic activity in the North Atlantic region, in East Africa, and in the Mediterranean region. Also during the Tertiary, most of the inland seas left the continents. By the end of this period the continents had the same general outlines they have today, but their relative positions were not the same.

During much of the Cenozoic the land level of the continents has risen gradually, which has brought about climate change, in some cases producing widespread grasslands. By the close of the Tertiary, mammals had come to dominate the land, again in size and not numbers. Cats, monkeys, whales, elephants, kangaroos, and birds all were well established by this time.

The decline of the reptiles, due to a general cooling during much of the Tertiary, triggered an explosive evolutionary expansion of those small mammals that had lived in relative obscurity for about 100 million years. These mammals increased in number and sought out nearly every available habitat on the land. Some took up life in the sea (whales and seals for instance), while others took to the air (bats, for example). Clearly, the Cenozoic quickly became the "Age of Mammals." Also early in the Tertiary nearly all of the main families of birds known to us today had become established.

The reptiles greatly increased their numbers and spread

widely over the land at a time when the two supercontinents of Gondwana and Laurasia were still joined. So it is not surprising that today we find fossils of reptilian forms fairly uniformly distributed over the various large land masses. This is because at the time they were so numerous there were no major geological barriers to prevent them from migrating from one end of the land to the other. This was also true of the earliest mammals. But by the time of the explosive evolutionary expansion of mammals during the Tertiary, the two supercontinents had broken up and produced those pieces we now call Australia, North America, and South America, all three of which are surrounded by sea.

Since those land masses are isolated from each other we would expect evolution to have followed different routes on each land mass, one reason being the different climates found on each. Australia has that unique group of mammals called *marsupials*, which are not found elsewhere. South America has its sloths and groups of grazing mammals not known to have appeared elsewhere. At one stage, however, a land bridge was thrust up and linked South America with North America, which permitted a two-way migration of various animal groups.

The great age of mammals peaked some two million or more years ago. At that time there were many giant forms—the mammoths and mastodons, five-meter(18-foot)-high ground sloths, giant bison, and two-meter(seven-foot)-long beavers. But for some reason these giants did not endure. By 8,000 years ago, North America's elephants, camels, horses, the dire wolf, and long-horn bison all were gone. The mammals familiar to us today are but a handful of leftovers from the great Age of Mammals.

What caused this tidal wave of ice-age extinction? Some have suggested a "prehistoric overkill" by the spread of skilled

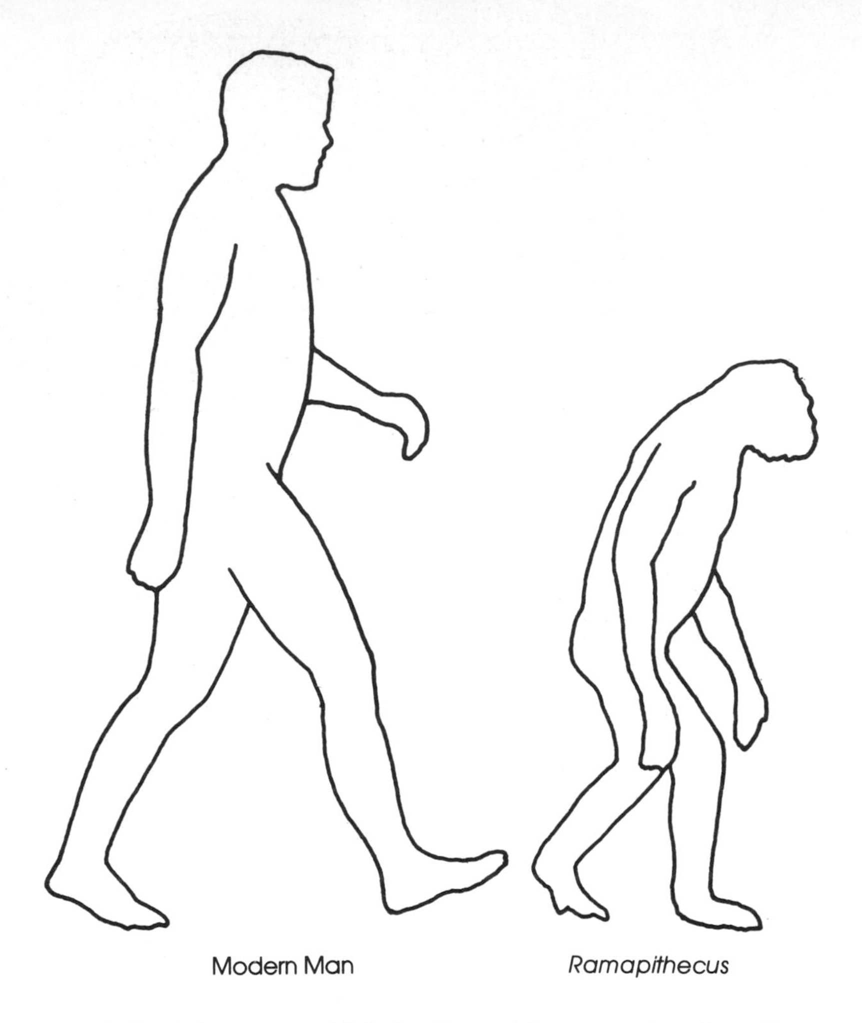

Anthropologists now think that Ramapithecus *may have been the direct ancestor of modern man, having given rise to that line of man-apes who eventually evolved into* Homo sapiens *about 500,000 years ago.* Ramapithecus *lived from about fourteen to ten million years ago before becoming extinct.*

---

hunters who developed new techniques of hunting by stampede and fire drive. Others point to climate change that accompanies a dying ice age. For example, according to A. Dreimanis, of the University of Western Ontario, the masto-

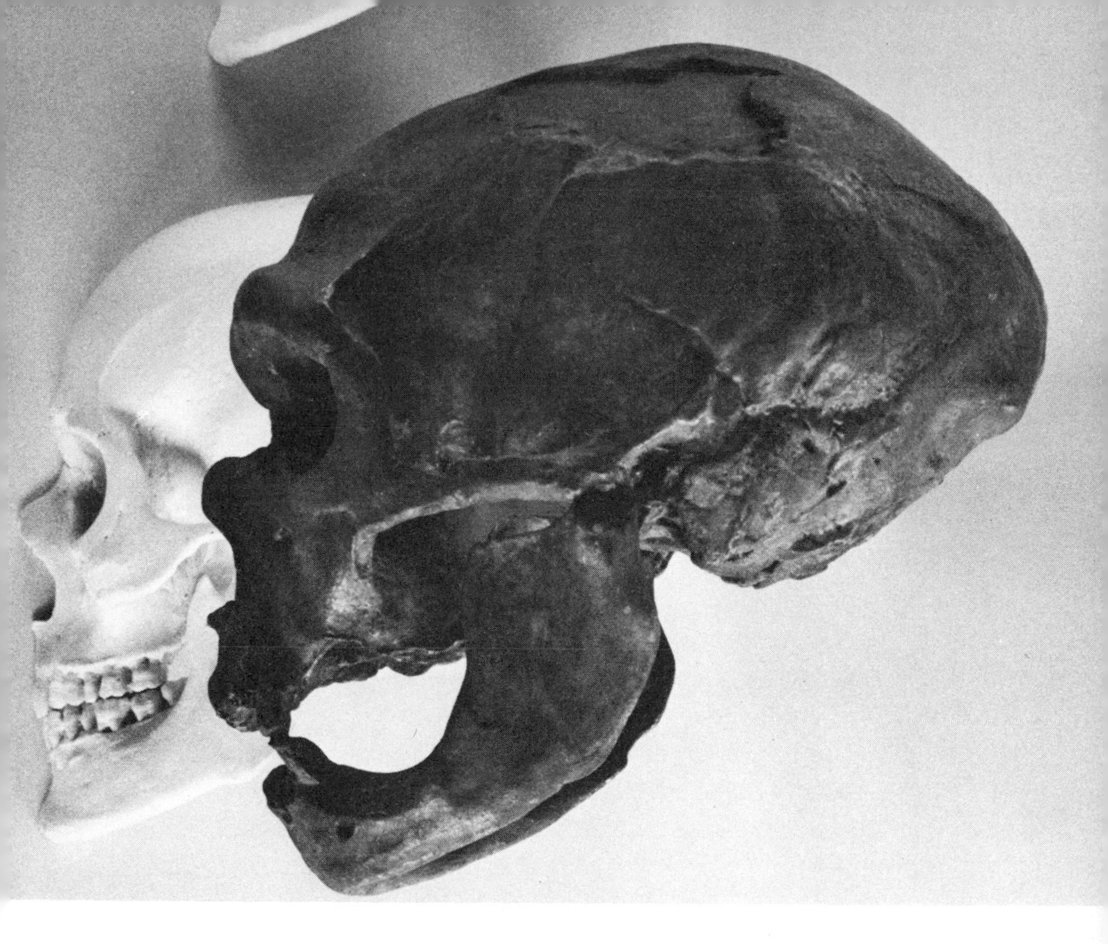

Neanderthal Man, who lived in Europe and Asia as long ago as about 100,000 years, was a member of Homo sapiens. *But notice the apelike features of his skull (foreground), a receding chin and jutting brow ridge, compared with the pointed chin and smooth brow ridge of modern man (background).* COURTESY: THE AMERICAN MUSEUM OF NATURAL HISTORY; PHOTO BY THE AUTHOR

---

dons became extinct as their spruce-forest habitats began to disappear about 11,000 years ago when the climate began to be drier. The mastodons became trapped in wet lowland refuges where spruce forests held out against the invading pine and hardwood forests. Eventually the lowland spruce refuges disappeared as well, and with them the mastodons.

A geological event that occurred during the Tertiary, some

45 to 50 million years ago, may have played a key role in the later evolution of man. At that time the Himalayan Mountains were thrust up by drifting action of the Indian subcontinent pushing up against Asia. These new mountains formed a barrier to global wind circulation, which gradually changed the climate. By about 14 million years ago climates that had been tropical in earlier times had changed to temperate climates. These regions of thinning and once tropical forests that had supplied fruits and nuts all year round eventually came to bear them only on a seasonal basis. This change in food supply may have caused some of the forest-dwelling apes to spend part of their time out on the grassy plains in search of supplementary food such as roots, seeds, and, in some cases, the meat of other animals.

Anthropologists reason that the apes who would have been most successful out of the forests were those who evolved into animals able to walk upright and see over the top of the tall grass in search of prey. Fossil remains of such a creature have been found. Called *Ramapithecus,* this manlike group of apes lived from about 14 to 10 million years ago before becoming extinct. It is *Ramapithecus,* anthropologists tell us, who very likely is our direct ancestor and who gave rise to that line of man-apes who eventually evolved into *Homo sapiens* about 500,000 years ago.

7

Ages of Ice

TERTIARY ICE SHEETS

It was also during the Tertiary that conditions triggered a series of outbreaks of ice that we call ice ages. It is not clearly understood what caused this widespread glaciation, which began with a gradual decrease in temperature in the mid-latitudes at the beginning of the Tertiary. One possibility is the migration of the continent of Antarctica to its present position at the South Pole. This would have increased winter snow, leading to mountain glaciation and eventually glaciation over the entire continent. Antarctica has been under a solid crust of ice for the past four to five million years. The ice-gripped continent then would have gradually cooled the surrounding ocean water, setting up a cold bottom current. Today just such a current flows out of the Weddell Sea toward the Equator. This cold water, which is only a few degrees above freezing, wells up to the surface and helps replace warm

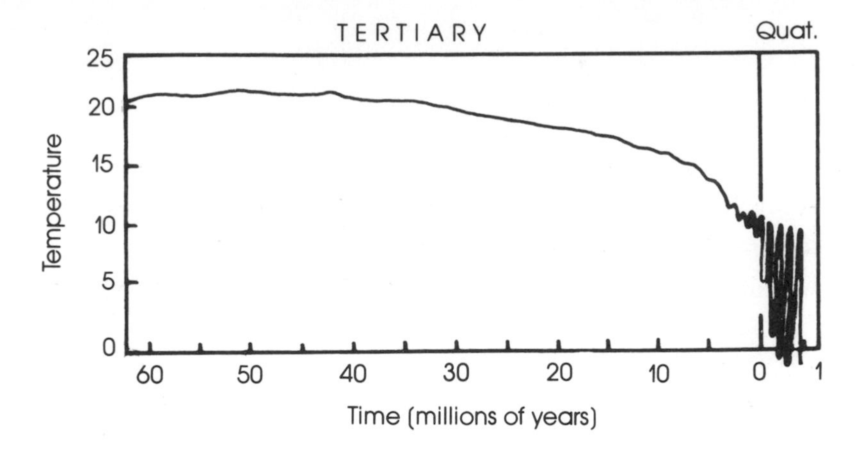

During the Tertiary, midlatitude temperatures gradually declined, although temperatures in the tropics seem to have remained unchanged. The suspected cause of the gradual decline at midlatitudes is the shifting of Antarctica to its present position. AFTER H. FLOHN

surface water blown westward along the Equatorial currents in the Atlantic, Pacific, and Indian oceans.

The gradual cooling of the Northern Hemisphere during the Tertiary seems to have been brought on by a slow mixing of the oceans' warm water with the new source of cold water from the Weddell Sea. Some change must also have occurred in the circulation of the atmosphere and in the amount of radiation received from the Sun and then lost back to space. Whatever the combination of circumstances, between about two and three million years ago, mountain glaciers began forming in the Sierra Nevada of California, in Iceland, and then later in Greenland, which is a source of a southward-flowing, cold bottom water.

THE PAST MILLION YEARS

As we attempt to reconstruct ancient climates we are treading on ever firmer ground the closer we come to present times. What can we say about the past million years?

Climatologists tell us that several ice ages have come and gone during that time. Over the past 700,000 years says Reid A. Bryson, there have been seven ice ages alternating with interglacial, warmer periods. It seems that we in the northern hemisphere may be near the peak of such a warm, interglacial period now. "To find a time as warm as the past few [thousand] years," Bryson tells us, "we have to go back through a long glacial period to 125,000 years ago, during the so-called 'Eemian interglacial.' " Each cycle of peak glacial activity—from one peak, through an interglacial period, then to the peak of the next glacial period—lasts about 100,000 years. From the end of one glacial period to the beginning of the next lasts about 10,000 years. The peak of the last glacial

---

Over the past 700,000 years there have been seven known ice ages, after which a period of warming (heavy lines) occurred. The most recent period of warming (heavy line at far right) has brought us to a stage where it is now warmer than it has been for more than 90 percent of the past million years. Evidence for these global glacial periods comes from measuring the oxygen content of deep-sea sediment cores. AFTER NATIONAL RESEARCH COUNCIL

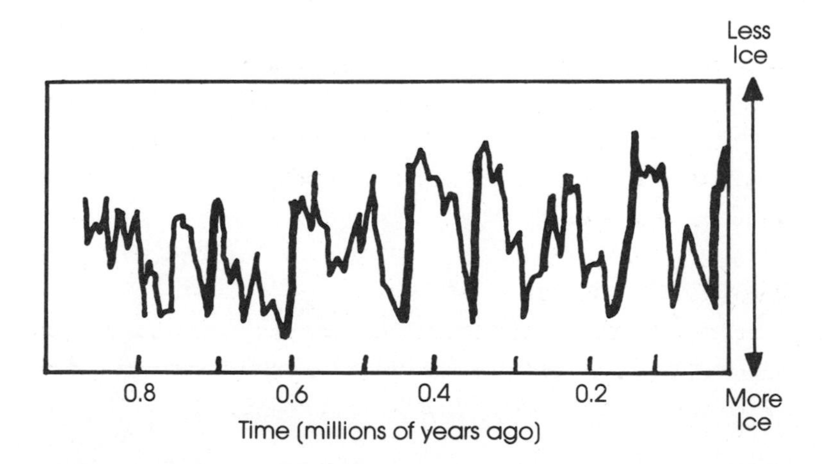

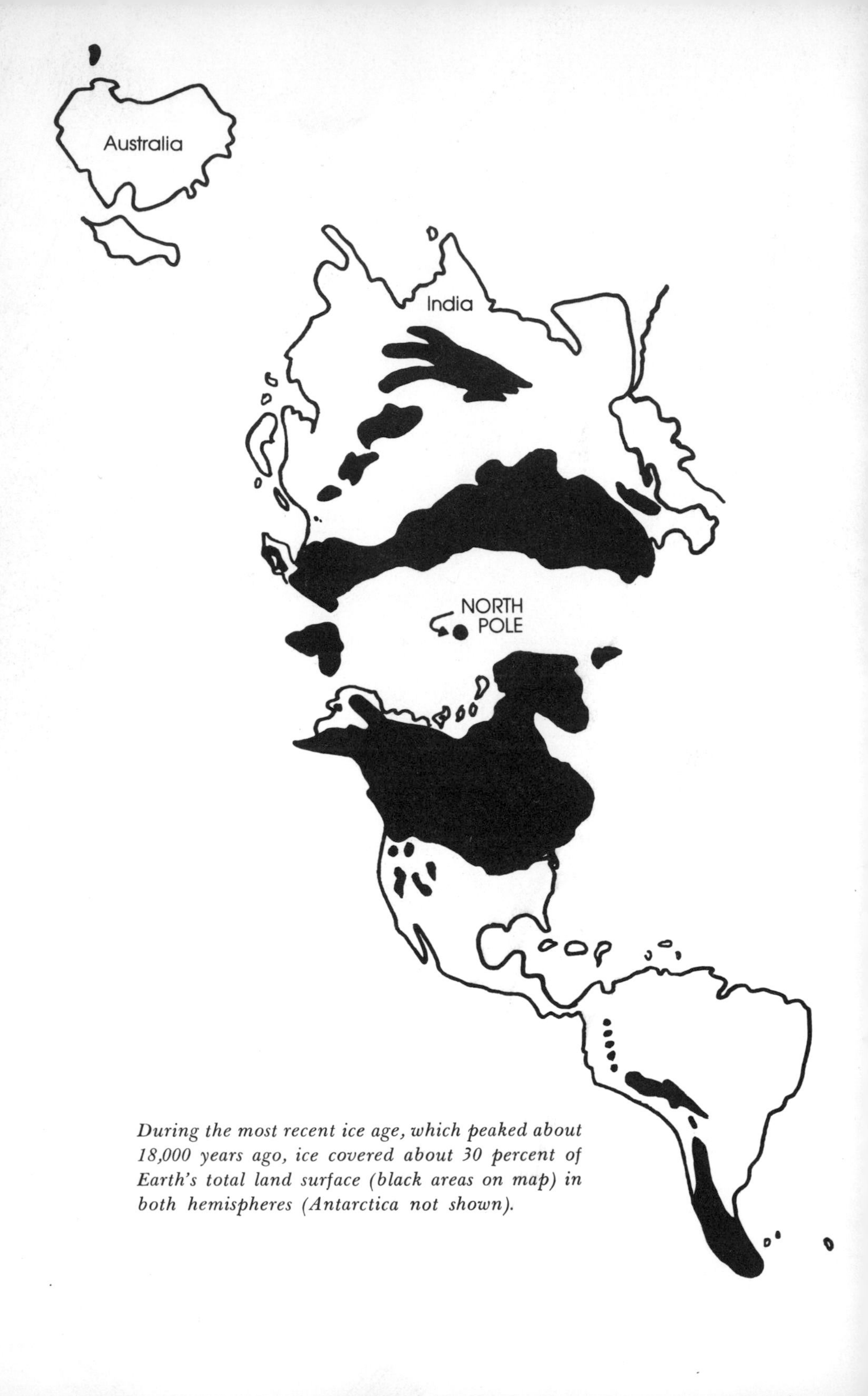

During the most recent ice age, which peaked about 18,000 years ago, ice covered about 30 percent of Earth's total land surface (black areas on map) in both hemispheres (Antarctica not shown).

Mountain glaciers flow toward the sea, meandering as they follow the steepest incline toward sea level. *See also page 116.*
COURTESY: THE AMERICAN MUSEUM OF NATURAL HISTORY; PHOTO BY THE AUTHOR

---

period occurred about 18,000 years ago, and it ended about 13,000 years ago. Evidence for these periods of alternating cold and warmth comes from oxygen–18/oxygen–16 readings of foraminfera skeletal remains found in core samples of the ocean floors. Throughout this million-year period both polar regions have been blanketed with ice. Ninety percent of this past million-year period has been colder than it is now and colder than it has been over the past several thousands of years.

During the last glacial period the world ocean level dropped about 100 meters (330 feet) as more and more evaporated ocean water condensed out as snow and so was withheld from the general circulation. In a still earlier ice age, sea level may have dropped by 145 meters (475 feet) but then may have risen to as much as 70 to 80 meters (230 to 260 feet) higher than the present level during the following interglacial period.

During the peak of the last ice age, about 18,000 years ago, ice covered a total of 32,000,000 square kilometers (20,000,000 square miles) of Earth's surface and formed in both the Northern and Southern hemispheres at the same time. That amounts to about 30 percent of the planet's total land surface. The low-latitude oceans meanwhile remained relatively warm. The Caribbean, for example, was a balmy 22°C (73°F) 18,000 years ago compared with 29°C (84°F) today. The average thickness of the ice was 1,200 meters (3,925 feet); in some places the maximum thickness probably reached 4,000 meters above sea level (13,000 feet). In the Northern Hemisphere the glacial activity seems to have begun in the mountains of northern Labrador, southern Greenland, and central Norway. These mountain glaciers then grew into ice sheets that spread south.

AS THE GLACIERS ADVANCE

We can imagine the process of accumulation and spreading as the glacial ice fans out in, for example, Greenland. During storm after storm the snows accumulate in thin layers, first in the mountainous regions above the snow line. As such snow layers become compacted they are called *firn*. Later the firn turns to ice, whose bottom layers spread ever downward and out toward the growing ice sheet's edges. At what speed we cannot be certain, but gradually the ice pushes ever outward over hundreds of miles, at first following routes determined by the topography of the land. At one stage of glacial growth the Greenland ice eventually reaches the west coast, where today it forms a frigid shoreline about 400 kilometers (250 miles) long.

In its progress toward the sea, the ice pushes and snakes its way through mountain passes and down long valleys, forming creeping rivers of ice. All the time the ice is pushing and picking up soil and grinding loose rock debris over the bedrock beneath. Meanwhile, much debris falls onto the top of these valley glaciers and is carried along. As the ice approaches confined regions and is funneled through them, the pace of its movement quickens compared with the slow movement of the inland ice. Called *outlet glaciers,* these rivers of ice eventually reach the shore, some continuing their advance along fjords, scouring them and depositing their rock and soil debris into the water.

Those rivers of ice that eventually flow to the sea and deposit thousands of icebergs are called "outlet glaciers." Some move along at about 15 meters (50 feet) a day. The outlet glacier shown here was photographed along the west coast of Greenland. U.S. COAST GUARD PHOTOGRAPH

Along other regions of the coast the advancing ice sheet inches its way outward from the coast. Gradually, one by one, large chunks calve and tumble into the sea as icebergs. Such calving of large bergs occurs as the end section of a glacier pushes its way into the water and is buoyed up. The resulting pressure causes a large section of ice to snap off along those zones of weakness called *crevasses*. Most such bergs are the by-products of the fast-moving outlet glaciers. We do not have exact figures, but some scientists who study glaciers estimate that the Greenland ice sheet today releases as much as 200

One U.S. Coast Guard annual census of icebergs reported a total of 40,232 bergs. Here, along the coast of Greenland, thousands of icebergs are visible, having recently calved off the ends of outlet glaciers. Here they are assembled in Baffin Bay and are slowly making their way southward for a three-year voyage into the shipping lanes off Newfoundland. However, many of the bergs will melt along the way. U.S. COAST GUARD PHOTOGRAPH

This mammoth iceberg was photographed off the Grand Banks of Newfoundland. Each year oceanographic research scientists conduct iceberg counts. Data collected over the years then serves as a reliable means of predicting the drift patterns of icebergs. U.S. COAST GUARD PHOTOGRAPH

---

cubic kilometers (50 cubic miles) of ice into the sea each year. According to geologist James L. Dyson, the Rink Glacier alone, on Greenland's west coast, "has dumped an estimated 500,000,000 tons of ice into the sea in a time span of a few minutes—and it repeats this feat about once every two weeks."

From 10,000 to 15,000 large icebergs calve into the sea from Greenland's shores every year. In 1943 United States Coast Guard iceberg census takers counted a total of 40,232 bergs. Some of Greenland's bergs are nearly two kilometers (about one mile) or more long and tower 90 meters (300 feet) into the air. The one shown here is 295 meters (950 feet) long and 125 meters (400 feet) above the water line. So to re-create the scene around Greenland some 18,000 years ago, we need only visit that desolate land today.

If the Greenland ice cap were to melt suddenly, the sea level would rise seven meters (24 feet). But "sudden" melting is not the rule in nature. To melt all of the polar ice we would have to experience for a period of 10,000 years, a gradual increase in world temperature typical of the rise over the past 100 years, according to geographer Howard J. Critchfield of Western Washington State College. Others disagree, saying that the time required would be only a few thousand years. The greatest known depth of Greenland's ice cap is 3,365 meters (11,000 feet). If all of that ice were spread evenly over the entire surface of the planet it would form a layer five meters (17 feet) thick. The Antarctic ice cap similarly reaches a thickness of about 3,060 meters (10,000 feet).

In North America during the last glacial period just about all of Canada was covered with ice, and the eastern United States was covered as far south as 38° to 39°N, near St. Louis, Missouri. Seemingly because of relatively little snowfall, the lowlands of northern Alaska and parts of the Canadian Archipelago, as shown in the diagram, did not accumulate glaciers. In the Southern Hemisphere the ice was confined mostly to the mountain regions and to high latitudes such as New Zealand. Drift ice at those latitudes was very common. On the land—especially Africa and South America—grasslands, steppes, and deserts spread at the expense of forests because

---

This cross-section of the Greenland ice cap shows the ice reaching a maximum depth of 3,360 meters (11,000 feet). If all that ice were spread evenly over Earth's surface it would form a layer five meters (17 feet) thick.

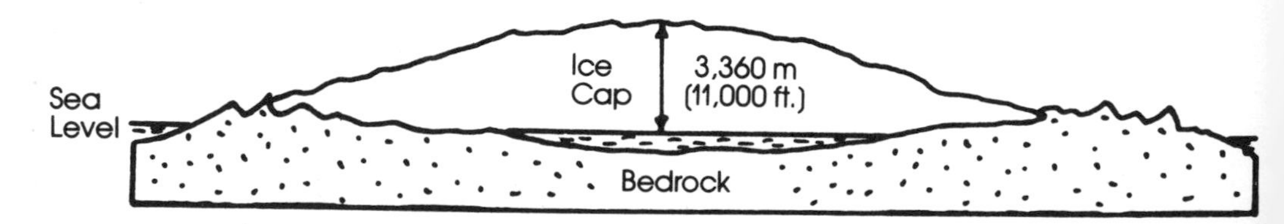

of a general drying. Coupled with the sprawling ice in both hemispheres, this change in vegetation caused a greater amount of the Sun's energy to be reflected back to space than is being reflected back today.

The mountain glaciers that formed in southern Alaska and in the Pamir-Hindukush-Karakoram part of central Asia did not grow into extensive ice sheets. In nearly all of the high mountain areas the snow lines crept down by 1,000 to 1,400 meters (3,270 to 4,580 feet) lower on the mountain slopes. Mountains along the tropics also had their snow lines lowered, by 700 to 900 meters (2,290 to 2,945 feet).

We might at first think that these massive blankets of ice would cause a *sharp* drop in the average world temperature, but this is not the case. The ups and downs of Earth's mean temperature from one geologic period to another seem to have amounted to only a few degrees Celsius rather than ten or more degrees. At least that is the general rule. But we can expect a sharper change from an interglacial to a glacial period. The average drop in mean temperature during the last ice age from the previous interglacial was only 5° or 6°C (about 10°F), but it was greater than that in middle latitudes.

The temperature change in the region of Greenland and similar areas with great ice domes, however, was greater and on the order of 12°C (21°F) compared with recent times. This sharper change was caused by air flowing down over the surface of the ice domes and being rapidly cooled. Coastal Ireland, France, and northern Spain had similar drops. In contrast, the temperature drop along the Pacific Coast of North America, at the same latitudes, was closer to the average of 5° to 6°C. This marked difference between the Pacific and Atlantic regions seems to have been caused by the initial lowering of sea level at the 40-meter (130-foot) stage. When the Pacific lowered by that amount the Bering Strait between Alaska and Russia was closed. This meant that relatively warm water from the Pacific could no longer flow into the Arctic Ocean. However, the flow of cold Arctic water down into the Atlantic continued.

A change in only two or so degrees Celsius in average world temperature seems to be enough to tilt the scales toward glaciation during an interglacial period, or toward an interglacial period from a glacial period.

We might suppose that such widespread ice coverage as occurred during the last glacial period would raise havoc in the plant and animal kingdoms and lead to the wholesale extinction of species. But apparently not—relatively few such extinctions seem to have been caused. It is true that several large land mammals—the mammoths, mastodons, ground sloths, and saber-toothed cats—did become extinct during the time we are concerned with. Although climate change has been suggested as a direct cause for some of the extinctions—for example, the mastodons—it is difficult to blame climate change on all of them.

One important effect of the advancing and retreating ice was a change in the distribution of plant and animal populations. For example, glacial deposits found in central and western Europe contain the remains of woolly rhinoceroses, mammoths, lemmings, reindeer, Arctic foxes, and moose, all species adapted to cold-weather environments. However, interglacial deposits in the same regions contain the remains of lions, rhinoceroses, hippopotamuses, and hyenas, all adapted to a warmer climate, a climate characteristic of Africa today. In the United States during the last glacial period reindeer and woolly mammoths lived in southern New England and moose roamed the New Jersey countryside. One animal, a creature of the age of ice, that did well biologically when on emerging about 500,000 years ago was *Homo sapiens*, or modern man.

At the peak of the last glaciation, as with the peaks of others, there was a dry period. Possibly these periods are caused by the cooler surface water of the oceans and an accompanying lessening of evaporation, which would result in smaller amounts of water vapor in the air. The evaporation rate may drop by 30 or 35 percent at such times. During these periods of dryness the winds pick up large amounts of fine dust, called *loess,* which over long periods gradually fall out of the atmosphere.

HOW ICE AGES BEGIN

No one knows for certain what triggers an ice age, although there are several theories. We will come back to more of these theories in the next chapter when we deal with the causes of climate change. All such theories fall into one of two categories: (1) Ice ages are set off by astronomical conditions, for example, a decrease in energy output of the Sun, or the Solar System passing through a nebula, a large cloud of space dust. (2) Ice ages are set off by events on Earth itself. For example—and this may be nothing more than coincidence—ice ages appear to occur during times of extensive mountain-building activity.

Some theories look to changes in ocean currents as the cause of ice ages. For instance, it is known that the Isthmus of Panama, linking North and South America, uplifted about two million years ago. When this huge land bridge was thrust up it blocked the warm currents flowing westward from the Atlantic into the Pacific Ocean. So an increased amount of warm Atlantic water was forced into the North Atlantic Ocean toward Newfoundland and Greenland. The then larger surface area of warm water would have led to an increase in evaporation, resulting in increased precipitation in the form of snow, enough snow to support the growth of ice fields. Some climatologists think that the northern ice sheets may be controlled by the Gulf Stream. According to this theory, as the great current of warm water shifts its position and becomes stronger or weaker from time to time, it causes an alternating spread and retreat of northern ice.

The ocean-control theory is an attractive one, although still only a theory. It assumes that once a massive buildup of ice begins there is a gradual cooling of the oceans. This cooling results in a gradual decrease in precipitation with the eventual result that the glacial region is starved of snow and stops advancing. It stops because its rate of melting is now greater than its rate of accumulation. This, then, is the arid stage mentioned earlier, a time when large amounts of loess enter the atmosphere. It has been suggested that this fine dust of mineral grains is deposited in thin layers on the continental ice sheets as it slowly settles out of the air. This causes a sharp reduction in the amount of solar energy reflected back to the atmosphere by the ice. The result is that the increased absorption of heat caused by the loess particles speeds melting. Although this may actually occur in certain places, it certainly did not occur in Antarctica and only very slightly in Greenland.

You can demonstrate this principle of melting by lightly sprinkling wood ashes over a patch of snow and then observing the difference in the rate of melting between your darkened patch and the surrounding, undisturbed snow.

THE PAST SEVERAL THOUSAND YEARS

We must not suppose that simply because we are now dealing with the period of written human history that we have highly detailed and reliable records of climate. We do not, at least not until the 1870s. For most of the period since the birth of Christ, documented climate change comes from manuscripts written for purposes other than describing climate, which often makes interpretation difficult. Although writers may have reported many details of drought, advancing glaciers, or a period of severe storms, periods of "normal" climate may not be mentioned at all. However, reports of wheat, corn, vineyard, and other such crop yields often can be used to fill in gaps. For instance, one indication that Europe was warm and dry in the seventh century is the heavy traffic over mountain passes in the Alps, passes now filled with ice. And a warm and dry period must have benefited England in the tenth and eleventh centuries since wine production there then reached its peak. Reports of floods and of human migrations, when coupled with other evidence, can also be used as climate indicators.

Since the retreat of the continental glaciers of the last ice age there have been several marked fluctuations of climate. Evidence of these fluctuations is based on a study of pollen records, tree growth-line records, and other sources. As the diagram shows, beginning about 15,000 years ago there was a marked general warming. Between 10,000 and 12,000 years ago there was very abrupt climate fluctuation. At that time the climate was still relatively cool and wet, a waning holdover from the dying glacial period, called the *Older Dryas.* Then there was a relatively sudden period of planet-wide warming, called the *Alleröd,* when the temperature rose about 6°C (9°F). At this time there seems to have been a dramatic warming of the oceans and a sharp change in the general circulation of the atmosphere. Evidence for the Alleröd comes from ocean-floor sediment cores, ice cores from Greenland, and records of the change in the level of lakes. Then came a dramatic readvance of ice around 10,800 years ago. In less than a century, according to the British climatologist H. H. Lamb, the ice came and wiped out huge areas of forests, and much of the earlier 6°C temperature gains were lost. Called the *Younger Dryas,* this new cold period once again transformed vast regions of Europe to sub-Arctic conditions of vegetation—small

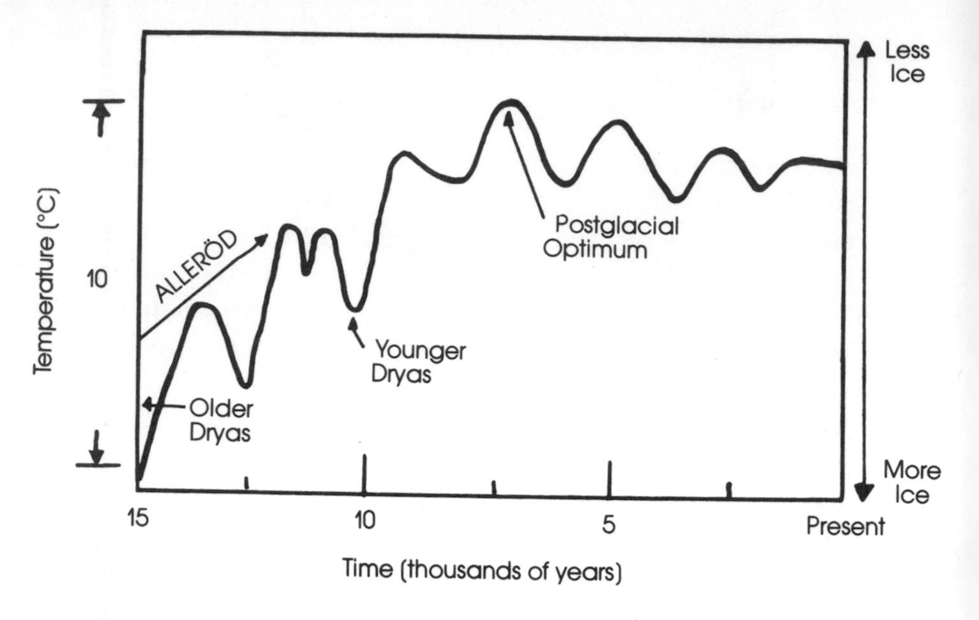

The last ice age peaked about 18,000 years ago. About 15,000 years ago a marked warming period began in the Northern Hemisphere and lasted until the Postglacial Optimum some 7,000 to 8,000 years ago. Notice the sudden advance of ice about 10,800 years ago, which wiped out huge areas of forests in less than a century. AFTER NATIONAL RESEARCH COUNCIL AND REID A. BRYSON

---

woody shrubs, moss, and lichens—creating treeless plains called *tundra.* For whatever reasons ice masses come and go, these went as suddenly as they had come and the following period was one of warming.

This planet-wide warming peaked sometime between 5,000 and 6,000 years ago, at which time world temperatures were as much as 3°C (5.4°F) higher than today. Large regions, including parts of North America and the USSR, were both warm and dry. Arctic Ocean ice withdrew considerably farther north than its position now, possibly to as far north as 80°. In places its winter limit now reaches about 70°N. While some regions were generally dry, others, including the Sahara Desert region and presently dry areas of the Near East, enjoyed a warm and moist climate and occasional heavy rains. Around the globe numerous glaciers left over from the Older Dryas were greatly reduced in size, some melting completely. As they did, the snow line retreated to higher levels on the mountains, reaching about 300 meters (980 feet) above the snow lines of those mountains today. The warming of this period—called the *Postglacial Optimum*—and accompanying melting caused the world ocean level to rise to its present level.

Interestingly, 6,600 years ago there was a brief and sudden fall in temperature. At the same time, a large volcano erupted in what is now Crater Lake, Oregon, spewing many tons of ash into the atmosphere. The ash spread eastward and most likely formed a thin veil that screened out small but significant amounts of heat from the Sun. In the next chapter we will have more to say about volcanic eruptions as possible causes of climate change.

As the diagram on the previous page shows, since the warming peak of the Postglacial Optimum about 6,600 years ago, there has been a general cooling with three sharp but brief dips in temperature.

THE PAST THOUSAND YEARS

Lamb has deduced the ups and downs of winter temperatures for eastern Europe over the past 1,000 years, as shown in the diagram. Notice the temperature curve for the period from about the year 900 to the year 1200. There are three peaks of warming that occurred during that time, which historians call the Middle Ages. During this period both Greenland and Iceland were enjoying a relatively warm climate, conditions there being much less harsh than they are today. Southern Greenland's average temperature probably was as much as 4°C (about 5°F) higher than it is today.

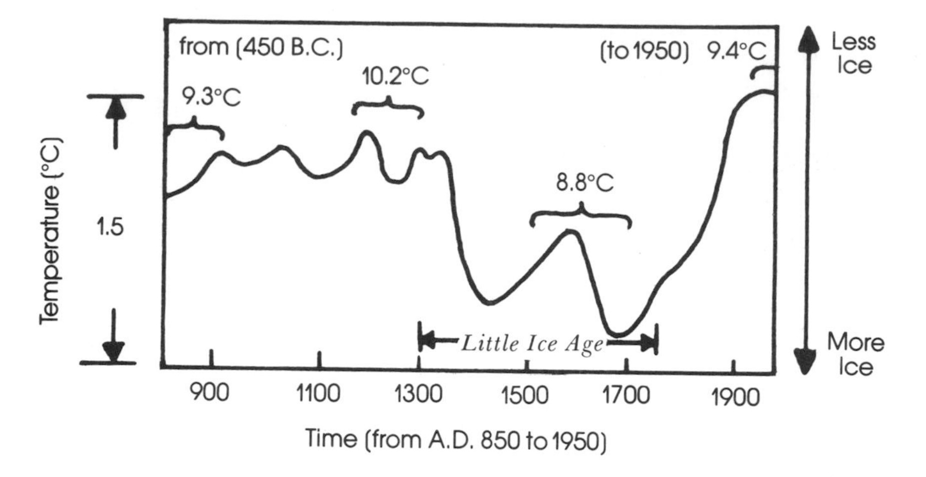

The diagram shows Northern Hemisphere temperature ups and downs from about A.D. *900 to about 1950. Notice the three warming peaks between about 900 and 1200. It was during this period that relatively warm seas permitted the Vikings to sail the waters between Iceland, Greenland, and America. Notice that from 450* B.C. *to about* A.D. *1000 the average temperature was about 9.3°C (49°F), then it rose to 10.2°C (50°F) for the period from about 1200 to 1300. Then there was a sudden dip to 8.8°C (48°F) during that period known as the "Little Ice Age."* AFTER NATIONAL RESEARCH COUNCIL AND H. H. LAMB

It was during the period from the 800s to the 1300s that a hardy group of adventurers, called the Norsemen, settled Iceland. The period of mild climate had led to a retreat of glaciers both on Iceland and southern Greenland and had opened a considerable amount of rich land for farming. During the first three centuries after the Norsemen settled in Iceland, there was scarcely a trace of drifting ice in the waters north of the island to hinder navigation. Erik the Red, followed later by many others, set sail in open boats from western Iceland and navigated to southwest Greenland. Here they set up colonies and for several centuries continued to carry on a brisk trade with Europe.

FREEZING OF THE NORSEMEN

Notice in the diagram what occurred from approximately 1300 to 1750. This period of cooling is known as the "Little Ice Age." As Europe's glaciers again began a forward march, as did the glaciers of Iceland and Greenland, floating pack ice began to make the established navigation routes between Greenland and Iceland hazardous. The route had to be moved ever farther southward as increasing amounts of drift ice were carried into the shipping lanes by the East Greenland Current. By the early 1400s trade between Greenland and Europe was stopped completely, partly for political reasons but also because of the hazardous conditions caused by drifting ice and a shift in the course of the Gulf Stream to the south.

For a period of about 100 years following the closing of the trade route with the homeland and Europe, the Norse colonies of southwest Greenland remained isolated. And it wasn't until the 1500s, when there was a brief period of slight warming, that European ships once again ventured to Greenland. On arriving, however, they discovered not a trace of the intrepid Norsemen. They had vanished.

The most likely cause of their failure to survive was being deprived of essential raw materials such as wood for shipbuilding, metal for toolmaking, and foodstuffs such as corn and flour. It now seems that the few Norsemen who did survive took up an Eskimo way of life, learning from the Eskimos who worked their way to southern Greenland to follow the walrus and seal, which were being driven farther south down the Davis Strait by increasing amounts of ice.

The telltale record left by the Norse settlements is a grim one. In 1921 the Danish archaeologist Poul Nörland began excavating the graves in a small cemetery of an old Viking colony at Herjolfsnes, which is located on Greenland's southwest coast. For 500 years the graves had remained undisturbed. There could be no doubt that the climate had grown harsh after the burial of these people. Skeletons, objects of wood, and even clothing were preserved, in spite of the long time they had been exposed to the soil.

As Dyson describes it:

> When they were excavated, the bodies were in permafrost [permanently frozen ground just beneath the surface soil], and the excellent preservation of the clothing is a sure sign that the ground in which it lay must have been frozen throughout most of the 500-year period of burial. Since the graves would not have been dug in the hard frozen ground —even today this is not done in permafrost regions—it must be assumed that the ground was not permanently frozen, at least not close to the surface, at the time the bodies were buried. The oldest burials were the deepest; later graves were dug to lesser and lesser depths as the permafrost zone moved upward, enveloping the bodies of those buried earlier. Further—and this leaves no room for doubt about the condition of the ground—the coffins, clothes, and even the bodies were enmeshed in plant roots which, of course, could not have penetrated into permanently frozen ground.
>
> So after the earliest Norsemen at Herjolfsnes were laid to rest, the summer thaw, under the influence of a cooling climate, penetrated to less and less depth, and finally, about the time Columbus began his epic voyages to the West Indies, the remains of the last surviving Norsemen in Greenland were claimed by the permanently frozen ground, in whose grip they remained until removed by the Danes in 1921. The extent of the frozen ground remains unchanged to the present time.

There can be no doubt that the Little Ice Age occurred, but it was a far cry from the harsh conditions of the last great ice age.

CLIMATE AND MADNESS

While the Norsemen were establishing their settlements in Iceland and Greenland during that mild period from about 900 to 1300, large numbers of people of western Europe from time to time were gripped by outbreaks of mass madness. Entire villages would suffer convulsions and hallucinations. In advanced forms the disease caused a darkening of the fingers and toes, which eventually fell off. Death was common among those afflicted by the dreaded disease. By the 1500s the disease had begun to die out as suddenly and mysteriously as it had appeared.

Late in the 1500s its cause was traced to a poison produced by a fungus (*Claviceps purpurea*) contained in kernels of rye. The fungus causes a blight that turns the kernels of stricken plants dark. Unaware of what they were doing, bakers of the time mixed the blighted rye in the flour they used to make bread. Anyone eating the bread then came down with the disease.

Beginning around 1150 and lasting three centuries or so, western Europeans were enjoying the same relatively mild winters that made the Vikings' Greenland colony possible. However, this period in western Europe brought steady, moisture-laden winds blowing out of the west off the Atlantic Ocean and spreading damp conditions far inland. Whenever this happens, fields remain forever wet and there is little sunshine for the grain harvest. Farmers in England, Denmark, and other regions of the stricken parts of Europe had to abandon their fields at such times of endlessly damp summers. These conditions, it turns out, are just those favored by the blight-causing fungus.

THE FARMERS WHO RAN AWAY

During this same period when many Europeans were suffering from madness indirectly brought about by climate, some-

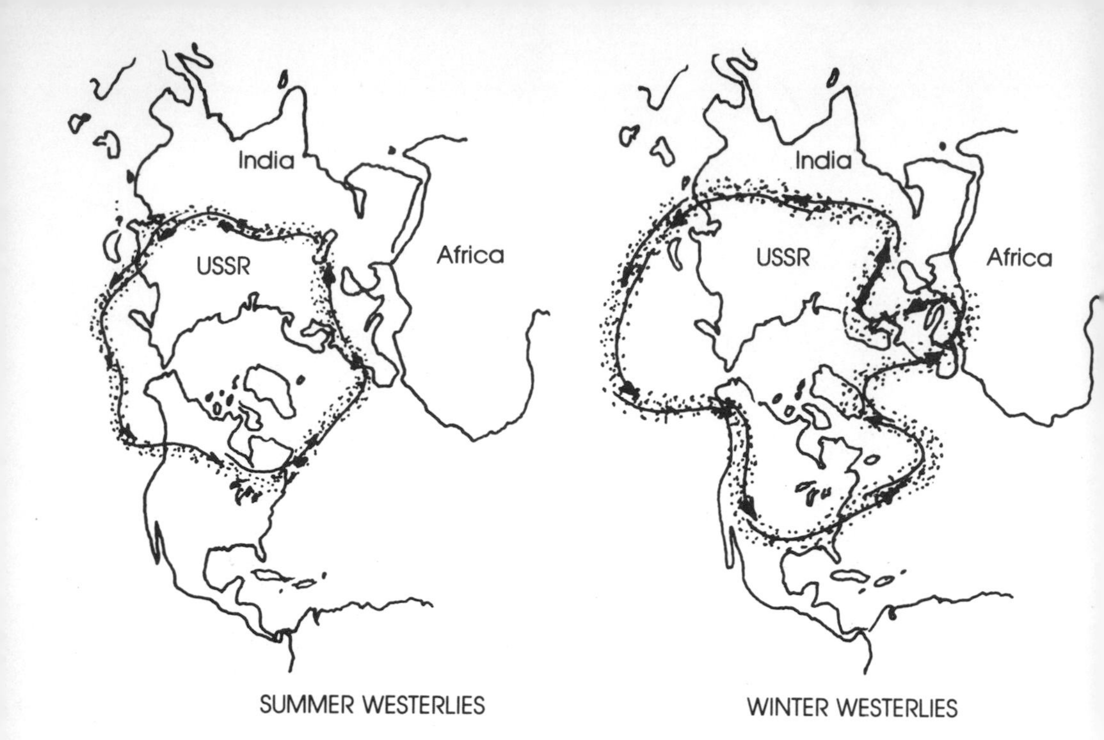

The prevailing westerly winds tend to change their flow pattern from summer to winter. In summer (left) they tend to form a relatively tight ring around the North Pole. In winter (left) the pattern changes as the westerlies tend to expand somewhat into lower latitudes and their loops broaden. AFTER REID A. BRYSON

---

thing interesting was taking place in the United States. At that time there were hundreds of small villages of farmers occupying that region we call the Great Plains, sprawling all the way from Iowa to Colorado. Archaeologists have enough clues about these early Americans to know that they hunted during the winter season and planted large areas of corn during the summer, as they had for centuries. By the 1500s only a handful of these once-thriving villages remained. The farmers had gone away and the villages were no more. What had happened?

By doing some rather interesting scientific sleuthing, Bryson and an anthropologist friend named David Baerreis produced the answer, which we will sketch out here. A more detailed account of it is given in Bryson's book, *Climates of Hunger,* which he prepared jointly with science writer Thomas J. Murray.

First of all, meteorological records going back several decades show that the prevailing westerlies are no more consistent than are the ocean currents. Both are subject to change. As the diagram shows, the westerlies tend to change their flow pattern from summer to winter. In summer they tend to form a relatively tight ring around the North Pole and go through a series of gentle loops. In winter the pattern changes as they tend to expand somewhat into lower latitudes and their loops become more meandering. During a period of expanded westerlies, cold air formed above the Arctic ice is permitted to flow farther south as the confining westerlies belt is slackened.

Bryson felt that the dying of the Greenland Norsemen, the disappearance of the Great Plains Indian farmers, and the cool, damp conditions of western Europe that brought on the rye blight might all be linked to a common cause.

As the diagram shows, the summer westerlies tend to flow across North America at a relatively high latitude. This northward migration of the summer westerlies permits warm, moist air from the tropics to flow right up against the lower limit of the westerlies. This warm, moist air is the source of rain over the Great Plains region. Warm, moist air also moves in off the Pacific. As it crosses the Pacific coast mountains and then the Rocky Mountains, this moist air tends to lose its moisture as it is forced aloft and cooled. On being cooled its moisture condenses out as rain that falls heavily on the western slopes of the mountains. Next, the air rushes down the eastern slopes of the mountain ranges and reaches the Great Plains region as relatively dry air. This "dry shadow" zone of the Rockies, as it is called, stretches eastward from the Dakotas through Iowa and into Illinois.

Now suppose that the normal seasonal expansion of the westerlies occurred on schedule but failed to return fully to its summer pattern the following year and that the winds were left in a slightly expanded position. And suppose further that the now expanded westerlies remained that way for two or three centuries.

Western Europe would be plagued with a continued period of cool and wet summers caused by strong winds blowing off the Atlantic. Greenland and Iceland would enter a cold period because of the southern expansion of cold Arctic air. Over North America the southern migration of the westerlies belt would sharply decrease the supply of warm, moist tropical air moving up from the south. Coupled with that, Bryson argues, would be a stronger flow of the westerlies over the Rockies with an increase in dry air sweeping across the Great Plains. In short, an onset and continuation of severe drought would occur there as the westerlies slightly expanded and remained that way.

Is this what happened to drive the Plains Indians away beginning around the year 1200? Bryson says yes. To find evidence for his theory he had to turn part-time anthropologist-archaeologist and so turned to his colleague David Baerreis. Their excavations at the so-called Mill Creek sites in Iowa, Nebraska, and South Dakota revealed what they had expected.

ARCHAEOLOGICAL SLEUTHING

Bryson and Baerreis had been looking for sites where ancient Indian settlements had stood for several centuries. Once such a site was found they made test digs to locate the community dump. Large mounds often mark such locations where one settlement builds right on top of an older one, and so on over the years. When the archaeologist uncovers the remains layer by layer, or settlement by settlement, he can then draw certain conclusions on how the people lived, what they ate, what tools they used, the crafts they practiced, and so on.

One thing these investigators knew was that the Plains Indians were hunter-farmers. In summer they planted corn and the rest of the year hunted several different kinds of game, including bison and deer. Bryson and Baerreis concentrated on collecting deer and bison bones and comparing the relative numbers of each, century by century. They were able to date these and other remains by carbon–14 dating.

Deer tend to be abundant when the climate brings enough rain to provide the leafy vegetation these animals browse on. Bison also do well during such times but they also continue to do well during times of relative dryness since they are grazing, not browsing, animals. During dry periods the deer tend to move away in search of moister areas. The bone counts indicated that "up to the year 1100 or so, deer bones ranked first," according to Bryson. "After that, the percentage of deer dropped, and bison bones became more prominent." The count also showed a sharp decline in the total number of bones after 1100.

Further study of pollen remains at the Mill Creek sites indicated what kinds of trees and grasses were plentiful or scarce over this period of two to three centuries. Again, the findings suggested general drying conditions. A predominance of trees that require moderate amounts of water was found around the year 1100, but later they were replaced by plants that favor a drier climate.

What effect did the long period of drought have on the corn farming of the Indians? According to Bryson: "As an index to corn production, we counted potsherds—pieces of broken pottery. We believed corn production and potsherds were related, because pottery would be needed to store, cook, and serve corn. Meat could be roasted and held in the hand.

"The numbers of potsherds remained high when bone counts first dropped. This hints that, while the drought must have hurt the corn farming, it hurt hunting even more. The potsherd count, if read as a reflection of the total number of people in the village, also suggests that the human population did not decline immediately.

"But with little food of any kind as the drought continued, numbers of bones and sherds both dropped rapidly after 1200, and by 1400 or so there were none, and no Indians either. The farmers were gone."

Bryson has no doubt the shifting westerlies brought on the climate change that drove the Indians away. But the question of where they went remains. We know the fate of at least one group, who for centuries had lived in western Nebraska on the upper Republican River, an area particularly hard hit by the drought. Farther south, across Kansas and into the Oklahoma Panhandle, the remains of other Indian settlements were discovered, settlements that showed unmistakable traces of Republican culture. The remains of these Panhandle Indian cultures had never been dated before. Could it be that they, too, died out at the same time as the Nebraska Indian cultures had? The radiocarbon dating of numerous samples showed just about the opposite—the Panhandle cultures had *begun,* not ended, around the year 1200. So at least some of the Great Plains Indians had migrated southward until they reached the lower limit of the expanded westerlies belt where moist air flowing up from the south provided them with adequate rain. And the migration was not one that lingered on over centuries. It has all the earmarks of having taken place in a short time span of about 25 years.

We will never know how many of America's early Indian

settlements perished in the great drought. But we do know that the drought was widespread. The evidence is clear that Indian communities in the southwest also were abandoned. According to Emmanuel LeRoy Ladurie, the cliff-dwelling Indians of Mesa Verde, Colorado, ran away or perished during the years 1271 to 1285. The exact dating is provided by tree growth-ring counts.

FURTHER EFFECTS OF THE "LITTLE ICE AGE"

During the period from about 1400 to 1850 there was another dramatic change in climate. The midlatitude winters gradually became longer, colder, and more severe, and the summers cooler and shorter. Again, the expanding westerlies seem to have been the cause. The overall drop in temperature was only one or two Fahrenheit degrees, not the 6°C (10°F) that triggers a major ice age. But that small drop was enough to bring a major change to those areas marginally evolved for growing oats and barley.

It doesn't take much of a temperature drop to shorten the growing season significantly. For each 1°C of cooling, the growing season is shortened by ten days. It cannot be overemphasized that *small* changes in *long-term* averages can be very important, especially at midlatitudes and higher, where the growing season tends to be short even in good times.

Mountain glaciers again advanced, some engulfing Swiss mountain villages. Such advances took place in 1600, 1640, 1740, 1810, 1820, and 1850. After that there was a planet-wide retreat of ice once again.

Try to imagine looking out your bedroom window and seeing, only a quarter of a mile or less away, a wall of ice 15 meters (50 feet) high and 105 meters (600 feet) wide inching its way toward you. This was the view that residents of the village of Chamonix, in the French Alps, had around the year

1600. By this time several mountain glaciers in the Alps had advanced way beyond their limits of a century earlier. Certain that the ice would overrun and crush their homes to rubble, many people left and took up life elsewhere. Others remained and tried to carry on in hopes that the threatening glacier would stop and once again begin to retreat. Many such people starved to death, for the shorter growing season, coupled with lower temperatures, either prevented their crops from maturing or killed them entirely.

After the 1850s, when the Alpine mountain glaciers again withdrew, only rubble and the geological telltale signs of glacier activity remained in some parts of the Chamonix Valley. Those Chamonix villages that survived the glacial advance of the Little Ice Age today have about one kilometer (about half a mile) of woods and glacial rubble between themselves and the present limit of the glaciers.

Historical records show that the winter of 1709 was especially fierce, killing people living in western Europe as if war had torn their land. According to Ladurie, in his book *Times of Feast, Times of Famine,* an Angiers priest of France wrote: "The cold began on January 6, 1709, and lasted in all its rigor until the twenty-fourth. The crops that had been sown were all completely destroyed. . . . Most of the hens had died of cold, as had the beasts in the stables. When any poultry did survive the cold, their combs were seen to freeze and fall off. Many birds, ducks, partridges, woodcock, and blackbirds died and were found on the roads and on the thick ice and frequent snow. Oaks, ashes, and other valley trees split with cold. Two thirds of the walnut trees died."

Thirty years later western Europe experienced another terrible winter. Belgium was especially hard hit. Again, Ladurie reports that there was "no spring, bad weather up till the middle of May, a short, cold, dull summer, a late wheat harvest spoiled by rain, wine harvests and fruit destroyed by the early frosts." As with the previous severe winter, the poor rebelled and rioted because there was so little food. According to Ladurie, the governor of Liège advised wealthy people who had ample stores of food to "fire into the middle of (groups of the poor people who were rioting). That's the only way to disperse this riffraff, who want nothing but bread and loot."

Winters throughout the Little Ice Age were generally not that severe, although most were more severe than anything we are experiencing now.

While the people of midlatitude western Europe were hard hit during this fairly recent period of cold, so were the people farther north in Scandinavia and Iceland. The Norsemen had grown grain in most of Iceland since about the year 900. With the onset of the long, cold period farming became increasingly hard for them and before long was restricted to southern Iceland. Even at a more southerly latitude the colder and longer winters, resulting in a shorter growing season, reduced their crops to only barley, which is adapted to a short growing season. By the 1500s the Icelanders seem to have abandoned grain-growing completely.

From records compiled of the changing course of the Gulf Stream beginning sometime after 1600, it would seem that the Icelanders were severely beset with cold, along with thick packs of drift ice. Hans Stolle, of the University of Wisconsin, has studied a sequence of old maps and other records indicating the Gulf Stream's changing course. As the diagram shows, between 1500 and 1700 the Gulf Stream had begun what was to be a major shift. While previously, as today, it flowed in a generally northeasterly direction up the North American coast and under Greenland directly to Iceland, during the seventeenth century it began a gradual southward shift, until about 1780 it was flowing in a slightly southerly direction.

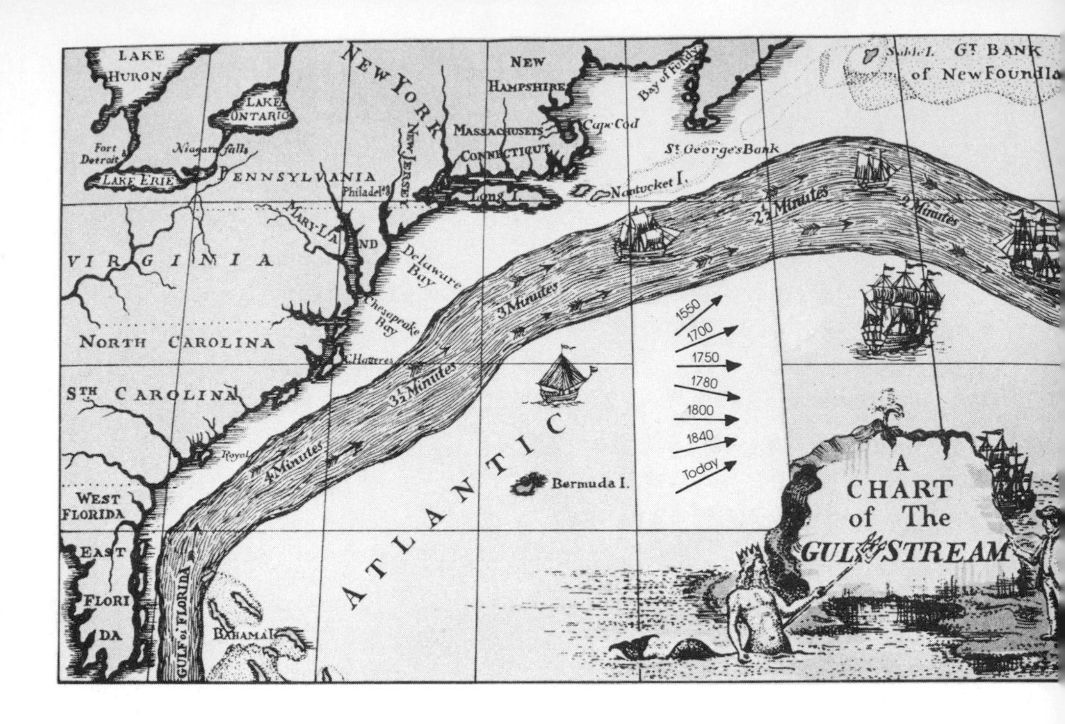

Benjamin Franklin made this map showing the course of the Gulf Stream in 1770. The arrows with dates above them show how the course of the Gulf Stream has changed over the years from 1550 to the present. DATA FROM H. STOLLE

The effect of this shift was to push the warm water of the southern North Atlantic even farther south, meanwhile permitting cold Arctic water to move farther south. The result was a southward invasion of drift ice around Iceland and cooler summer and colder winter winds from the expanded westerlies. It wasn't until well into the 1900s that the Gulf Stream resumed its nearly northeast course of four centuries earlier.

The United States seems to have been less hard hit than western and northern Europe during the Little Ice Age. Because North America was not settled by technologically oriented people until well into the 1600s, we have fewer records than do the Europeans of climate conditions early in the Little

Ice Age. However, pollen records suggest that after about 1400 conditions became cooler and/or wetter, according to Bryson. Other records kept by the army in the mid-1800s show that temperatures for that period averaged about 1.9°C (3.5°F) lower than over a similar time period covering the 1930s and 1940s, with September showing a difference of 3.8°C (6.9°F). In regions that tend to have relatively short growing seasons even when times are favorable, a shortening of the growing season by 20 percent (or about a month) can have serious consequences in food production. As Maine farmers can tell you, a drop in temperature of only a degree or two can mean a killing frost early in September and the loss of several vegetable crops. Still other records for this same mid-1800s period show a tendency toward more northerly winds, a result of the expanded westerlies.

CLIMATE CHANGE SINCE THE 1800s

As we continue our reconstruction of climates up to the present, we are on much firmer ground when we reach the late 1800s. It was during this time that a sufficient number of weather stations were established which collectively could provide systematic global averages of temperature, humidity, wind, precipitation, and other weather readings.

Since the late 1800s, the tendency has been a general warming at the rate of 0.0008°C a year, which would amount to a rise of 0.8°C (1.4°F) from about 1850 to 1950. In 1883, however, an event occurred that caused a brief dip in world temperature. A monstrous eruption of the Krakatoa volcano in Indonesia spewed tons of ash into the atmosphere. Caught up by the winds, the ash screened out some of the Sun's energy. The eruptions of Krakatoa and other volcanoes probably have been responsible for temporary temperature dips measured over several years.

What has happened since about 1950? According to several researchers who have been studying Northern Hemisphere climate conditions over the years, a general cooling has been occurring since 1945 and is continuing. Since that time, according to Bryson, the average cooling for the Northern Hemisphere, above 50°N latitude, amounts to 0.5°C (0.9°F). From 1951 through 1972, according to the German meteorologist Martin Rodewald, the temperature of the North Atlantic dropped rather steadily. In that short, 20-year period its temperature dropped one-sixth of the total drop for that same ocean during the last great ice age!

Bryson is convinced that we are headed for another ice age. In an interview reported in the March 1976 issue of *Mother Earth News*, Bryson said: "We've been in the current interglacial period for approximately 10,800 years now. . . . The question is, how soon will we find ourselves in the next ice age? One hundred years from now, or 9,000 years from now? The odds are very small for 100 years and approach a certainty for 9,000 years. There is, to put it another way, just the barest hint of a possibility that we could start a transition into a glacial epoch during the next century."

WHEN THE ICE COMES

If Bryson is right and the ice is coming, what will it be like? James L. Dyson, in his book *The World of Ice*, paints the following scene:

> What can we say about Chicago or whatever metropolis is sprawled around the southern rim of Lake Michigan at the time of the next ice invasion? The die has already been cast. When the ice again cuts off the Straits of Mackinac and isolates Michigan from the other lakes, all its water will go out through the Chicago outlet and into the Mississippi, if tilting of the Earth's crust has not already caused it to do so.

... Chicago and other lakeside cities will not be submerged under rising waters. If the volume of outflowing water becomes too large for the channel to accommodate, it will simply be enlarged by dredging. By that time earth-moving equipment will have been developed to the point where deepening of river channels and the making of new ones will be mere child's play—or the channel will be made larger by an army of troglodytes wielding picks and shovels! In any event the water would cause few problems. An occasional iceberg that had floated down from the edge of the glacier might get stuck in the channel and cause local flooding, but these trouble spots would quickly be eliminated.

There will, however, be some other events that will have much greater impact on the citizenry of the times. Generations of people will come and go while the ice front advances the length of Lake Michigan. For each one of these generations the changes, because of their slowness, may scarcely be apparent, but during this time Chicago, without moving an inch, will become a city of the sub-Arctic, as first one climatic zone and then another retreats from around it. A shorter and shorter growing season will drive the land of tall corn to the south, and even the dairy herds of Wisconsin—if the people of those times are still using so inefficient a machine as a cow to manufacture their milk—will be inching their way into Illinois and Kentucky.

Long before the ice reaches the Straits of Mackinac much of the lake traffic will have disappeared because of the exhaustion of the iron mines, but now, with the glacier in Lake Michigan itself, all shipping on the lake will have vanished. The shifting sands of shore dunes may be moving again, this time through the ruins of vast steel mills. Slowly but surely the city will be strangled by the destruction of its hinterland.

Not everywhere, on the other hand, will Nature be unkind to man. The southward migration of the Polar Front and Prevailing Westerlies will bring more water to wet the world's arid lands. Each generation of ranchers and farmers in the western desert basins [of the United States] will have a little more irrigation water than the one before it. There will be more snow in the mountains and more rain in the basins. Lakes will begin to expand and playas and salt flats will slowly be covered with permanent water as new lakes are born. The plains east of the mountains, too, will benefit from the new pluvial age.

In the Sahara, in the great deserts of interior Asia, and in other vast dry regions the same changes will take place—more snow in the mountains, more rain in the lowlands. Lakes will expand and new ones will be born.

Past events tell us that in some arid regions there may be more water than men will want. Lakes Bonneville and Lahonton will be re-created, and lands previously made productive by increased rain and by water from the mountains will be claimed by the rising lake waters. [The above mentioned lakes covered vast areas of the western United States some five million years ago. Lake Bonneville, for example, covered an area of 32,000 square kilometers (20,000 square miles) and was about 300 meters (1,000 feet) deep. Its remains today are marked by Great Salt Lake, Utah Lake, and Sevier Lake.]

When the new pluvial age starts, so also will begin the slow creep of Bonneville's waters up toward the wave-cut beaches of the old Provo and Bonneville shorelines and the level of the ancient outlet into the headwaters of the Snake River at Red Rock Pass. But it is unlikely that many generations of the valley inhabitants will watch these waters rise over fertile fields without doing something about it. This time the water will not rise until it is 800 feet deep at the site of the Mormon Temple in Salt Lake City, as it was when old Lake Bonneville flowed out through Red Rock Pass. Regional planners will have determined a critical elevation above which they will not allow the lake to rise. When the water reaches this level the excess waters will be pumped through huge aqueducts for sixty miles along the route of the old outflow and dumped into the headwaters of the Portneuf River to continue their journey through the Snake and Columbia Rivers to the Pacific. Other giant pumping stations might force water over the Wasatch Range to the Colorado in order to help hold this future Lake Bonneville in check.

Not all climatologists agree with Bryson. But we will save the extremely interesting business of Earth's future climate for the last chapter when we come to grips with the ways in which man's activities on this planet may be nudging climate change in one or more directions. It is time now that we turn our attention to the natural causes of climate change.

8

What Causes Climate Change?

It is certain that climate changes. The agents that conspire to bring about those changes are at present illusive. Or are they?

Earlier we mentioned that explanations for climate change can be arranged in two major groups—astronomical events that are external to Earthly affairs; and distinctly Earthly events, such as activities of the atmosphere and oceans and crustal movement. Let's look at astronomical events first to find out to what extent climatologists regard them as agents that bring on climate change.

DOES THE SUN'S ENERGY OUTPUT VARY?

For many centuries various primitive groups have looked on the Sun as a god and, therefore, as the height of perfection. Greek mathematicians of more than 2,000 years ago also looked on the Sun as a model of perfection, a natural object forming a "perfect" circle. But the more we find out about the Sun, the more reasons we discover for regarding it as less than 100 percent predictable, although more of a steady-state object than one characterized by random behavior.

As early as 400 B.C. Chinese astronomers were regularly observing and recording the appearance of dark spots moving along the Sun's equatorial belt of gases. In 1611, Galileo became the first European astronomer to study these "blemishes"

Sunspots, electrical storms generated beneath the Sun's surface layer of gases, tend to occur in cycles of about 11 years. They are an indicator of variations in the Sun's activity, which in turn has been shown to produce climate change on Earth. THE HALE OBSERVATORIES

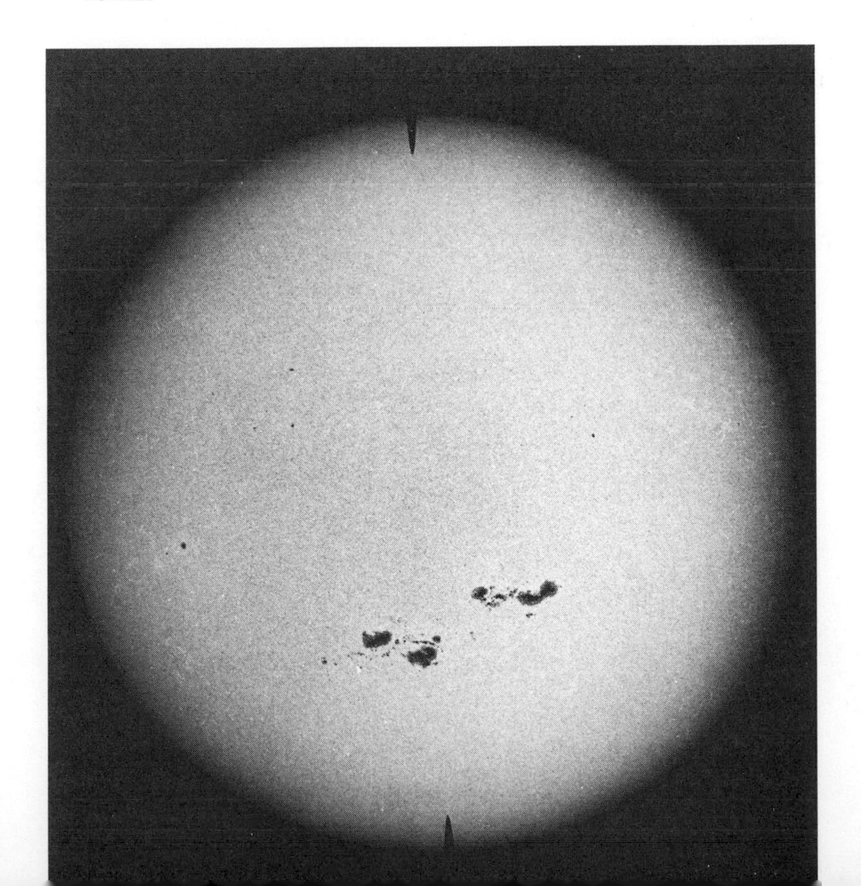

on the Sun's surface. Today we think these disturbances, called *sunspots,* are electrical storms occurring within the Sun's surface gases. They appear as dark spots only because the disturbed areas of gas are cooler than the surrounding surface gases.

Just before the turn of the present century, the English astronomer E. Walter Maunder made a discovery that other astronomers could scarcely believe. A search through old books and journals convinced him that from about 1645 to 1715 sunspots had all but vanished from the Sun, along with other solar activity, such as that responsible for producing the colorful auroras in Earth's atmosphere that are often seen at high northern and southern latitudes. Just a few years before this period, however, when Galileo was observing the Sun, sunspots had been in evidence. And they were observed again later in the 1700s. Maunder concluded that during a single year in this century we count more sunspots than were seen during that entire 70-year period ending in 1715.

Sunspots were observed to come and go in cycles, building up to a peak of activity and then trailing off again. The cycle from one peak to the next took an average of 11.2 years. When there were lots of sunspots there was a flurry of other solar

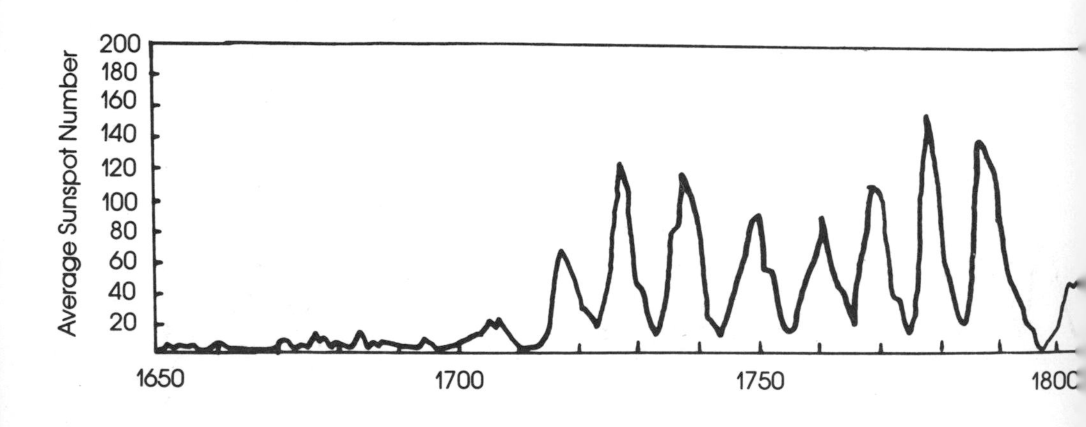

activity also. During an active 70-year period on the Sun as many as 1,000 auroras are seen. Yet Maunder said there was one period of 37 years when there wasn't any record of a single aurora being reported anywhere on Earth.

Auroras were not commonly reported in ancient times, although there had been human settlements in Scandinavia and Iceland since the time of the Norse settlements. It wasn't until 1550 that reports of sightings rose steeply. But such reports were numerous only for about 100 years, until that lean period of 70 years now called the *Maunder sunspot minimum.* Then the period after 1716 proved to be the beginning of another active period of solar activity, including both sunspots and auroras. It is interesting that sunspot activity was very low during the latter part of the Little Ice Age, and very likely throughout most of that period. It also is interesting that the warming period after the Little Ice Age occurred when sunspot activity increased.

The graph shows a succession of peak periods of an active Sun from the year 1650 to 1976. Notice that a neat 11-year cycle of sunspots is not the rule. Sometimes there is a span of only eight years between peak periods, other times as long as 17 years. Notice also the period of 50 years when very few sunspots were reported. AFTER J. EDDY

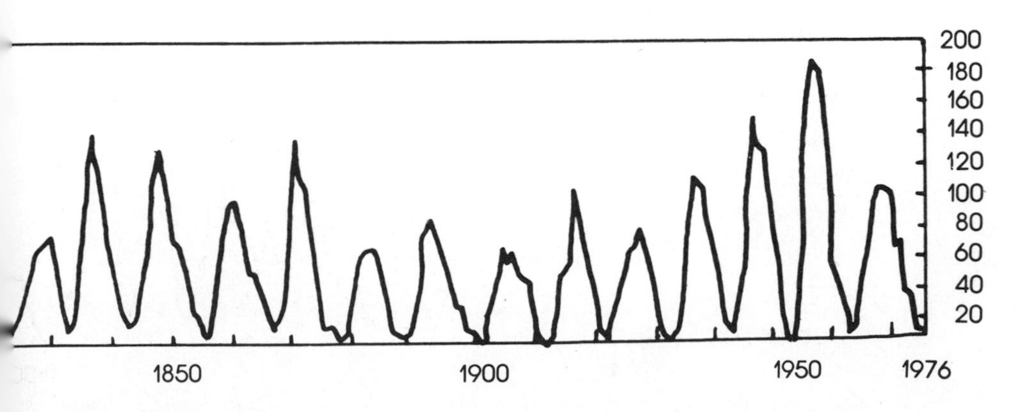

Astronomer John A. Eddy, of the High Altitude Observatory of Boulder, Colorado, is convinced that "the present-day frequency of sunspots and auroras is probably unusual, and that since the seventeenth century the activity of the Sun has risen steadily to a very high level—a level perhaps unequaled (over the past million years)."

Eddy further reports that examination of bristlecone annual growth rings, coupled with carbon–14 dating, gives us a measure of the change in solar activity extending back some 7,000 years. Eddy has shown that over most of that period glaciers have come and gone in pace with decreases and increases in solar activity. "Every rise in solar activity . . . matches a time of glacier retreat." He concludes: "These early results in comparing solar history with climate make it appear that changes on the Sun are the dominant agent of climate changes lasting between 50 and several hundred years."

Physicist Willi Dansgaard, of Copenhagen University, who has studied ice cores of the Greenland ice cap, is also convinced that periods of ice come and go with periods of lesser and greater energy output of the Sun. Dansgaard sees two such solar energy cycles, one peaking about every 78 years, and the other peaking about every 181 years. His long-range forecast is lowering temperatures through the early 1980s, then a gradual warming until the year 2015, which will bring us back to the average temperature of 1960. Then it will start getting cold again, and colder, for the next 50 years or so.

VARIATIONS IN EARTH'S ORBIT

As Earth orbits about the Sun its attitude in space varies in three significant ways. In the 1930s, the Yugoslavian geophysicist N. Milankowitch suggested that these three astronomical aspects of Earth combine and so cause periodic climate change.

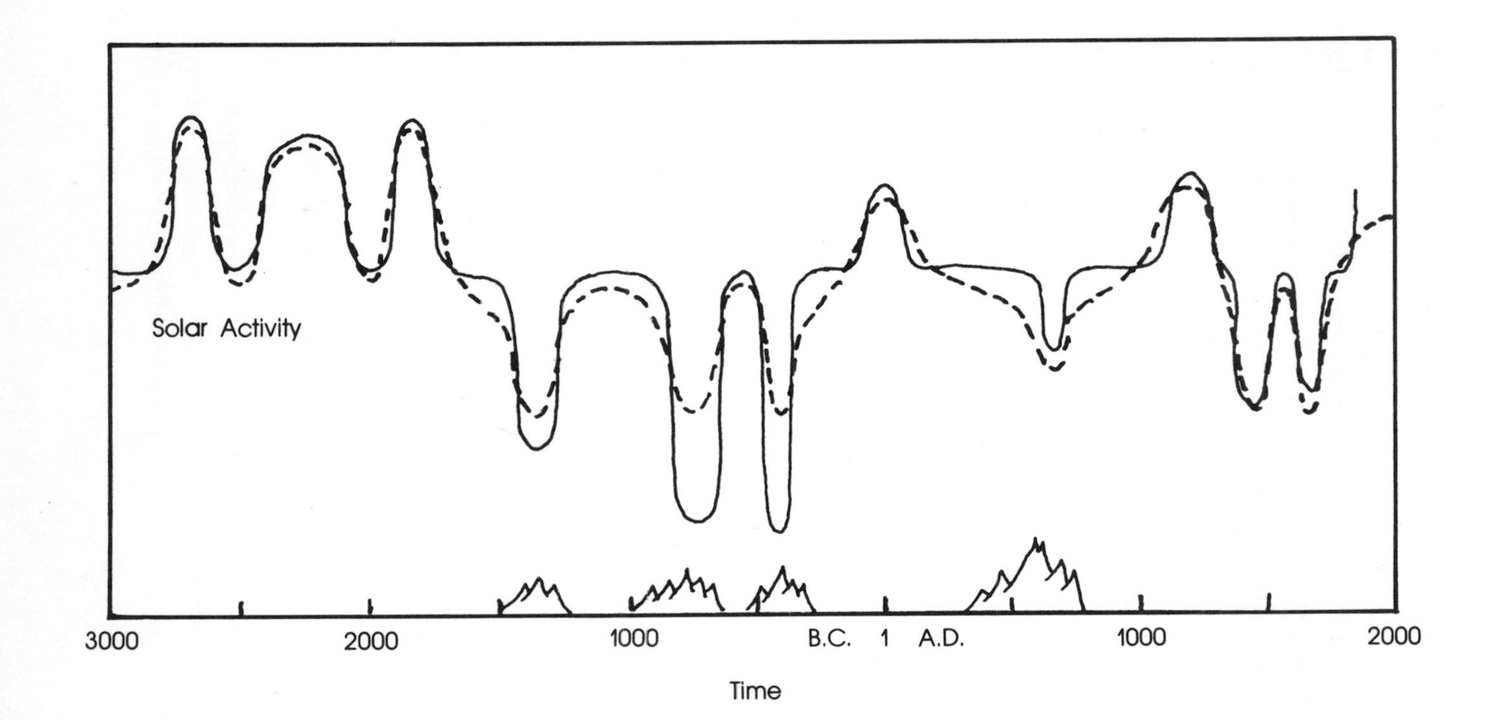

It now appears that changes in the Sun's energy output are the major cause of climate changes lasting between 50 and several hundred years, as shown by the graph. The solid line represents solar activity over the past 5,000 years, based on the abundance of carbon-14 in the growth rings of bristlecone pine trees. The broken line represents solar activity based on "a possible sunspot cycle." The sequence of four "glacial mountains" on the bottom line represents times when Alpine glaciers advanced. AFTER J. EDDY

Earth's axis is inclined by 23.5° with respect to the plane of its orbit about the Sun. We call this tilt its *obliquity,* and it is Earth's obliquity that causes our changing seasons. Like all other things in nature, Earth's obliquity changes. Its range of change has been estimated to be between 22.1° and 24.5°. The greater the tilt the greater the seasonal contrast at a given time. The less the tilt, the less difference there will be. The change in obliquity from least to greatest and back to least again occurs in cycles of about 41,000 years.

Precession is another way in which Earth's attitude in space changes. Tilted over at its present angle of 23.5°, Earth wobbles like a slowly spinning top, completing one wobble-cycle every 25,800 years. As discussed in the second chapter, 10,500 years ago our Northern Hemisphere winter occurred at a time when Earth was most distant from the Sun. Theoretically, winters in the Northern Hemisphere then should have been colder than they are now, and summers hotter.

A third way in which Earth's attitude in space changes with respect to the Sun, and so can bring about climate change, is its varying mean distance from the Sun, called its *eccentricity.* Earth's eccentricity varies from zero to a value of about 0.06 once every 93,000 years. When at its greatest eccentricity and most distant from the Sun, Earth receives an estimated 20 percent less solar radiation than when we are closest to the Sun. From the standpoint of climate change, this is a significant amount when you consider that a drop by only 13 percent would bring on a super ice age, covering Earth's entire surface with a blanket of ice 1.6 kilometers (one mile) thick. A rise of 30 percent would bring on a heat wave that would destroy virtually all Earth life.

Three scientists working on Project Climap, which analyzed hundreds of ocean bottom cores taken from the Southern Hemisphere, have come to the conclusion that changes in

Earth's orbit have been the basic cause of the advancing and retreating of ice over the past two million years. The scientists are a Columbia University geologist, J. D. Hays; a Brown University oceanographer, John Imbrie; and a Cambridge University Quaternary Research Specialist, N. J. Shackleton. Their ocean-floor cores contain climate records of the past 450,000 years. They claim to have found peaks of climate change occurring regularly at 23,000-year periods, which would tend to fit the 25,800-year cycle of precessional wobbles. Another series of climatic peaking occurs every 42,000 years, which would tend to fit the 41,000-year cycle of obliquity shifting. And a third series of climatic peaks occurs about every 100,000 years, which tends to fit the cycle of eccentricity change. Recall Bryson saying that the time between peaks of ice periods was about 100,000 years.

What conclusions do the scientists reach about Earth's future climate? "The long-term trend over the next 20,000 years is toward extensive Northern Hemisphere glaciation and cooler climate," they report.

The *simplest* explanation for the fundamental cause (if there is *one* cause) of a long-term climate change is varying energy output of the Sun. The varying solar energy we receive now seems to be due to two things—a Sun that changes from time to time, and changing motions of Earth. Although scientists are still not in agreement about the Sun's role in climate change, the hypothesis is attractive to some because of its simplicity. As "all of Nature abhors a vacuum," all of science deplores a complex hypothesis.

DUST AS A CAUSE OF CLIMATE CHANGE

When you are lying on the beach on a hot summer day and a cloud passes between you and the Sun you immediately feel a temporary cooling until the cloud is gone. If the Solar System should pass through a cosmic dust cloud in space, it is likely that a similar cooling would be felt on Earth since even a thin veil of space dust would prevent some of the Sun's energy from reaching us. The period Earth remained in a cooler state would, of course, depend on the size and density of the cosmic dust cloud. Has such an event ever occurred?

The British astronomer W. H. McCrea, of Sussex University, says it has. The Solar System revolves about the central hub of our galaxy once each "cosmic year," which is 250 million years long. McCrea says that during its journey around the Galaxy, the Solar System passes through at least two regions (spiral arms) of dense dust. When this happens the Sun's surface heats up as it attracts large amounts of dust into itself. This solar warming, McCrea says, increases Earth's precipitation and cloud cover. The increased cloud cover reflects a more than "normal" amount of solar energy, which results in a general cooling at Earth's surface. McCrea says that the Solar System emerged from a cosmic dust cloud about 10,000 years ago and that we should have clear sailing around our galaxy for the next many millions of years—a long-range forecast indeed.

We are on somewhat firmer ground when we ask if clouds of dust raised on Earth can bring on climate change. They can and certainly have. Ash layers found in Antarctica ice cores show that for a period of about 13,000 years, beginning 30,000 years ago, there was intensive volcanic activity that threw fine ash into the atmosphere. During that time world temperatures lowered by about 3°C (5.5°F). There seem to have been waves of volcanic activity, according to H. H. Lamb, from 3500 to 3000 B.C., again from 500 to 200 B.C., and again from A.D. 1500 to 1900, which fits in well with the Little Ice Age.

In 1815 a volcano known as Mount Tambora in Indonesia erupted and cast an estimated 150 cubic kilometers (36 cubic miles) of ash into the atmosphere. Clouds of the airborne ash were so thick that an area extending 480 kilometers (300 miles) from the volcano was in total darkness for three days. In the United States and Europe, the next year was called "the year without a summer." Temperatures dropped from 1°C (1.8°F) to 3°C (5.5°F). In some places it rained every day—except for three or four days—from May to October. In New England it snowed in June. In 1816 there were frosts every month of the year. Again, this is a reminder of the effects only a very slight drop in temperature can have.

It is suspected that several especially severe winters around the late 1800s may have been caused by the massive eruption of the volcanic island of Krakatoa in the Sunda Strait in 1883.

According to Bryson, massive eruptions during the 1880s made the Northern Hemisphere colder. Then there was an-

---

H. H. Lamb and others suspect that periods of intense volcanic activity are related to periods of cooling since fine volcanic ash and dust tend to block out solar radiation. The graph shows two such related periods—intense volcanic activity from about 1550 to 1700 (the "Little Ice Age") and a corresponding period of cooling in the early 1800s, at which time there was continued intensive volcanic activity. AFTER H. FLOHN AND H. H. LAMB

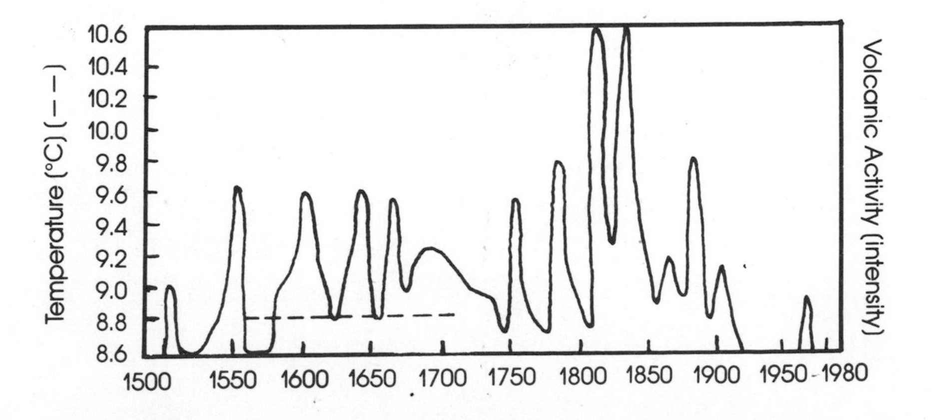

other active period from about 1904 to 1920. And there was a third active period beginning in 1963. "We've tabulated some 5,000 volcanic events and there's a very definite [agreement with periods of cooling]," Bryson says. Several large eruptions of this period that have poured tons of ash into the atmosphere include Mont Pelée in the West Indies in 1902, Katmai in Alaska in 1912, Agung in 1963, Taal in 1965, and Mayon and Fernandina in 1968.

According to Lamb, ice ages and volcanic activity may well be involved in climate cycling. During an ice age a large quantity of ocean water is locked up as ice on land. As large amounts of this ice eventually melt and return to the oceans as water, the land is relieved of great weight, which thousands of years later may result in periods of volcanic activity. Long periods of volcanic ash filling the atmosphere then bring on an extended period of cooling and another ice age.

Other climatologists, however, do not see a relationship between volcanoes and periods of cooling. So the volcano theory seems to be open to debate.

MOUNTAIN-BUILDING AND CLIMATE CHANGE

Times of major long-term climate change seem not to have been haphazard. Instead, say some investigators, they have occurred on a sort of geological schedule about once every quarter of a billion years, as noted earlier. According to this theory, there have been four periods of ancient major glaciation when regional ice sheets were formed: one about one billion years ago; another about 750 million years ago; one 480 million years ago; and another 240 million years ago; the most recent occurred one million years ago. According to the British geographer, C. E. P. Brooks, "the same ordered sequence has been observed in the evolution of Earth's surface features, where it has been termed 'the rhythm of geologic time.' " Alternating with long periods when Earth's crust has been at rest have been relatively brief periods of intense disturbance resulting in the thrusting up of mountain ranges. Brooks tells us that these greatest periods of mountain-building took place in association with the greatest periods of glaciation. The Alps were thrust up during the Tertiary Period just before the most recent age of ice. During the late Pennsylvanian and early Permian there was another major period of mountain-building, this time in southern Wales, northern and central France, southern Germany, Bohemia, and southern Russia. Widespread volcanic outpouring accompanied the folding. Then a bit later, says Brooks, came another major period of ice. He also cites two earlier mountain-building periods—one about 500 million years ago and the other about 750 million years ago—each presumably associated with major periods of ice.

Brooks says that the last two ice ages, at least, followed the periods of maximum mountain-building activity by "some

---

Periods of major mountain-building occur in close relation with the periods of greatest glaciation, according to one theory. The graph here shows four such corresponding periods occurring one-quarter of a billion years apart. The solid line represents mountain-building activity while the broken line represents periods of major glaciation. AFTER C. BROOKS

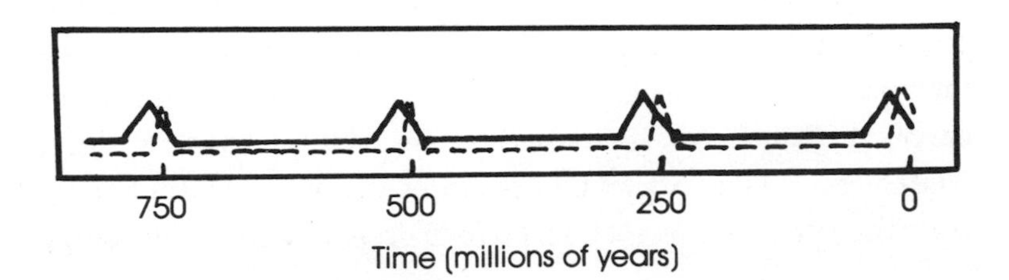

millions of years." He attributes this "lag period" to the then warm oceans requiring a long period of time in which to lose their heat before glaciation could begin. According to those favoring mountain-building as a cause of major climate change, the newly thrust up mountains alter atmospheric-circulation patterns and hence ocean-current patterns.

Still others suspect that the major cause of climate change is periods of mountain-building reinforced by reduced periods of solar activity. They feel that neither force alone is enough to initiate a full-scale ice age. Such a twin cause would mean that the two forces would have to be working together.

CONTINENTAL DRIFT

The drifting about of the continents also has been cited as a cause of major long-term climate change. As the enormous crustal "plates" on which the continents rest slide about on the molten rock beneath and grind up against one another, they thrust up mountains in one place and leave enormous depressions elsewhere. This activity changes the shape and vertical features of the land and the shapes of the oceans. The result is a change in sea level and the way currents flow, with a resulting change in the distribution of heat and moisture northward and southward of the Equator. It is hard to imagine major shifts in the positions of the planet's land masses occurring without altering climate in some way, since both atmospheric and oceanic circulation patterns surely would be affected.

As attractive as the continental drift theory of climate change may appear, it seems unable to account for the warm interglacial periods of the present ice age or for the glacial advances. Recall that it seems to be essential for relatively large land masses (Greenland and Antarctica, for example) to be near the polar regions in order to accumulate large masses of ice. It just happens that during the several interglacials of the present ice age Greenland and Antarctica both have held their present positions, or very nearly so.

CARBON DIOXIDE

One of the important roles played by carbon dioxide in Earth's atmosphere is to provide a greenhouse effect by preventing long-wave (heat) radiation given off by the ground from escaping up through the atmosphere. A large increase in the amount of carbon dioxide would tend to increase the greenhouse effect and so cause a general warming. A large decrease would tend to bring on a general cooling, or so it would seem. One theory is that after periods of mountain-building the weathering of rock might reduce the carbon dioxide content of the atmosphere by 50 percent. Such a large reduction, according to the theory might bring about a temperature drop of about 4°C (7.2°F), enough to trigger an ice age.

The amount of carbon dioxide in the atmosphere from one century to the next depends on several complex factors: volcanic activity (a source of atmospheric carbon dioxide); the weathering of rocks; how much or how little carbon dioxide the oceans are able to store; and, in today's world, the increasing amounts of carbon dioxide released into the atmosphere by automobiles, factories, and other of our activities. Our altering the land by the wholesale destruction of forests and extensive surface mining, for example, now appears to be a more important factor in the release of carbon dioxide than we believed earlier.

Only since 1958 have we been monitoring the accumulation of CO_2 in the atmosphere. Since the Industrial Revolution in the mid-1800s, man has increased the CO_2 content of the atmosphere from 10 to 15 percent, a quarter of the increase occurring since about 1970. It seems that of all the CO_2 released by our burning of fossil fuels and our cutting of forests, only 50 percent stays in the air. The oceans and forests, especially the tropical rain forests, seem to absorb and store the rest. Tropical rain forests appear to store nearly half of all the carbon locked up in our land vegetation.

We will take a more detailed look at the carbon dioxide story in the next chapter, when we consider how man's activities may be altering world climate.

THE SURGING ANTARCTIC ICE SHEET

A. T. Wilson of Victoria University, Wellington, New Zealand, has offered an interesting theory that is now being tested. He says that the Antarctic ice sheet goes through alternating periods of growth and shrinking. When the ice sheet is growing, the Northern Hemisphere is in an interglacial period; when the ice sheet shrinks we are in a glacial phase. Here is what Wilson thinks may happen.

When the seas are relatively warm and evaporation rates relatively high, the Antarctic ice sheet thickens due to increased precipitation. Heating from within the planet's interior melts the bottom layer of the ice sheet and so enables it to slide outward in all directions and so cover a larger area. This produces an ever-larger ice shelf around the continent. The larger surface area of ice increases the amount of solar radiation reflected back to space by the planet. The result is a gradually decreased temperature, which triggers glacial growth in the Northern Hemisphere. The growing Northern Hemisphere ice cover further reduces the amount of solar radiation absorbed at Earth's surface and further reduces world temperature. The now-thinned Antarctic ice sheet (thinned because its expansion is more rapid than its snow accumulation) becomes colder and stops its rapid sliding when its base ice layer freezes once again.

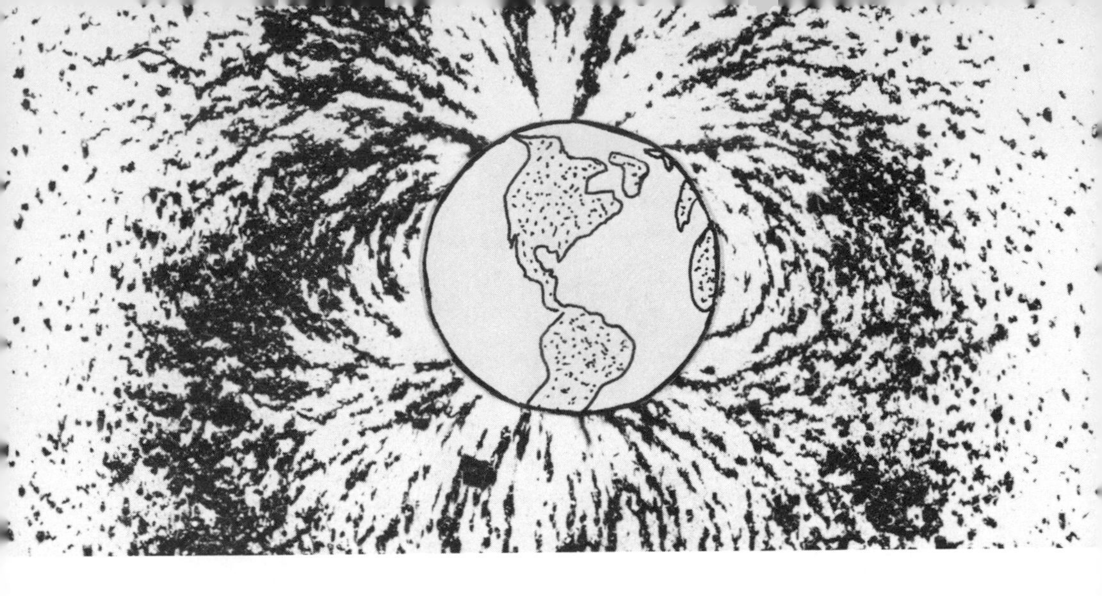

Like a bar magnet, Earth has a magnetic field looping around the planet from the North Magnetic Pole to the South Magnetic Pole. It has been suggested that changes in the intensity of Earth's magnetic field may be associated with periods of climate change.

Rapid calving of icebergs gradually reduces the surface area of the ice sheet, which results in a gradual warming due to less solar radiation being reflected away. It is at this time that the fully developed Northern Hemisphere ice begins to melt and continues the warming trend by exposing more and more ground and ocean surface to heat absorption. The warming waters around Antarctica then start another buildup of ice and so begin another cycle.

EARTH'S MAGNETIC FIELD

Goesta Wollin, of Columbia University's Lamont-Doherty Geological Observatory, has suggested that there may be a relationship between Earth's magnetic field and major climate change. Like a bar magnet, Earth has a magnetic field looping around the planet from the North Magnetic Pole to the South Magnetic Pole. The field is thought to be set up by Earth's rotation and electrical currents generated in the planet's metallic liquid core, with the system acting as a dynamo.

Measurements show that Earth's magnetic field is not constant but strengthens and weakens from time to time. Wollin suggests that there is a link between the magnetic field changes and major climate changes. He says that during those periods when the field is strong the climate tends to be relatively cold. This suggests that a relatively strong magnetic field may set up a shielding effect and so reflect away a significant amount of solar radiation. If Wollin is right, then changes in Earth's liquid core trigger climate change by regulating the amount of solar radiation reaching Earth's surface. As with Wilson's hypothesis, this one also must be investigated further.

These are only a few of the many theories offered to account for climate change. To date, no one theory by itself can account for the many large and small changes in climate that the new science of paleoclimatology is uncovering.

On what basis do we favor one theory over any number of others? First, any theory attempting to account for an ice age must explain what conditions brought on the beginning of ice accumulation. It must also convincingly explain how the ice was able to advance and then retreat and then advance again. And in the end it must account for the disappearance of ice at the end of the ice age. And, as mentioned earlier, the theory must be a model of simplicity rather than a chain of possible but unprovable situations.

Will we ever find the answer to the causes of climate change? According to Yale University climatologist R. F. Flint, "Our strong curiosity, our increasing manpower, and the rapid development of our technical skills lead me to expect that the theory of climatic variation will be with us before the end of the twentieth century."

9

Climates of the Future

MAN AND SHORT-TERM CLIMATE CHANGE

Up to this point we have considered *natural* causes capable of bringing about climate change. These include long-term influences such as variations in the Sun's energy output and continental drift, and shorter-term influences such as dust veils cast into the atmosphere by volcanic activity and altered patterns of the westerly wind belt. It is now time to consider man's role in bringing about climate change. The question is: *Is* our industrial activity—from farming to factories—influencing climate change?

In searching for answers to that large question we must keep in mind that there are dozens of bits and pieces to the climate puzzle, all pushing climate this way and that and often in opposite directions. So far, no one has come up with a single comprehensive theory of climate that can show how those dozens of pieces operate in relation to each other, and whether

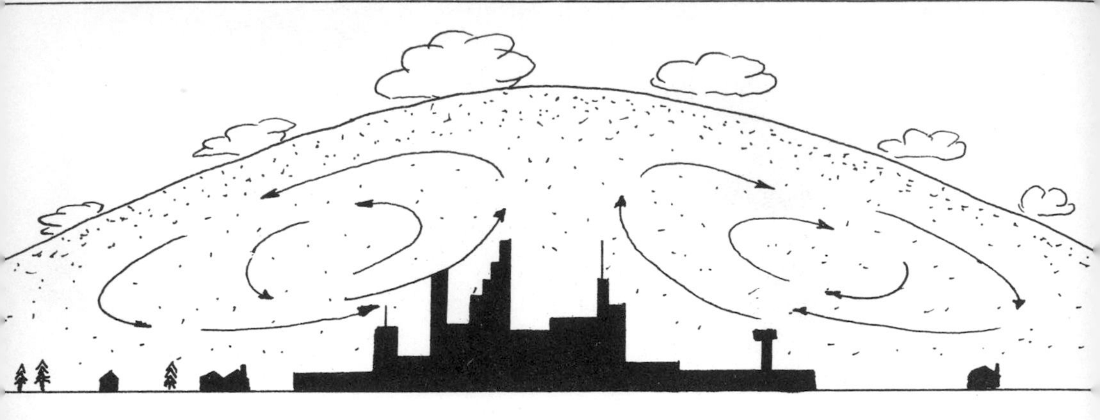

Cities usually are warmer than the neighboring suburbs by an average 1° to 2°C (about 2° to 3°F). They are warmer because their extensive areas of asphalt and concrete absorb and store heat. Dust and smoke in the city air tend to collect and form a "dust-dome," which gives a city its own local climate. The dome persists until broken up by wind or rain. AFTER W. LOWRY

man's activity, in fact, is presently contributing to climate change. Although such activities are known to bring about local climate change—such as in large cities—effects on global climate remain largely unknown. Lacking a workable "model" of climate, we are hard put to understand how climate changes, not to mention predicting how it will change over the next dozen centuries. Says MIT meteorologist Jule Charney: "I don't think we can predict climate now and I wouldn't trust anyone who said he could. The atmosphere is just too complex to take some of these vague statistics and try to use them to predict with." In spite of the difficulties, climatologists nevertheless are trying to predict what kind of climate change we are headed for and when we may expect it. As some have put it, "Are we going to freeze or fry?"

Earth's atmosphere works as a heat engine. It transfers heat from one region (the Equator) to other regions (the poles). If this pattern of heat distribution is changed, then climate must change, even if the total amount of solar radiation striking the top of the atmosphere remains unchanged. The question we now want to ask is whether any of our human activities are tampering with the planet's atmospheric heat engine, and whether such activities are changing the amount of heat that arrives at Earth's surface after passing through the atmosphere.

PARTICLES AND CARBON DIOXIDE

We dump many pollutants into the atmosphere each day at an ever-increasing rate. Among those pollutants are numerous particles and carbon dioxide.

There are both natural and man-made sources of particles that act as atmospheric pollutants. Among the natural sources are ash particles from volcanoes and forest fires started by lightning. Among man-made sources are particles continuously spewed out of an ever-increasing number of factory chimneys, automobiles and aircraft exhausts, and about 60 million tons a year of smoke from "slash-and-burn" farming techniques used in agriculturally primitive regions. Add to that the uncounted tons of dust kicked into the air daily in these same regions where, according to Bryson, "every person, every cow, every goat, every plow is followed by a cloud of dust. That may not seem like enough particles to change something as complex as Earth's climate, but just multiply all those separate little clouds by the hundreds of millions of people and animals and machines that make them."

There are fine particles and larger blobs of matter in the air. It is the fine particles that hang in the atmosphere the longest and reflect solar radiation more. A particle floating in the lower atmosphere has an average lifetime of three to four days before it is flushed out by rain. The lifetime is shorter in the rainy tropics than at the arid poles. Fine volcanic-ash particles may remain in the atmosphere for several years. It is the Northern Hemisphere that is most plagued by particle pollution since that is where virtually all of man's industrial activity takes place.

All of this atmospheric particle pollution, says Bryson, is causing a cooling that began around 1946 and continues today in the Northern Hemisphere north of about 50°N. The result, he claims, is an expansion and increased looping of the westerlies belt of winds and a cooling of the Arctic by a noticeable amount. "This increase in stirred-up particulate matter seems to be increasing the contrast between the hot and the cold sides of the Northern Hemisphere's atmospheric heat engine. Which, in turn, is altering much of the hemisphere's climate, especially in those same semiarid and marginal countries whose subsistence agriculture is kicking a great deal of the dust into the air in the first place. These countries live or die on monsoon rains and, because of the dust they are now creating, those monsoons seem to be drying up and becoming increasingly erratic."

In spite of Bryson's claims, say some climatologists, there is no convincing evidence that increased dust has altered climate *globally*, or for that matter that man has altered *global* climate.

The source of carbon dioxide (CO_2) is the burning of the fossil fuels petroleum, coal, and wood, and the worldwide destruction of forests. The role played by forests in affecting the amount of CO_2 in the atmosphere at a given time is important. According to George M. Woodwell, director of the Ecosystems Center at the Marine Biological Laboratory in Woods Hole, Massachusetts, "The emphasis is on the forests because they are extensive in area, conduct more photosynthesis worldwide than any other type of vegetation, and have the potential for storing carbon in quantities that are sufficiently large to affect the carbon dioxide content of the atmosphere." Woodwell also goes on record by saying that "it is difficult to avoid the conclusion that the destruction of the forests of the world is adding carbon dioxide to the atmosphere at a rate comparable to the rate of release for the combustion of fossil fuels."

Ever since the Industrial Revolution, which began in the mid-1800s, we have been releasing increasing amounts of CO_2 into the air, most of it in the last decade. Because of world population growth, and the industrial growth required to serve it, each year we increase the amount of CO_2 released to the air by about 3.5 to 4.0 percent. And it appears that we will

The graph shows the increase in global CO_2 concentration in the atmosphere since 1958. This record was made at the Mauna Loa (Hawaii) station of the Scripps Institution of Oceanography and is the most accurate continuous record ever made. The up-and-down pattern of the curve is due to plants consuming large amounts of CO_2 during the growing season but not during winter. AFTER G. WOODWELL

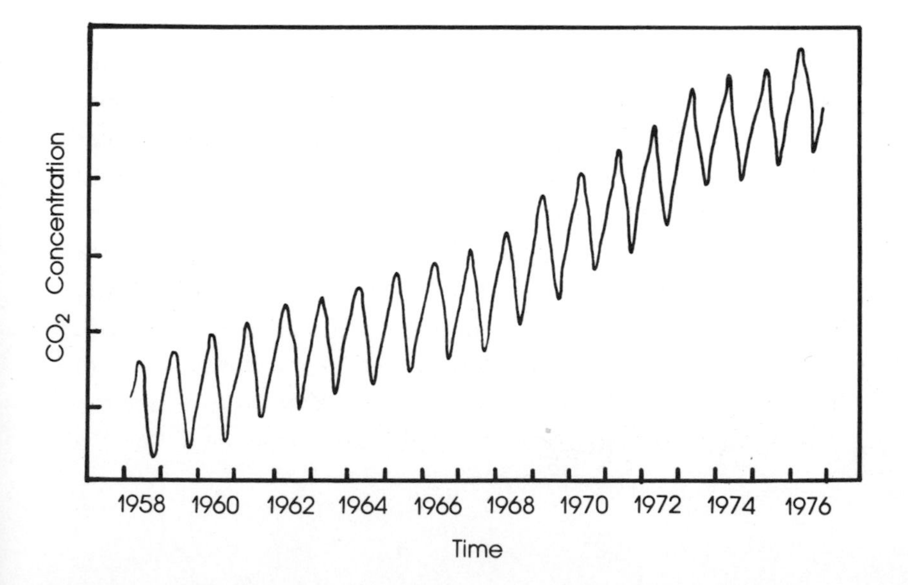

continue to do so until around the year 2000. By that time we will have nearly doubled the amount of atmospheric CO_2 from 0.03 to 0.06 percent. Also by about the year 2000 all but a small percent of our fossil fuel supply will have been used up. Increasing the amount of CO_2 in the atmosphere tends to increase the greenhouse effect by trapping the long-wave (heat) radiation from Earth's surface. A doubling of the CO_2 concentration would tend to increase the average surface temperature of the planet by 2°C (3.6°F). Such a large temperature change is enough to bring about a relatively rapid change in climate. One result of such a rapid onset of warming would be an enlargement of the arid regions of the world, which would significantly affect agricultural production.

Raising the CO_2 content of the air seems to have an interesting side effect—that of increasing the amount of water vapor. This increased amount of water vapor would further trap heat radiation from Earth's surface and so tend to add to the general heating trend. But a second side effect has not been mentioned—that of an increased amount of water vapor leading to an increased amount of cloud cover. An increased amount of cloud cover of only 2.4 percent could lower the average surface temperature by about 2°C and so cancel out the increased CO_2 greenhouse effect! An increasing amount of fine dust in the atmosphere, like a larger cloud cover, also would have a shielding effect, blocking out still more solar energy. This might result in a net loss of surface heat, and hence a period of cooling.

To complicate the matter of a general cooling *versus* a general heating, earth scientists Paul E. Damon, of the University of Arizona, and Steven M. Kunen, of the University of Utah, report a warming trend in the Southern Hemisphere, although they say that their data are "scanty." They report that the Northern Hemisphere cooling trend is "out of phase" with a

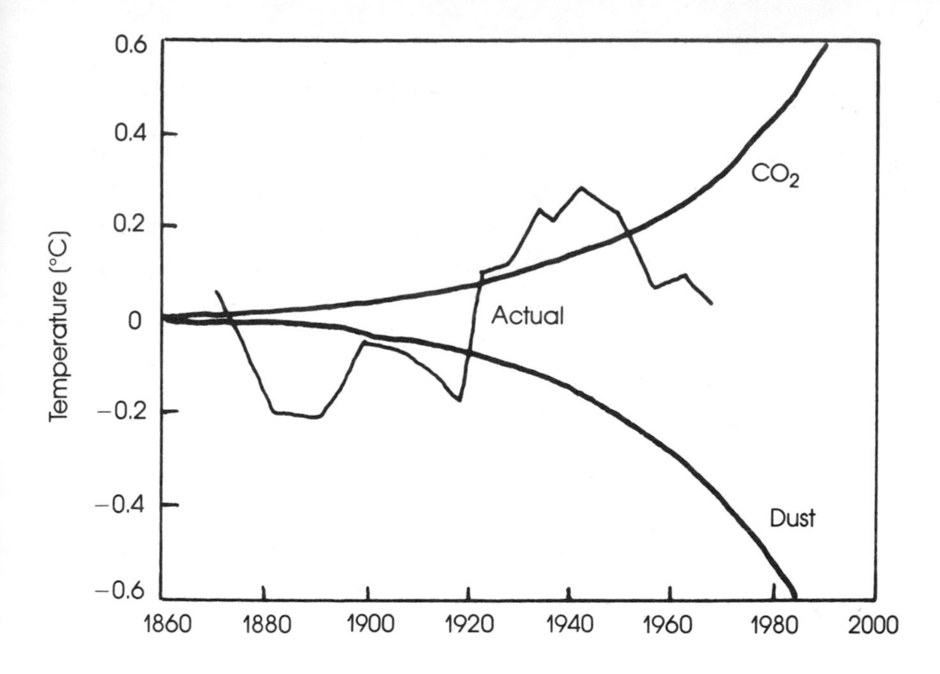

The graph shows the warming curve that in theory would occur due to the greenhouse effect triggered by increasing amounts of carbon dioxide released to the air by man's activities. Also shown is the cooling curve that in theory would occur due to dust released into the air by man's activities. The two effects would seem to cancel each other out. The actual temperature curve occurring since about 1860 reflects changes too large to be explained by human activities, some climatologists say. AFTER M. MITCHELL

---

warming trend at high latitudes in the Southern Hemisphere. They suspect that CO_2 is the cause and that it has touched off a general global warming trend that has begun in the Southern Hemisphere. Columbia University earth scientist Wallace S. Broecker agrees. He says that Greenland ice cores suggest that the present Northern Hemisphere cooling since the mid-1940s is simply a temporary fluctuation that will soon "bottom out." So far, he says, it has overridden the CO_2 greenhouse effect. But over the next decade or so the cooling trend should stop and then there should be a rapid warming trend lasting several decades. He expects this warming period to produce global temperatures higher than any in the last 1,000 years.

Two other earth scientists, Sherwood B. Idso of the United States Water Conservation Laboratory in Phoenix, Arizona, and Anthony J. Brazel, a geographer at Arizona State University, also look to a warming trend due to the combined effects of atmospheric dust and CO_2. Their experiments show that "initial increases in atmospheric dust concentration tend to warm the planet's surface." But when still more dust is added to the air, a cooling trend begins. However, this extra amount of added dust must be a very large amount, they say, ". . . so large that any particulate pollution of the lower atmosphere by man will have a tendency to increase surface temperatures." So man-generated dust, they conclude, instead of offsetting the warming tendency of increased carbon dioxide, will add to the warming trend.

These conflicting speculations about the direction our future climate will take are an excellent example of how various bits and pieces of climate operate to push and pull each other, often in opposite directions, but sometimes in the same direction. To date no one can say for certain what the long-term effects of pouring increased amounts of dust and CO_2 into the atmosphere will be.

INDUSTRIAL HEAT

Man's numerous industrial and transportation activities release large amounts of heat into the atmosphere. According to one estimate, the amount is about 1/15,000 the energy absorbed from the Sun; according to another, 1/1,000. Some climatologists say that that amount is nothing to worry about. They add, however, that the time to begin worrying is when man begins to release 1 percent of the total solar input, and that time, they tell us, will be in about 100 or more years at our present growth rate. According to the Russian climatologist M. I. Budyko, it will be sooner if there is a wholesale reliance on nuclear power. Since 1970, we have been releasing 5.7 percent more heat into the atmosphere each year.

What will be the effect of all this man-produced heat on climate? One result will be a global temperature rise of about 1°C (1.8°F), which is enough to start a major climatological upset on a global basis. But again, no one can say exactly what the results might be, and climatologists W. W. Kellogg and S. H. Schneider, of the Climate Project of the National Center for Atmospheric Research, remind us of the dangers of isolating one piece of the climate puzzle from the others.

We might at first suppose that if we add heat to the atmosphere we could sit back and wait for the temperature of the atmosphere to rise. We might even suppose we could estimate by how much the temperature would rise by knowing how much heat we were pouring into the atmosphere and how much solar radiation the atmosphere receives. Not so, since there are many other pieces of the climate puzzle acting in relation to each other—CO_2 and water-vapor greenhouse effects, changing amounts of dust in the atmosphere, and so on.

As another example, the increased heat might evaporate more water, which then could produce a wider cloud coverage. This could result in less solar radiation reaching the surface and so counteract the artificial warming trend. Now suppose that the heat input were concentrated in Greenland or on the Antarctic ice cap. This could lead to a reduction in the size of the ice cap and to less solar energy being reflected back to space, which would produce still more warming. But what if the increased cloudiness canceled out the decreased ice area, or one of the many other bits and pieces of climate came into play? "The range of possible interactions is staggering," say Kellogg and Schneider, again a reminder that we have no comprehensive theory that includes the many interacting variables leading to climate change.

SPRAY CANS AND SUPERSONIC AIRCRAFT

Every time we press the button of an aerosol can of deodorant, lubricant, fly killer, or whipped cream, we release into the atmosphere a certain amount of a substance known as Freon, or halocarbons, which contains chlorine (Cl). And every time one of the giant supersonic passenger planes cruises through the stratosphere it releases quantities of the chemical nitric oxide (NO), one atom of nitrogen bonded to one atom of oxygen.

Both the chlorine and nitric oxide find their way into that layer of gases in the stratosphere called the *ozone layer*. Ozone is a special form of oxygen having three (O_3) instead of two (O_2) atoms. The ozone layer is essential to maintain the present forms of animal—and presumably, plant—life on Earth. It acts as a shield against the high-energy ultraviolet radiation from the Sun. Without this protective shield, we would be exposed to the full force of solar ultraviolet radiation and would be severely burned and develop skin cancer.

It has been shown beyond doubt that the free chlorine from Freon combines with and breaks down ozone. But some climatologists are quick to add that it is uncertain whether the ozone may be replaced by natural means. It has also been shown that the nitric oxide released by the supersonic transports also breaks down ozone. What happens first is that the nitric oxide combines with the ozone and breaks it down to nitrogen dioxide (NO_2) and oxygen (O_2). Next, the nitrogen dioxide combines with an oxygen atom and produces more nitric oxide, plus oxygen. That means that there is now more oxide available to break down more ozone.

ENVIRONMENTAL EFFECTS OF MAN-MADE GROUND EMISSIONS

Pollutant and Source	Observed Trend	Potential Atmospheric Effect	Time Scale of Importance
Carbon dioxide (CO_2) from combustion of fossil fuels.	Up to more than 20 percent in last 100 years.	Increased global temperatures leading to melting of polar icecaps, sea level increase, perturbations of marine biology.	Thorough assessment needed. May be a problem over next 50 years.
Fluorocarbons (e.g., Freon) from aerosol cans, refrigeration systems, etc. Nitrogen oxides from high-flying aircraft (and perhaps rom fertilizers).	Fluorocarbons are now detectable throughout the atmosphere. Nitrogen oxides are a natural component. Stratospheric measurement program being established to determine levels and trends.	Reduction of the global stratospheric ozone layer and perturbation of the atmosphere's radiation balance. Analysis of current trend in ozone is not yet definite due to natural variability.	According to recent assessment by National Academy of Sciences, action probably needed within several years.
Krypton-85 rom nuclear fuel eprocessing and power lants.	Building up proportionally with nuclear power generation.	Modification of the atmosphere's electric field, which may cause modification of the hydrologic cycle.	Thorough assessment needed, may be a problem over next 100 years with growth of nuclear power industry.
ulfur compounds rom fossil fuel ombustion.	Not well-established, but concentration may already be too high on occasion.	May affect regional precipitation chemistry and acidity on regional to subcontinental scale.	May presently be a problem which would be aggregated by further coal burning.
ust om combustion, ash/burn agriculture, nd improper land onservation.	Not well-established because of evolution of sources and particle sizes with controls.	Initial response is temperature change (sign dependent on location and source type), precipitation modification. Problem mainly on subcontinental, but possibly up to global scale.	Further evaluation needed as improved data available.
eat and water eleases to the tmosphere from the nergy generation rocess (thermal ollution, cooling wers, etc.).	Increasing with energy generation.	Temperature and precipitation modification on local and regional scale.	Evaluation needed in regions of concentrated energy generation (e.g., energy parks, etc.)
ceanic oil slicks om tanker cleaning, c.	Not known.	By changing the reflectivity and evaporation characteristics of large oceanic areas, the earth's energy balance might be perturbed in an unknown way.	Assessment needed as capability for evaluation improves.

Another ozone destroyer is the gas nitrous oxide (N_2O), produced in ever larger amounts by the increased use of nitrogen fertilizers. Those who look to "technological miracles" to save the starving millions occupying arid lands of the globe advocate limitless use of nitrogen fertilizers to increase crop yields. So it is projected that the use of this industrially produced fertilizer will increase by hundreds of percent over the next 25 years!

Destruction of Earth's ozone layer, according to a report of the National Research Council (NRC), entails the threat of "drastic" climate changes. According to Veerauhadran Ramanathan, of NASA, the halocarbons absorb long-wave (heat) radiation reflected by Earth's surface and so tend to produce a greenhouse effect, as do CO_2 and water vapor. The NRC report estimated that the greenhouse effect produced by halocarbons might contribute an increase of about 0.5°C (0.9°F) over a 50-year period, equivalent to that produced by the anticipated buildup of CO_2. The NRC strongly recommended that spray cans be banned, but manufacturers of the cans keep right on producing them, (except, at least, in Sweden, where Freon cans have been banned). By doing so, the manufacturers of these cans are conducting a worldwide experiment with the environment, the results of which no one can tell. From 1971 to 1974, the Naval Research Laboratory reported a 67 percent increase of chlorine released into the atmosphere by spray cans. Without some kind of control, we can expect the production of spray cans containing halocarbons to increase year by year.

Some time ago, Harold Johnston, of the University of California at Berkeley, estimated that a fleet of 500 giant supersonic passenger aircraft flying an average of seven hours a day could destroy one half of the planet's ozone supply within one year. One result, he said, is that "all animals of the world would be blinded if they lived outdoors during the daytime." More recent estimates of MIT meteorologists say that if a fleet of such aircraft were to fly ". . . at an altitude of 20 kilometers (12.4 miles) in the midlatitudes of the Northern Hemisphere, a signifi :ant depletion of about 12 percent in total stratospheric ozone would be realized." They add that on an annual basis about 16 percent would be destroyed in the Northern Hemisphere. An additional 8 percent would be destroyed in the Southern Hemisphere even though no aircraft were flying there. This last point brings into focus an environmental problem that becomes more important and far-reaching each year: Why should one manufacturer, one industry, or one nation be permitted to degrade the environment to such an extent that nations and peoples far removed are affected?

Other chemists have been leaking nitrogen oxides into the air for decades with no apparent harmful effects on the ozone layer. So why worry about high-flying supersonic aircraft? The fact is we do not know what the results would be. In view of present warnings, it would be foolhardy for any two nations to start a race to see who can be the first to have a large fleet of supersonic aircraft operating in the ozone layer of the atmosphere without first doing everything possible to find out if it would be safe. But by all appearances, just such a race has begun.

HOW TO MAKE A DESERT

Unsound use of the land coupled with climate change is causing deserts to creep outward in many parts of the world. Africa, Asia, Australia, and North and South America all are experiencing *desertification*. In many such regions there is a serious shrinking of available farmland and land for grazing.

As the sprawling Sahara Desert in Africa creeps ever southward, forests gradually are destroyed and give way to savanna, broad grasslands of tall grass with scattered trees. Eventually the savanna loses its trees and can support only steppe vegetation of grasses. Steppe vegetation is the last stage before the land is claimed by the desert. Measurements made between 1958 and 1975 show that the Sahara has shifted southward by an average of about 90 to 100 kilometers (56 to 62 miles) in the last 17 years. That is an average rate of 5.5 kilometers (3.4 miles) a year.

Deserts also are expanding in parts of southern Africa, including Botswana, Kenya, Tanzania, and Ethiopia. Parts of Argentina and large stretches of Mexico and the southwestern United States also are giving way to desert. What causes this highly destructive invasion of deserts?

According to Erik Eckholm and Lester R. Brown, both of the Worldwatch Institute, "One of the most dramatic and, in human terms, costliest examples of desertification in the United States is that of the huge Navajo Indian Reservation in northern Arizona and New Mexico. Encouraged by the U. S. government to become sheep farmers after their nineteenth-century subjugation, the Navajos proved to be adept shepherds. But as the flocks multiplied in the absence of proper range-management techniques, the land—and ultimately the people living off it—paid an enormous price. Locations described by mid-nineteenth-century travelers as lush meadows are today vistas composed of scattered sod remnants amid shifting sands and deep gulleys. Only a small fraction of the potential economic benefit is being harvested from these dusty, sagebrush-dotted lands that were once largely carpeted with grass.

"In one zone that range specialists recently calculated could safely support 16,000 sheep at most, 11,500 Navajo people with 140,000 sheep were trying to wrest an existence."

The story of Africa's Sudan is the same. Since 1957 the number of livestock in that province has grown sixfold with the result that the grasses and shrubbery are being put under great pressure to survive, let alone support the growing livestock population. Since the year 1900, the population of North Africa's arid lands has grown sixfold. Meanwhile, since 1930, vegetation has continued to be destroyed at an increasing rate in Morocco, Algeria, Tunisia, and Libya.

Overgrazing by livestock and grain farming on unsuitable land are a large part of the cause. According to range specialist H. N. LeHouérou, the result "is the loss of more than 100,000 hectares (270,000 acres) of range and cropland to desert each year." The story in western Rajasthan, India, is the same. From 1951 to 1961 "the area available exclusively for grazing dropped from 13 million to 11 million hectares (32 million to 27 million acres), while the population of goats, sheep, and cattle jumped from 9.4 million to 14.4 million," according to M. S. Swaminathan. Those who have visited the western and central regions of India say that the land looks like a lunar landscape.

It is in just such poor regions of the world—India, Africa, and South America—that human population growth is the highest. So by adding more people to the land, and more livestock, and carrying out more farming to feed ever more people, the problem must become worse year by year. Even in the best of times conditions in these areas are bad, with most of the people existing at near starvation levels by our standards. In the worst of times—times of drought—thousands die of starvation and disease associated with malnutrition.

It is the monsoons, those seasonal winds that bring life-giving rain each summer to the Sahel region of Africa and to India, that spell the difference between starvation and survival for the teeming millions inhabiting these regions. With an expansion of the westerlies belt, according to Bryson's dust

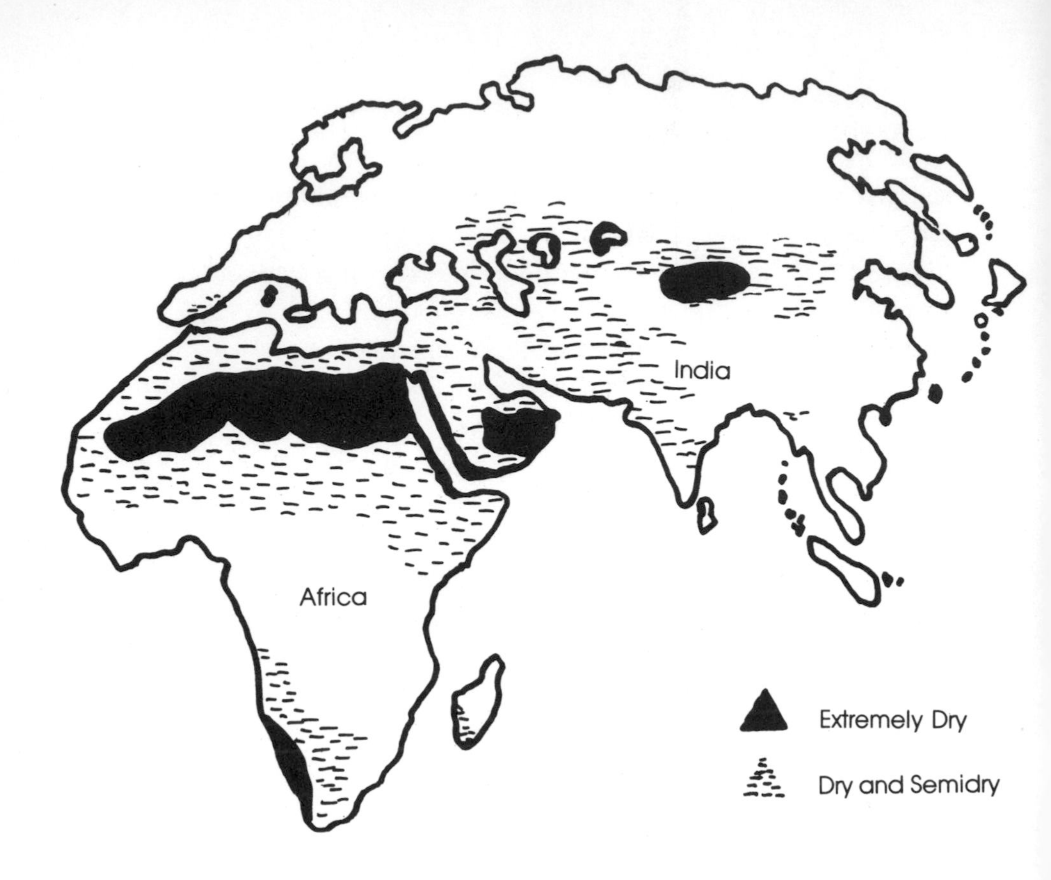

The map shows areas of dry conditions discussed in the text.

theory, the monsoons are prevented from pushing far enough north and releasing their rains. Since the mid-1950s, says Bryson, the monsoons have stayed farther south than before. Their failure to move north in the late 1960s and early 1970s brought a six-year-long drought that destroyed the pasturelands and grains of more than 20 million people. Helplessly, they stood by and watched their rivers and wells dry up and fill with sand. According to *Time* magazine correspondent Lee Griggs, at least three million nomads—mostly Fulani and Tuareg tribesmen—have lost entire herds of cattle, sheep, goats, and even camels. According to *Time*'s New Delhi correspondent James Shepherd, "In the Kutch district of drought-stricken Gujarat [West Bengal], peasants patiently wait for dogs and vultures to finish picking at the carcasses of dead cattle. The hungry gather up the bones and sell them to mills where they are made into bone dust, a kind of fertilizer." More than one third of the livestock in the drought-stricken areas starved to death, as did more than 100,000 of the people. Were it not for a million tons of relief food sent to these people by 34 nations, as many as six million might have died.

There were other consequences as well. Four million people were herded into refugee camps near the cities, where conditions were far from satisfactory—few jobs were to be had and epidemics broke out due to poor sanitary conditions. The long period of drought has been cited as part of the cause of the civil war in Ethiopia that resulted in the downfall of Emperor Haile Selassie in 1974.

Can we blame climate change on this period of drought? In 1974 and 1975 the monsoons came back, but untold damage had been done to the land during the years before. When the refugees returned to their homeland they found little more than dust and the remains of dead livestock. Commented University of Toronto climatologist F. Kenneth Hare: "I don't believe that the world's present population [of 4.1 billion] is sustainable if there are more than three years like 1972 in a row."

DROUGHT AND CLIMATE CHANGE

As all climatologists will tell us, climate change has occurred in the past. Few, however, would be willing to go on record by saying that we are now going through a period of climate change and that the recent droughts are a direct result. Unfortunately, no one knows and no one is able to predict whether droughts follow a 20-year cycle, a 200-year cycle, or are now-and-then events occurring when several bits and pieces of climate just happen to fall into a certain relationship to each other.

Jule Charney looks to local conditions giving rise to desert formation, which is associated with drought. Satellite observations show that more heat radiation is reflected back to space by the Sahara Desert than is absorbed from solar radiation. So the Sahara is a region of "negative radiation balance" and has a radiation deficit. The strong reflecting property of desert surfaces, he says, helps preserve their dryness by encouraging warm, dry air to sink over those deserts. This sinking dry air, Charney adds, prevents cloud formation and so makes rain scarce. Similar local conditions in the Sahel tend to have the same effect. But an additional local condition there—that of animals overgrazing the land—also contributes to drought conditions. Charney concludes that we cannot overlook the importance of local conditions, in addition to global ones, in contributing to drought.

Russell Schnell, an atmospheric scientist, suspects that rainfall over the Sahel (and other similar regions) during times of drought tends to be unlikely even when rain clouds are present. For a cloud to rain, it must be invaded by tiny particles of matter around which the minute cloud droplets of water can collect, and these particles must grow in size until they are heavy enough to fall out of the cloud as rain. Schnell suspects that such tiny rain-making particles over the Sahel consist of microscopic-size bits and pieces of decayed plant matter carried up into the air by the wind. Overgrazing of the land, he says, makes such rain-making particles scarce, thus contributing to drought conditions. Dry conditions on the ground then make the vegetation cover even scarcer than before, which in turn makes the grazing animals compete even more for what little vegetation remains, which in turn results in still fewer rain-making particles, and so on. Only when the grazing animals are removed or starve to death can the vegetation recover and once again produce a sufficient number of rain-making particles while also providing food for a limited number of grazing animals. And so the cycle of drought-recovery-drought repeats itself, aided by local conditions. In the event that recovery of vegetation is not possible because the topsoil has been blown away, then the land is turned to "permanent" desert.

It may be nothing more than coincidence, but most of the grazing animals of the Sahelian populations died in the drought years of 1972 and 1973, which relieved the land of heavy grazing pressure. In 1974 welcomed rains quickly restored large areas of vegetation cover once again.

Again, it is difficult to single out only one condition to explain something as complex as a drought over a region of many thousands of square kilometers. But it is not difficult to follow the observed chain of events that occurs: (1) In good times the animal populations are high and the grazing pressures strong. (2) Then the monsoons fail. (3) The vegetation cover thins out until there is not enough food for the grazing animals. (4) Soon the land becomes overgrazed. (5) There is now an increase in solar energy reflected off the land, which tends to add to the dry condition, now in drought stage. An increased amount of dust also enters the atmosphere. (6) Drought conditions continue until global atmospheric circulation patterns change for the better, or until the animal populations are so reduced in size that a vegetation cover can return.

The lesson in this sequence of events, whatever their cause(s), is clear to any ecologist: Anywhere on this planet man must not overwork the fragile ecosystems by trying to take more out of them than they are able to give. How clearly that simple truth is written in the sands of the Sahel and elsewhere.

When we try to take from an ecosystem more than it can give we risk reducing the productivity of the ecosystem to ever lower levels. Ultimately we may destroy it altogether for a period of one or several generations.

Although some climatologists suggest that desertification is being aided by a climate change now, others say no. F. Kenneth Hare says there is "no firm basis for claiming that the extreme weather events of the 1970s are part of a major climatic variation." According to records, rainfall over North Africa seems to have remained pretty much the same over the past 100 years, as it has over the Middle East for the past 5,000 years.

What is certain is that droughts come and go. Are they brought on largely by the expansion and looping patterns of the westerlies wind belt, as Bryson maintains? And could the length of time a drought condition lasts, and how often droughts occur, be related to widespread desertification of the land? Some climatologists say yes, that there may well be a reinforcing effect, with droughts encouraging more desertification and increased desertification encouraging drought conditions.

THE DROUGHT PROBLEM GROWS

A drought condition, anywhere in the world, commands an increasing amount of attention as the number of people starving to death increases. With the populations of Africa and India increasing at rates well above the world average, we can expect increased social unrest with the ever-growing number of deaths by famine during future periods of drought; and they are bound to occur. Some have suggested that the richest nations of the world, such as the United States, provide surplus grain to the African and Indian nations during times of drought. Indeed, we have done so in the past and probably will again in the future. But how much good can we really do in the light of those nations' mushrooming populations? What it boils down to is just how many mouths, other than our own, will we be able (or *willing*) to feed come the next crunch. Bryson has much to say on this subject:

"Let's say that Americans each consume a ton of grain every year. If we lived at the level of India's population and ate only a quarter-ton each year, that would make three-quarters of a ton of grain available per person. So, for our 200 million citizens, that means we could suddenly ship an additional 150 million tons of food to the rest of the world. And—at a quarter-ton each—that would feed 600 million people [which is nearly the population of India].

"Now, in the first place, this would be impossible. We're bigger than the Indians. Our climate is harsher. We simply couldn't exist on the Indian diet.

"In the second place, we wouldn't have that much excess grain to ship anyway. Because if all Americans ate that little, we'd begin to act just like the people in India act. We'd sit around a lot just the way they do. Not because we were lazy, but because we wouldn't have any energy to waste. When you sit quietly, you produce about 150 watts of energy . . . but when you're doing hard work, your body has to put out up to 300 watts. And when you eat as little as the average person in India eats, you have no choice: You sit around a lot. And if we did that here, our production, obviously, would go down considerably. We'd consume less food . . . and we'd also produce a lot less.

"In the third place, I don't think this—even if it could be done—is any kind of a realistic solution at all as long as the population of these poorer nations continues to grow the way it does. Just look at India again . . . [Its] population increases about 15 million a year. And it has an absolute minimal food supply. So we say, 'They're short of food and they can't afford to buy any, so let's give them some of ours.' And we give them four million tons. At $250 a ton, that's a big commitment . . . but we give it to them.

"And then next year, they've got *another* additional 15 million to feed. And the following another 15 million. And the year after that yet another 15 million. Now, instead of shipping over four million tons, we've got to send 20 million tons. Just how long can that go on?

"If *any* nation in the world were to make this completely impossible—for the reasons just mentioned—sacrifice, the United States is the country that would do it. Americans are, by and large, a generous people . . . and that generosity has been played upon by a great number of the world's peoples. Uncle Sam, in fact, has become far too indulgent a 'parent' to far too many 'children' during the past 30 years or so. He now has a great number of other nations which expect him—one way or another—to give them a big and unwarranted 'allowance' in addition to whatever they can earn for themselves. . . .

"For a number of reasons, this idea that the United States has some obligation—or even the *ability*—to feed all the other nations while many of those other countries make no systematic effort to ensure their own food supply is rather unrealistic, to say the least.

"And besides that, I'm doubtful—given the current total capital and food supply and population of the world—that this rather romantic 'share-and-share-alike' idea has any merit anyway. If you'd take all the world's food right now and divide it absolutely equally among all the world's people, nobody's portion would come up to the FAO's recommended minimum standard. Is this any kind of solution? How do you ever expect to amass enough capital and energy and technology and seed stock and so on to produce more food tomorrow when no one has enough to even fill his or her stomach today?

"The alternative to these times of mass starvation and death is to keep population near or below the number that can be supported in the *worst* of times, not in the best of times and not even in 'average' times."

A prominent Indian population expert has remarked that most of his upper-class countrymen "would be perfectly happy to see fifty percent of the lower class Indian population disappear." India's Minister of Agriculture told a concerned world press in 1975 that his country's famines and the deaths resulting from them "ought to be thought a blessing rather than a curse."

10

Climate Control—Who Wins?

Up to this point we have talked about climate changes brought about by natural forces. We have also considered whether some of man's daily activities, such as releasing increasing amounts of carbon dioxide, heat, and a variety of chemicals and solid substances into the atmosphere, are triggering either short-term or long-term climate change.

In this chapter we face another possibility: deliberate large-scale engineering schemes that have been proposed, schemes that surely would initiate climate change on a local basis, and possibly on a global basis. Some such schemes also might be used as countermeasures to offset climate trends regarded as "undesirable" by some, but by no means all.

Before considering such schemes, let's first examine two case histories of large engineering projects in order to get at least a glimpse of some unexpected consequences of performing technological "miracles."

CASE OF THE UNWELCOMED DAM

You don't have to think very hard to come up with a long list of ways in which man changes the surface of the planet. When he creates cities, he puts up high buildings and the people live at the bottom of an atmospheric sea of pollutants. He cuts mile after mile of green forests for timber, which he uses to build his homes. He clears billions of acres of land for farmlands to grow the food he needs. He drills and digs beneath Earth's surface to remove petroleum and coal, which he uses to power his machines. And he removes from Earth's crust untold tons of iron and other ores, which he uses to build those machines. He also changes the face of the land by building great dams to generate electrical power. In doing so, he creates large man-made lakes behind the dams and cuts off or slows the flow of water to settlements downstream from the dam.

Much of what man does to the landscape is done with the best intentions, at least for the economic or social good of a given group. But man's technological miracles sometimes backfire and produce unwanted results that turn out to be economically or socially harmful. While there are numerous cases of engineering schemes backfiring in unexpected ways and tipping the natural balance of the environment, there are as yet no parallel case histories of climatological schemes, but they may not be long in coming. Meanwhile we will have to draw our lessons from what ecologists are learning about the results of man's technological manipulations of nature.

Before 1958, twice each year the waters of the Zambezi River, in southeastern Africa, overflowed their banks at normal flood time and deposited layers of rich alluvial soil over the river land. Thousands of Africans who had been practicing farming along the river valley for many years had come to depend on the annual floods and the fresh supply of fertile soil. It meant that year after year they could cultivate their crops without having to worry about overworking the land.

Land farther back from the river's shores was poorer. Either it had been overgrazed by livestock, or it had been overfarmed and was low in the mineral nutrients needed by food plants. Life for these river farmers was hard, even in the best of times, and their ignorance of proper farmland use (crop rotation and contour planting, for example) made their lives even harder than need be.

But all of this was about to be changed—not for the better but for the worse—by a technological miracle. In 1958 a huge dam, the Kariba Dam, was built across the Zambezi River at Kariba Gorge. Its main purpose was to generate electrical power for people living many miles away. When the man-made lake that backed up behind the dam eventually reached the full mark in 1963, it covered an area of more than 2,740 square kilometers (1,700 miles). It was the largest man-made lake in the world, and its great size brought significant climate change—higher humidity, more even temperatures, and increased rainfall. But what other effects were there?

People living along that part of the riverbank that was overrun by the sprawling new lake had to move away and build new homes. That caused crowded conditions along other parts of the river and put an even greater burden than before on the river-valley farmlands. According to Thayer Scudder, an anthropologist who has studied these Africans' way of life, those who planned the dam did not look kindly on the farming families who had to be moved. "The population to be re-

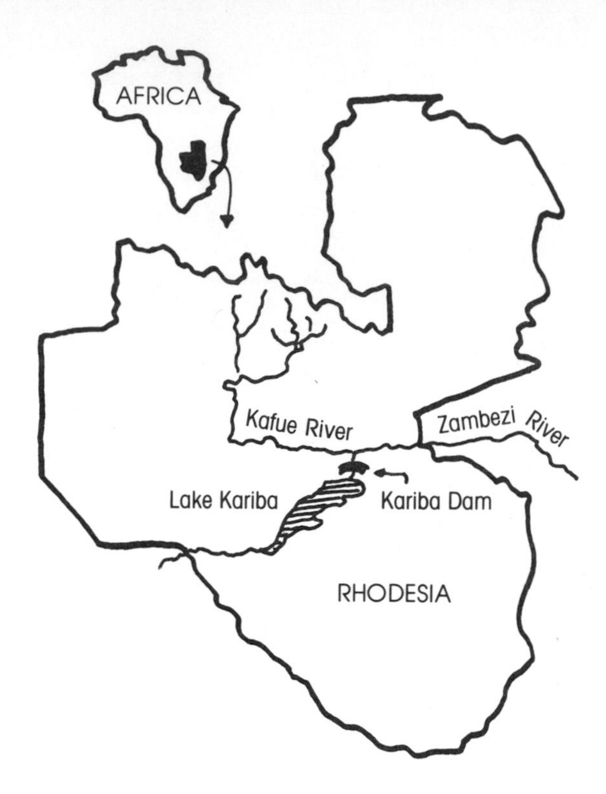

Location of the Kariba Dam and the large lake that formed behind the dam.

located," he wrote, "was seen, not as a resource, but as an expensive nuisance, whose very existence was unfortunate."

For three years after the Kariba Dam was completed, there were no annual floods along the river's banks between the dam and the Kafue River. The main purpose of the dam was to form a lake for power generation—not to supply the downriver farmers with flood water. When the flood waters failed to come, many farmers began to plant the low-lying regions during the wet season, something they had never done before, and for a very good reason. The timing would have been all wrong. The natural flood waters began washing over the land at just about the time crops planted during the wet season would be reaching their peak. And that is just what happened in April, 1962.

The farmers had planted during the wet season because there had been no flood waters for the three years since the dam had been built, because the dam gates had not been opened. But the operators of the dam decided to release enough water to duplicate the natural pattern of flooding. Within one day the new low-land crops were covered with three meters (ten feet) of water. The crops, of course, were completely washed out, causing a food shortage among the farmers and among the people in the nearby village of Kadabuka. The same thing happened again in February, 1963.

Throughout the rest of 1963 and 1964 the sluice gates of the dam were opened and shut several times. As a result, none of the low farmlands could be seeded during the best growing season. The flow of the river water was too uncertain. This every-now-and-then pattern of opening and closing the sluice gates was kept up through 1966. "It is hard to imagine how those regulating the flow of water through the dam could have acted in a way more [harmful] to down-river [farming]," Scudder says.

Some authorities feel that planners of the Kariba and other dams often close their eyes and minds to problems the dams can and do bring. They see only the quick benefits, in this case electrical power for areas far removed from the land. In the case of the Zambezi farmers, well over 10,000 people had to be relocated along other parts of the river, and will probably have to be relocated again and again as they continue to overtax the land.

M. Farvar, of the Center for the Biology of Natural Systems, has this to say about the future of dams the world over: ". . . One can foresee that all the major rivers of Africa, Asia, and Latin America will be dammed, along with many of the lesser ones. The construction of Kariba started [something] that will no doubt alter the African landscape and affect the lives of millions of people."

He goes on to say that the people who build such dams usually place little importance on the farming that is upset as a result of the dams. That is because the farms are nearly always too small to produce enough food to be sold and so be an important source of money. Instead, the crops grown usually are barely enough for the farming families themselves. But what happens when the farmers are flooded out? Who is to feed them if they cannot feed themselves? Either there is famine and they starve, or the government must pay huge sums of money to relocate them, feed them, and otherwise care for them. So numerous, delicate, and complex are the bits and pieces of a given ecosystem within the environment that a large dam can create more problems than it was supposed to solve in the first place.

Indeed there is a lesson here for those who would deliberately encourage mammoth technological schemes to change one aspect of climate in order to "benefit" a particular nation. But what of neighboring nations? A climatological blessing to one nation may well turn out to be a climatological disaster to a neighboring nation.

Stephen H. Schneider points up this lesson by citing a hypothetical case in his book, *The Genesis Strategy*. Suppose there happened to be an extended period of drought in the grain-producing region of Russia, such as the one that occurred in 1972. Soviet climatologists are summoned by the government and asked what can be done to break the drought. They come up with a plan to melt the thin layer (three meters, or ten feet) of ice covering the North Polar Arctic Sea and so expose a vast reserve source of moisture.

LET'S MELT THE ARCTIC ICE CAP

One possibility for doing this has been worked out by an atmospheric scientist, Halstead Harrison, of the University of Washington. He imagines sowing the ice-covered Arctic sea area with black soot, which would absorb solar energy and cause widespread melting of the ice. Some scientists believe that a 20 percent decrease in the reflection of solar energy over the ice field would melt the ice completely in about three years. Harrison says it would take a fleet of 500 Boeing 747s each making two flights a day over the ice field for a period of 50 days. During that time they would spread ten million tons of soot, one ton for each of the ten million square kilometers (six million square miles) occupied by the ice cap. The cost, he says, would come to about two billion dollars, not an impossible sum for the Russians to raise.

Would such a scheme actually work? At this stage no one can say. There is at least one doubter. University of Arizona meteorologist Louis J. Battan says that the "utterly fantastic" amount of soot required to do the job clearly makes the idea a "hopeless one."

What would be the results, aside from the Russians possibly getting the much-needed rain? There undoubtedly would be severe side effects that would be harmful to other parts of the globe. The open Arctic water would most likely increase the polar region temperature substantially, with January temperatures rising by as much as 15°C (27°F). This would mean an increased rate of evaporation, resulting in increased snowfall and possibly setting the stage for another ice age for northern Canada and Europe. That much warming of the Arctic Sea surely would affect global climate and regions in low northern latitudes.

It would appear obvious that attempts to change the climate should not be the sole decision of any one nation since the consequences are global and almost certainly would lead to national and international conflicts.

Yet the Russians have already made a tentative move in this direction. In 1971, concerned over a 2.5 meter (eight-foot) drop in the level of the Caspian Sea over a 35-year period, they proposed to use 250 15-kiloton nuclear explosives to blast a 113-kilometer(70-mile)-long canal and change the course of the north-flowing Pechora River so that it would link up with the south-flowing Kolva River and so replenish the Caspian Sea. Three nuclear charges were set off in a test to see if the plan was realistic. They were planted about 120 meters (400 feet) deep and about 150 meters (500 feet) apart. The two blasts cleared a ditch 700 meters (2,300 feet) long and 335 meters (1,110 feet) wide and up to 15 meters (50 feet) deep. The Russians reported that the tests had successfully "demonstrated the idea's feasibility."

They neglected to mention the possible effects of depriving the Arctic Sea of the Pechora River's supply of fresh water. Climatologists now suspect that the Canadian and Russian rivers flowing into the Arctic Sea contribute to its permanent ice cover since fresh water freezes more readily than does salt water. If those Canadian and Russian rivers were diverted southward, as the Russians seem to want to do to the Pechora, there might well be a gradual and increasing reduction in Arctic Sea ice.

What other schemes have been proposed to alter climate?

LET'S DAM THE BERING STRAIT

Former President Ford reportedly discussed with USSR Chairman Brezhnev in Vladivostock a plan to build a giant dam across the 97-kilometer(60-mile)-wide Bering Strait, between Alaska and Siberia, an idea proposed in 1959 by the Soviet engineer P. M. Borisov. Water would then be pumped out of the Arctic Sea at the dam site into the North Pacific Ocean. As a result of the withdrawal of Arctic waters there, the southward-flowing cold current off the west coast of Greenland would be reversed and so allow warm Gulf Stream water to be drawn up from the North Atlantic into the Arctic Basin and gradually to melt the sea ice. Again, while it is certain that the global climate would be changed by such a scheme, it is not certain which direction climate would take after the initial warming of the north polar cap region.

Still another proposal to break up the Arctic ice is to explode "clean" nuclear devices beneath the ice and "stir up saltier, warmer water from below," an idea first proposed in 1958 by the late Harry Wexler of the United States Weather Bureau. Wexler said that nuclear bombs exploded in the Arctic Sea would force heat and moisture high into the atmosphere over the polar region. According to Battan, "this procedure would cause clouds of ice crystals to form. They would act as a shield preventing the escape of Earth's radiation and the trapped heat rays would be expected to warm the lower atmosphere."

Any scheme to reduce or completely eliminate the Arctic ice would reduce the temperature difference between the North Pole and the Equator, which would lead to a change in the general circulation of the atmosphere, thus affecting a wide region of the globe. Warns Battan: "At the present time, most meteorologists would agree that warming the Arctic by a small amount would change the global weather and climate. Unfortunately, nobody knows *how* it will change. Will the deserts be brought into bloom and the swamps dried up? Or will the swamps be even more inundated and deserts enlarged? Will the farming regions of the world get more or less rain and snow and when will it fall? Will the ocean surface rise and flood the low-lying cities of the world? Will the changes in general circulation initiate another ice age? No one yet knows the answers to these and a great many other related questions. Until we do, or at least can take a good guess, we better be careful tinkering with the global atmosphere."

MAKING RAIN

Widespread cloud seeding to cause moisture-laden clouds to rain might also bring about climate change. Cloud seeding has been successfully carried out many times on a local level and is a proven means of wringing water out of the atmosphere under certain conditions. From the point of view of climate, extensive cloud seeding—if it could be carried out on a large scale—would lead to two things: a change in precipitation patterns and a tendency to warm the atmosphere where the seeding took place. The warming would come from heat released as water droplets in the clouds reached the freezing level and turned to ice.

TAMING HURRICANES

A possibility of modifying local climates plagued with hurricanes is to find a means of lessening the force of these violent tropical storms by artificial means. Although we are not even close to being able to tame a hurricane, several schemes have been proposed. Hurricanes form over the ocean and feed on a continuing source of warm, moist air. The reason a hurricane weakens and dies over the land is that it is deprived of this source of warm, moist air.

One scheme proposed coating the ocean surface ahead of a hurricane with oil and then setting it afire. The air in the fire zone would create a low-pressure area that theoretically would send the hurricane off in a direction where it would not damage lives and property. Another proposal is to airdrop large numbers of tiny plastic bubbles over the top of a hurricane.

This might produce a greenhouse effect and trap heat in the upper part of the storm system. It can be argued that this new pattern of heat distribution would weaken the hurricane.

The most direct way to tame a hurricane might be to deprive it of its source of ocean surface heat. Underwater explosives set off several kilometers ahead of the hurricane's path would send cool water up to the surface and so cool the surface water by several degrees.

At the present time no one can say if any of these schemes would work. If one should prove to work and then be put into regular use, it might touch off an international hassle. For example, drought-prone Mexico often benefits from much-needed rain produced by hurricanes that sweep in near Florida and sometimes into the Gulf of Mexico. So one nation's disastrous storm is another nation's liquid manna from heaven. Who is to decide which it is?

LET'S MAKE AN AFRICAN SEA

There have been numerous engineering proposals which, if ever carried out, would almost certainly alter climate in such a way that several nations would be affected directly and global effects would be bound to result.

Around 1935 the German architect Herman Sörgel drew up an ambitious project that would have brought major climate changes to a large part, if not all, of Africa. It involved Lake Chad, the shallow and swampy remains of what 10,000 years ago was an impressive, sprawling, fresh-water "sea." Lake Chad, fed by the Shari and Logone rivers, and now and then by other rivers when they are not dry, now covers an area about 9,600 square kilometers (6,000 square miles) in the central Sahel during the wet season, but its shoreline varies seasonally since it lacks an outlet and loses water by evaporation. The Lake is a little more than half the size of Lake Erie. At its glory the Chad Sea covered some 30 times the area that it does today.

Sörgel's plan was to re-create the Chad Sea by damming the Congo River at a point some 1,930 kilometers (1,200 miles) due south of Lake Chad. The dam was to be built across a section known as the Chenal, which is only a kilometer and a half (about a mile) wide in places. Such a dam would eventually back up the Congo's waters and, aided by other lakes that

The map shows Congo Lake, the Chad Sea, and the course of a new outlet river that the German engineer Herman Sörgel envisioned in his ambitious plan to re-create the Chad Sea by building a dam across the Congo River.

feed into the Congo above the dam, would slowly flood the Congo Basin. The result would be a mammoth lake, Congo Lake, covering an area as large as the combined areas of California, Nevada, and Oregon.

What would happen to Congo Lake when it filled up? Sörgel had it all worked out. He had planned for a number of "drainage holes" positioned at advantageous points around the lake. Each such hole would be made up of several concrete tunnels up to nine meters (30 feet) in diameter and would have a turbo-generator at the other end. The main drain of the lake, however, would be located north of where the Ubangi River makes its sharp turn. This major outlet would flow in a northwesterly direction and join the Shari River that presently feeds the dying Lake Chad. Sörgel imagined the time when Lake Chad would be restored to its days of former glory 10,000 years and more ago.

But why did Sörgel want to go to all this trouble? Lake Chad today is a land-locked lake with no outlet, but the Chad Sea would swell to the stage where it created an outlet to one of the oceans. Sörgel's philosophy ran something like this: "If water has to have an outlet it is always wise to provide one. Otherwise it may go in a direction which, though predictable, may be undesirable." Sörgel reasoned that the northwest extension of the Chad Sea would come close to the Ahaggar Plateau. That's where he would build the outlet and so create a large river that curved northward through Algeria and finally eastward, emptying into the Mediterranean in Tunisia's Gulf of Gabès. Such a river, according to Sörgel, could be navigated by small steamers and power boats, which could enter the Chad Sea and then navigate along the Sahel to the Ubangi.

Several questions immediately arise on hearing of such a proposal. First, could it actually be done? With present-day technology it no doubt could. But a more important question is whether it would be economically worth it. A third question is whether Sörgel's dream would be worthwhile in human terms. Over a half century or more, as the Chad Sea would be filling up and the "Second Nile"—as Sörgel called the river that would flow into the Mediterranean—was forming, several million people would be displaced and would have to relocate. As a result of climate change brought about by the Chad Sea, possibly large areas of what was left of the Sahel would become productive farmland. But to come up with meaningful answers to these questions would require several years of research on the part of climatologists, geologists, engineers, economists, and many others with different specialties.

THE ATLANTROPA PLAN

Man, it seems, cannot resist altering the environment, either accidentally or deliberately. When an engineer looks at a map and sees any narrow geographical feature he starts clicking his calculator and reaches for his T-square. If the narrow feature happens to be a land bridge linking two large land masses, he will plan to cut through to build a canal, such as the Panama Canal and Suez Canal. If the narrow feature happens to be a strait separating two land masses, he will plan to build a bridge or tunnel to link the two land masses, such as San Francisco's Golden Gate Bridge or New York's George Washington Bridge. Or he may decide to build a dam.

The narrow gap of water forming the inlet to the Mediterranean Sea and known as the Strait of Gibraltar—or the Pillars of Hercules in classical times—has long intrigued engineers. Possibly more than any other mammoth engineering project, the "Atlantropa Plan" to dam up the entrance to the Mediterranean has fascinated engineers, politicians, agriculturalists, city planners, and just about everyone else.

The dreamer of this ambitious plan again was Herman

Sörgel. He proposed it in March, 1928, when he was employed by the Bavarian government. At first, people thought that he must be joking, so far-reaching were the results of the plan as he described them. He called his plan *Mittelmeer Senkung,* which means "Reduction of the Mediterranean." The Mediterranean Sea, he said, is a recent sea. About 50,000 years ago (he was not sure of the exact figure), it was about 930 meters (3,000 feet) lower than it is today, which meant that there was no Mediterranean Sea then. Instead there were two large lakes —one east of Sicily and the other west. Europe and Africa were then linked by three isthmuses: the Spain-Morocco isthmus, the Tunisia-Sicily isthmus, and one joining Greece to North Africa. Sörgel envisioned all of this former "extra" Mediterranean land as "fruitful and possibly even inhabited." When the last glacier melted, he went on, sea level rose and the present Mediterranean Sea was formed. Building a dam across the Strait of Gibraltar would enable us to regain that lost land, and with benefits beyond our dreams, he said.

Engineers today agree that indeed the level of the Mediterranean would drop if the Strait of Gibraltar were blocked off. The reason is that the Mediterranean loses more water through evaporation than it receives from the rivers that feed the sea and from rainfall. Two-thirds of the lost water is replaced by the inflow of a surface current from the Atlantic. Beneath this inflowing surface current is a cold-water current flowing out of the Mediterranean, a current we will return to in a moment. A dam across the Strait of Gibraltar would lower the Mediterranean by a meter (about three feet) or more a year. But as the map shows, a dam also would have to be built across the Dardanelles to keep out the Black Sea.

The Gibraltar dam would be a huge effort, 29 kilometers (18 miles) long and about 310 meters (1,000 feet) high from its deep, underwater base to its top. A railroad and automobile

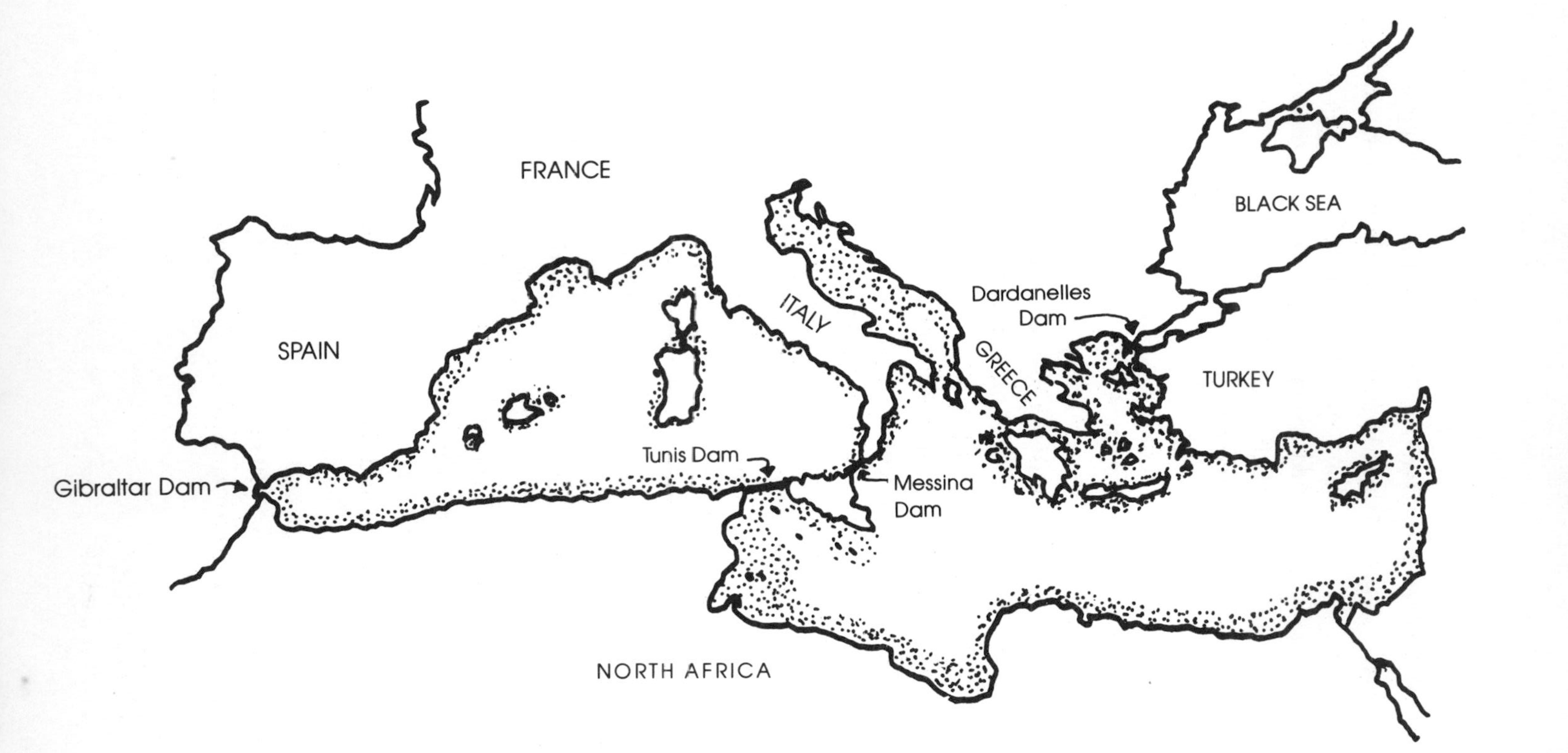

Sörgel also drew up a plan that would reclaim a vast amount of land (dotted areas) from the Mediterranean Sea. In short, he proposed to lower the level of the Mediterranean by about 100 meters (330 feet) by building dams across the Strait of Gibraltar, across the Strait of Messina, another from Sicily to Tunisia, and another across the Dardanelles.

highway would run along the top of the dam and so link Europe with Africa. The top of the dam, according to Sörgel, would have to be 51 meters (165 feet) wide and its base ten times that width to hold up under the tremendous inward push of water from the Atlantic.

Sörgel estimated that ten years after the dam was completed, the level of the Mediterranean would lower by ten meters (33 feet). At this stage numerous hydroelectric turbines could be installed to produce enormous amounts of electrical power.

At the end of a century the level of the Mediterranean would be lowered by 100 meters (330 feet). At this stage another dam would be built, this one across the Strait of Messina between Sicily and the Italian mainland. Still another dam would be built across the narrow stretch from Sicily to Tunisia. Thus the eastern Mediterranean would be isolated from the western sector. In effect, two enormous lakes would be formed. By this time dams would have been built across every river mouth and would be producing almost unlimited electrical power. Meanwhile, a total of 145,000 square kilometers (90,000 square miles) of new land would have emerged along the shoreline. Italy would enlarge by half its size again; Corsica and Sardinia would become a single land mass; and Sicily would nearly double its size.

At this stage the western part of the Mediterranean would be maintained at the new level by permitting water from the Atlantic to flow through the Gibraltar dam from time to time. Meanwhile the eastern sector would be allowed to drop by an additional 102 meters (330 feet). This probably would take less than a century, after which time the eastern half could be stabilized at its new level by periodic flows of water from the Black Sea and from the western Mediterranean.

The large amount of water—350,000 cubic kilometers (84,000 cubic miles)—kept out of the Mediterranean would have to go elsewhere, to all of the other oceans. As a result, sea level everywhere (except in the Mediterranean) would rise by about one meter (about three feet). The final result in the Mediterranean would be a gain of a total of 354,000 square kilometers (220,000 square miles) of new land. From the point of view of generating almost limitless amounts of electrical power, Sörgel said that the Atlantropa Plan could be stopped when the level of the Mediterranean had been reduced by only 15 meters (50 feet). The ultimate goal of Atlantropa, he said, was to fuse Europe and Africa, and in his 1938 book, *The Three Big A's,* he wrote at length about *A*merica, *A*sia, and *A*tlantropa. He also described the extensive series of locks that would permit shipping to go on as usual.

There is no doubt that many benefits would be gained were the Atlantropa Plan to be put into action. In addition to the enormous gain in land area and electrical power, the climate of northern Europe almost certainly would be made warmer. This would happen because that deep, cold-water current flowing out of the Mediterranean into the Atlantic would have been stopped. With that current blocked the Gulf Stream would be permitted to flow in closer to the coast and up the English Channel. There would certainly be major climate changes, but what the far-reaching climate change would amount to is largely guesswork. Some nations would benefit, but there are bound to be others who would be losers.

What are some other disadvantages? For one, all of the present seaports in the Mediterranean would be left high and dry. Trieste would be 480 kilometers (300 miles) from the sea with the maximum reduction in sea level mentioned. Also, those areas 90 or so meters (about 300 feet) below sea level would tend to have a climate resembling that of the Dead Sea area now, which is not a pleasant climate. And there would always be a possibility of the main dam at Gibraltar collapsing. It has also been suggested that the great weight of water removed from the Mediterranean's floor might touch off a new series of volcanic and earthquake activity, like that which has plagued the northern Mediterranean shores many times in the past. The larger and more variable the natural forces man attempts to manipulate, the more uncertain are the results of his manipulations. Sörgel's dream projects are on such a gigantic scale that it is at present impossible to sort out the numerous interacting consequences.

When asked to comment on Sörgel's two mammoth schemes, Bryson had this to say: "I really find it difficult to be even moderately polite about such irresponsible schemes as Sörgel's suggestions. Neglecting the totally impossible capital outlay of re-creating every Mediterranean port, what about the loss of agricultural land from incision of the Rhone, the Po, the Nile, etc., with lowered base level? Sheer folly even if no climatic change occurred or a good change occurred. Likewise with the Chad Sea. *No one* knows what the climatic effect would be —and I hope no one suggests the experimental method to find out."

It would be possible to fill many more pages in describing dozens of schemes to change climate directly or indirectly through ambitious engineering schemes similar to those described here. It would be miraculous if any scheme such as damming the Bering Strait, the Strait of Gibraltar, or the Congo, or a systematic taming of hurricanes would benefit all. Some would be bound to suffer at the expense of others' gains. But that has always been so. Anticipating such plans at this stage of our severely limited knowledge of climate, not to mention our frighteningly limited ability to get on with each other as nations, would be foolhardy. We simply cannot afford to tamper with the global system of climate for the simple reason that *any* such tampering would inevitably affect the well-being and life-styles of many people. Such deliberate tampering would be the ultimate in irresponsibility.

This does not mean that someday Herman Sörgel's dream might not be pursued, but not until we have a world organization of states willing to work together for the mutual benefit of all mankind. Considering the present state of the world that day is not just around the corner.

WHERE DO WE GO FROM HERE?

What we must do meanwhile is carefully consider the consequences of our large-scale actions that may lead to significant changes of the atmosphere. Bryson has already sounded one alarm. The temperature variation in the Northern Hemisphere during this century, he says, is accounted for by an increased amount of man-made dust and carbon dioxide released into the atmosphere by primitive agricultural practices and industrial growth. While carbon dioxide accounts for 3 percent of the temperature variation, dust accounts for 90 percent, he says. The net effect, he maintains, is to reduce temperature, which causes the westerlies to expand and take a more looping pattern. The results: "Drought in the monsoon lands and elsewhere, shorter growing seasons in the world's main food-producing areas, and more highly variable weather around the world."

Bryson is convinced that the monsoons will not regularly return to India and Pakistan during this century. If so, history will be repeating itself, but Bryson fears that no one at the government level is willing to heed its lessons. "They seem unwilling even to *listen*," he says.

Not all climatologists agree with Bryson, but my purpose here has not been to take sides. Rather it is to point out the *possible* consequences of our actions as a species in influencing climate change. Natural forces, unaided by man, will continue to change the global climate as they have done for hundreds of millions of years, and it seems that we are helpless to halt or reverse a major climate trend. What we may be capable of, however, is nudging climate along in a direction already dictated by natural forces by significantly altering one or more of the many variable bits and pieces of climate. So while we are not in a position to control climate, it now seems that indeed we may be in a position to influence climate. That in itself is a tremendous power to possess. How we will use it remains to be seen.

Bibliography

Following is a selected listing from the numerous books, periodicals, and other published materials referred to during the research stage of this book. Many of these materials are of a highly technical nature and will be beyond the scope of those young readers for whom this book is intended. Nevertheless, I list them for those students advanced enough, and interested enough, to want more detailed information about various major topics than appears in this book.

ABELSON, PHILIP H. "Energy and Climate," (an editorial). *Science,* 2 September 1977.

ALYEA, FRED N.; CUNNOLD, DEREK M.; and PRINN, RONALD G. "Stratospheric Ozone Destruction by Aircraft-Induced Nitrogen Oxides." *Science,* 11 April 1975.

BATTAN, LOUIS J. *Harvesting the Clouds.* New York: Doubleday, 1969.

BROOKS, C.E.P. *Climate Through the Ages.* 2d rev. ed. New York: Dover, 1970.

BRYSON, REID A., and MURRAY, THOMAS J. *Climates of Hunger.* Madison: The University of Wisconsin Press, 1977.

———. "World Climate and World Food Systems III: The Lessons of Climatic History" *IES Report 27.* Institute for Environmental Studies. University of Wisconsin at Madison, November 1974.

BUDYKO, M. I. *Climatology.* New York: Academic Press, 1974.

CALDER, NIGEL. *The Restless Earth.* New York: Viking Press, 1972.

———. *The Weather Machine.* New York: Viking Press, 1974.

CLIMAP Project Members. "The Surface of the Ice-Age Earth." *Science,* 19 March 1976.

CRITCHFIELD, HOWARD J. *General Climatology.* 3d ed. Englewood Cliffs, N.J.: Prentice-Hall, 1974.

DAY, JOHN A., and STERNES, GILBERT L. *Climate and Weather.* Reading, Mass.: Addison–Wesley, 1970.

DONAHUE, THOMAS M. "The SST and Ozone Depletion," (letter). *Science,* 28 March 1975.

DYSON, JAMES L. *The World of Ice.* New York: Knopf, 1962.

ECKHOLM, ERIK, and BROWN, LESTER R. "Spreading Deserts: The Hand of Man," *World Watch Paper 13.* Worldwatch Institute. August, 1977.

EDDY, JOHN A. "The Case of the Missing Sunspots." *Scientific American,* May, 1977.

EDINGER, JAMES G. *Watching for the Wind.* New York: Doubleday, 1967.

EMILIANI, CESARE. "Ancient Temperatures." *Scientific American,* February, 1958.

ENGLAND, J., and BRADLEY, R. S. "Past Glacial Activity in the Canadian High Arctic." *Science,* 21 April 1978.

GALLANT, ROY A. *How Life Began: Creation Versus Evolution.* New York: Four Winds, 1975.

———. *Beyond Earth: The Search for Extraterrestrial Life.* New York: Four Winds, 1977.

GRIBBIN, JOHN. *Forecasts, Famines and Freezes.* New York: Walker, 1976.

GROOTES, P. M. "Carbon–14 Time Scale Extended: Comparison of Chronologies." *Science,* 7 April 1978, and 12 May 1978.

HAYS, J. D.; IMBRIE, JOHN; and SHACKLETON, N. J. "Variations in the Earth's Orbit: Pacemaker of the Ice Ages." *Science,* 10 December 1976.

HOYT, JOSEPH BIXBY. *Man and the Earth,* 2d ed. Englewood Cliffs, N.J.: Prentice-Hall, 1967.

HSU, KENNETH J. "When the Black Sea Was Drained." *Scientific American,* May, 1978.

IDSO, SHERWOOD B.; and BRAZEL, ANTHONY J. "Planetary Radiation Balance as a Function of Atmospheric Dust: Climatological Consequences." *Science,* 18 November 1977.

KERR, RICHARD A. "Carbon Dioxide and Climate: Carbon Budget Still Unbalanced." *Science,* 30 September 1977.

KNOX, JOSEPH B. "Man's Threat to His Atmosphere." Santa Barbara: The Center for the Study of Democratic Institutions, *The Center Magazine,* October/November, 1976.

KORMONDY, EDWARD J. *Concepts in Ecology.* 2d ed. Englewood Cliffs, N.J.: Prentice-Hall, 1976.

——— (coauthored with ROBERT S. LEISNER). *Pollution.* Dubuque, Ia.: Brown, 1971.

LAMB, H. H. *Climate: Present, Past, and Future.* London: Methuen, 1972.

LAPORTE, LÉO F. *Ancient Environments.* Englewood Cliffs, N.J.: Prentice-Hall, 1968.

LOWRY, WILLIAM P. "The Climate of Cities." *Scientific American,* August, 1967.

LADURIE, E. L. *Times of Feast, Times of Famine.* New York: Doubleday, 1971.

MATSCH, CHARLES L. *North America and the Great Ice Age.* New York: McGraw-Hill, 1976.

MAUGH, THOMAS H. II. "The Ozone Layer: The Threat from Aerosol Cans Is Real." *Science,* 8 October 1976.

MCALESTER, A. LEE. *The Earth.* Englewood Cliffs, N.J.: Prentice-Hall, 1973.

Mother Earth News, March, 1976, p. 7, "Interview with Reid A. Bryson."

OPIK, ERNST J. "Climate and the Changing Sun." *Scientific American,* June, 1958.

PLASS, GILBERT N. "Carbon Dioxide and Climate." *Scientific American,* July, 1959.

SCHNEIDER, STEPHEN H. *The Genesis Strategy.* New York: Plenum, 1976.

SHAW, ROBERT H., ed. *Ground Level Climatology.* Washington, D. C.: American Association for the Advancement of Science, 1967.

STOKES, WILLIAM LEE. *Essentials of Earth History.* Englewood Cliffs, N.J.: Prentice-Hall, 1960.

STUIVER, MINZE. "Atmospheric Carbon Dioxide and Carbon Reservoir Changes." *Science,* 20 January 1978.

WOODWELL, GEORGE M. "The Carbon Dioxide Question." *Scientific American,* January, 1978.

Glossary

ABSOLUTE AGE: The dating in years of an object of geological or biological importance. Absolute age can be determined by several radiometric dating processes.

ALGAE: Aquatic or land plants including, for example, seaweeds. They may reproduce sexually or asexually and exist in unicellular or multicellular forms. Algae contain chlorophyll and so are capable of photosynthesis.

AUTUMNAL EQUINOX: The time each year, about September 21, when the Sun crosses the celestial equator from north to south, and when the hours of sunlight and darkness are nearly equal everywhere on Earth.

BLACK DWARF: The remains of a burned-out star that has undergone gravitational collapse and is no longer radiating energy. The Sun after passing through the red giant and then white dwarf stages, will end its "life" as a black dwarf.

BORA: A cold local drainage wind of the Adriatic that blows in excess of 130 kilometers (80 miles) per hour.

BRACHIOPODS: Aquatic animals, such as lamp shells, that have two-valved shells and resemble mussels. During adult life they live fixed by a stalk or by one shell. Although abundant during the Paleozoic, they are small in number and species today.

BRYOZOANS: Small aquatic animals that live attached and have tentacles with which they feed.

CALORIE: The amount of energy required to raise the temperature of one gram of water 1°C (1.8°F).

CAMBRIAN: That geological period lasting some 70 million years and occurring between 500 and 570 million years ago. Shallow Cambrian seas abounded with sponges, trilobites, brachiopods, and other early forms.

CARBONIFEROUS: The Pennsylvanian and Mississippian periods combined, lasting some 65 million years and extending from 280 to 345 million years ago. It was the time when large coal deposits were being formed. Amphibians ruled the land at this time.

CATASTROPHIC HYPOTHESIS: Any hypothesis in astronomy that has a planetary system, such as the Solar System, being formed as the result of stellar collisions or the like.

CENOZOIC: That geological era, including the Quaternary and Tertiary periods, that dates from 65 million years ago to the present. Most of the inland seas left the continents during that time and mammals became the dominant land animals.

CEPHALOPODS: That class of mollusks including octopus, squids, and cuttle-fish.

CHINOOK: A strong, dry, warm wind developing along the lee slope of mountain ranges, for example in Wyoming and Montana, where these winds blow down off the Rocky Mountains.

CLIMATE: A region's weather averaged over a long span of time. From the Greek word *klima,* meaning "slope or incline," and referring to the degree of slant of the Sun's rays relative to Earth's surface.

CORIOLIS EFFECT: An apparent force tending to deflect winds and currents due to Earth's rotation. It is maximum at the poles and zero at the Equator.

COSMIC YEAR: The length of time it takes the Sun to make one complete circuit about the Galaxy, a time span of 500 million years.

CRETACEOUS: That geological period lasting some 71 million years and extending from 65 to 136 million years ago. The dinosaurs became extinct during this period and primitive mammals appeared.

CRINOIDS: Marine organisms that have existed since Cambrian times. They usually live attached to other objects by stalks and have long, branched, feathery arms. They include the feather stars and sea-lilies.

DENDROCHRONOLOGY: Dating past events in Earth's history by using the annual growth rings of trees. Such geological clocks can serve as climate indicators going back about 8,000 years.

DESERTIFICATION: The spreading of desert conditions with the result that less of the land is made available for agriculture.

DEVONIAN: That geological period lasting some 50 million years and extending from 345 to 395 million years ago. Most of North America was covered by shallow seas during this time and a bewildering variety of fish arose.

DOLDRUMS: That belt of light or calm and variable winds occurring at the Equator.

DRAINAGE WINDS: Those winds resulting from the downward flow of cold air sweeping down the slopes of high plateaus and gathering in the valleys and fjords and then reaching the coast as gentle or moderate breezes.

ECCENTRICITY: A long, stretched-out orbit of a planet or other celestial object circling about a second object is said to be "eccentric." Eccentricity is found by measuring the distance of either focus of the elliptical orbit from the center of the ellipse and dividing by the length of the semimajor axis. Eccentricity usually is expressed as a decimal fraction.

FIRN: Granular snow one or more years old, through which air and water can pass.

FOEHN: A strong, dry, warm wind developing along the lee slope of a mountain range. Foehns are most frequent and strongest along the northern slopes of the Alps.

GEOLOGIC TIME: The portion of time occurring before written history began.

GLACIER: Any mass of moving land ice formed out of compacted snow. There are eight principal forms of glaciers.

GONDWANA: A continent formed during Earth's very early history, when a large supercontinent broke into a northern half and a southern half, the latter of which was Gondwana.

GRAPTOLITES: Fossilized skeletons of extinct colonial animals found in Cambrian, Ordovician, and Silurian rocks.

GREENHOUSE EFFECT: The heat-trapping action of the atmosphere due to the blocking of long-wave radiation reflected from Earth's surface.

GULF STREAM: A northeasterly flowing current of relatively warm water flowing up the eastern coast of the United States and across to Britain and farther northward.

The Gulf Stream branches near Britain and loops southward and then westward, forming a closed loop.

HALF-LIFE: That period of time during which one half of the number of atoms of a radioactive (parent) element change into atoms of a different (daughter) element.

HORSE LATITUDES: The high-pressure belt of air forming at about 30°N and S latitudes.

HYDROLOGIC CYCLE: The water cycle, in which water from the oceans and land evaporates and enters the air as water vapor. The water vapor then condenses as water droplets and forms clouds, which release water in the form of rain, snow, and ice.

ICE AGE: Any extended period of time during which a substantial portion of Earth's surface is covered by "permanent" ice. There have been seven known major ice ages during the past 700,000 years, with the last ice age reaching its peak about 18,000 years ago.

ICE CAP: An ice sheet such as that covering Greenland and Antarctica.

INSOLATION: Short for "incoming solar radiation," that portion of the Sun's energy entering Earth's atmosphere.

JURASSIC: That geological period lasting some 54 million years and extending from 136 to 190 million years ago. A period of relative quiet. Dinosaurs were numerous; feathered birds appeared, as did small mammals.

LAURASIA: A continent formed during Earth's very early history when a large supercontinent broke into a southern half and a northern half, the latter of which was Laurasia.

LITTLE ICE AGE: That period from roughly 1300 to the early 1700s during which mountain glaciers advanced and a number of severe winters occurred.

LOESS: Silt with smaller amounts of very fine sand and/or clay.

MESOSPHERE: That layer of atmosphere immediately above the stratosphere and below the thermosphere.

MESOZOIC: That geological era containing the Cretaceous, Jurassic, and Triassic periods. The Rocky Mountains were formed, crocodiles appeared, and flowering plants became common.

MISSISSIPPIAN: That geological period lasting some 20 million years and extending from 225 to 280 million years ago. Active mountain building occurred in Oklahoma and Arkansas. Amphibians made their appearance as the major land animals.

MONSOON: An atmospheric circulation system that develops in accordance with the yearly changes in the temperature difference between the oceans and land. The Indian monsoon is the best known example.

NEBULAR HYPOTHESIS: Any hypothesis in astronomy that accounts for the formation of a planetary system, for example, by supposing that the first stage of such a system occurred as a vast collection of gas and dust, which later condensed as a star with accompanying planets.

OBLIQUITY: The amount (23.5°) by which Earth is tilted in space with respect to the plane of its orbit.

ORDOVICIAN: That geological period that lasted some 70 million years and extended from 430 to 500 million years ago. It was a rich period for marine life since about 70 percent of what is presently North America was flooded.

OUTLET GLACIER: Any river of ice draining an ice sheet, usually through a fjord.

OZONE: A gas composed of three atoms of oxygen (O_3) as opposed to the oxygen we breathe (O_2). A layer of ozone in the upper atmosphere protects living organisms by filtering out a substantial portion of the ultraviolet radiation entering the atmosphere from the Sun.

PACK ICE: A large area of floating sea ice, such as that occurring in the Arctic Ocean.

PALEOCLIMATOLOGY: The study of ancient climates.

PALEOZOIC: That geological era containing the periods from Cambrian to Permian times and spanning a time period of some 345 million years. A long era that saw much mountain building and during which reptiles and amphibians arose, as did many other forms.

PANGAEA: A large supercontinent that during Earth's very early history broke into a northern portion, Laurasia, and a southern portion, Gondwana.

PENNSYLVANIAN: That geological period spanning some 45 million years and extending from 280 to 325 million years ago.

PERMIAN: That geological period lasting about 55 million years and extending from 225 to 280 million years ago. A generally drying climate during this period caused many plant and animal species to become extinct, but favored the success of reptiles.

PHOTOSYNTHESIS: That ability of green plants to synthesize the sugar glucose out of carbon dioxide and water from the atmosphere in the presence of sunlight.

PLANKTON: Usually very small plants and animals that drift passively in the sea and inland bodies of water. These organisms form the first link in the food chain and are eaten by fishes and whales.

POLAR EASTERLIES: Belts of winds occurring at extreme latitudes in both hemispheres. They blow out of the northeast in the Northern Hemisphere and out of the southeast in the Southern Hemisphere.

PRECAMBRIAN: That long geological period lasting some

3,900 million years and extending back from 570 million years ago to Earth's formation as a planet, some 4,500 million years ago. The first living forms—simple algalike and funguslike organisms—arose during the Precambrian.

PRECESSION: Earth's wobbling on its axis, which makes one complete wobble once every 25,800 years.

PREVAILING WESTERLIES: Those winds blowing out of the west from about 30° to 60° N and S latitudes. Those in the Northern Hemisphere blow out of the southwest, and those in the Southern Hemisphere blow out of the northwest.

PSILOPSIDS: Oldest land plants known and occurring during the Devonian.

QUATERNARY: That geological time period spanning the past two million years.

RADIOMETRIC DATING: Determining the absolute age of a substance by the study of the ratio of stable daughter elements to their radioactive parent element.

RELATIVE AGE: The age of an object of geological or biological importance measured in relation to other such objects. For example, determining that object A is 2,500 years older than object B tells us only the relative age of the two objects and nothing about the absolute age of either object.

SEDIMENTARY ROCK: Rock formed from clay, lime, sand, and gravel—and sometimes plant and/or animal remains—that have been squeezed under great weight and pressure for long periods of time. Sedimentary rock makes up about 75 percent of the land area of the world.

SILURIAN: That geological period lasting some 35 million years and extending from 395 to 430 million years ago, during which life seems to have taken its first hold on land.

SOLAR CONSTANT: The amount of solar energy striking a one cm^2 area of Earth's upper atmosphere in one minute, which amounts to very nearly two calories. The solar "constant" turns out not to be constant but is greater during some geological periods than during others.

STRATOSPHERE: That layer of atmosphere lying above the troposphere and below the mesophere. The stratosphere is Earth's second air layer and extends from a height of about 12 kilometers (seven miles) to about 45 kilometers (28 miles).

SUMMER SOLSTICE: The northernmost point reached by the Sun as it travels along the ecliptic, which occurs about June 22. The summer solstice point lies in the constellation of Gemini and marks the longest day of the year.

SUNSPOTS: Great dark spots (up to 97,000 kilometers, or 60,000 miles, across) that break out periodically in varying numbers on the Sun's surface. Sunspots are thought to be great outbursts of gases that break out from deep inside the Sun. As the outrushing clouds of gas rise high above the Sun's surface, they cool and so appear dark against the lighter surface of hotter gases. Maximum activity tends to occur about every 11 years, but these periods of activity vary.

TERTIARY: That geological period lasting some 63 million years and extending from two to 65 million years ago. Most of the inland seas left the continents, and grasslands became widespread. Mammals became the dominant land animals and anthropoid apes evolved.

THERMOSPHERE: The top layer of Earth's atmosphere, which begins at a height of about 80 kilometers (50 miles).

TILLITE: A sedimentary rock composed of cemented, nonsorted sediments carried or deposited by a glacier.

TRADE WINDS: The two wind belts extending from the margin of the doldrums to about 30° N and S latitude. In the Northern Hemisphere they blow out of the northeast and in the Southern Hemisphere out of the southeast.

TRIASSIC: That geological period lasting some 35 million years and extending from 190 to 225 million years ago. Thecodonts, ancestors of the dinosaurs, arose during this period, as did turtles and crocodiles. Seaways covered the western edges of North and South America.

TRILOBITES: Extinct marine animals abundant from Cambrian to Silurian times and probably related to the ancestors of present-day crustaceans.

TROPOSPHERE: That layer of atmosphere extending from the ground to a height of about 12 kilometers (seven miles). It is where most of our weather occurs.

VARVE: Two contrasting layers of sediments deposited in one year's time.

VERNAL EQUINOX: That time, about March 21, when the hours of daylight and darkness are very nearly the same all over the globe.

WATER VAPOR: Water in the form of a gas.

WESTERLIES: See Prevailing Westerlies.

WINTER SOLSTICE: The lowest point reached by the Sun as it travels along the ecliptic, which occurs about December 22. Winter Solstice point lies in Sagittarius and it marks the shortest day of the year.

Index